BRANDED
BEAUTY

BRANDED

BEAUTY

HOW MARKETING CHANGED THE WAY WE LOOK

Kogan
Page

MARK TUNGATE

Publisher's note

Every possible effort has been made to ensure that the information contained in this book is accurate at the time of going to press, and the publishers and authors cannot accept responsibility for any errors or omissions, however caused. No responsibility for loss or damage occasioned to any person acting, or refraining from action, as a result of the material in this publication can be accepted by the editor, the publisher or the author.

First published in Great Britain and the United States in 2011 by Kogan Page Limited

120 Pentonville Road	1518 Walnut Street, Suite 1100	4737/23 Ansari Road
London N1 9JN	Philadelphia PA 19102	Daryaganj, New Delhi 110002
United Kingdom	USA	India

www.koganpage.com

ISBN   978 0 7494 6181 2
E-ISBN 978 0 7494 6182 9

British Library Cataloguing in Publication Data

A CIP record for this book is available from the British Library.

Library of Congress Cataloging-in-Publication Data

Tungate, Mark, 1967-
  Branded beauty : how marketing changed the way we look / Mark Tungate. – 1st ed.
      p. cm.
    ISBN 978-0-7494-6181-2 – ISBN 978-0-7494-6182-9 1. Cosmetics industry. 2. Branding
(Marketing) 3. Advertising–Cosmetics. I. Title.
  HD9970.5.C672T86 2011
  381'.4566855–dc23
                                        2011021594

Typeset by Saxon Graphics, Derby
Print production managed by Jellyfish
Printed and bound by CPI Group (UK) Ltd, Croydon, CR0 4YY

*For Géraldine, Daphné, Carmen,
Carol and Tracie – the most important
women in my life*

CONTENTS

Contents

ACKNOWLEDGEMENTS

There are some beautiful people out there, and many of them helped me with this book. Most of them I cannot list, as they wished to remain anonymous – but they know who they are. Those I can name are Simone Brochard of NY Adorned, Caroline Crabbe of Cosmetic Valley, Indi Davis of Aesop, Cassandra Moonen of Clarins, Camille Velut of IFF and Sabine de Seze of *Cosmétique Magazine*, as well as François Kermoal who put me in touch with her. A big thanks, too, to everyone quoted within these pages. I should not forget Jon Finch of Kogan Page, whose patience and enthusiasm in the face of my ever-sliding deadline seemed limitless. A very special thanks to Bruno Sellés of Vasava in Barcelona, whose cover design has given this book a special radiance and uplift.

Finally, a special word of thanks to my wife, Géraldine, who was never less than supportive despite the stress of a house move right in the middle of this enterprise. She is the most beautiful of all.

INTRODUCTION

'The tyranny of beauty.'

There are more people outside the art gallery than in. They flock on the narrow Parisian street, smoking and sipping red wine from plastic cups, the boys cartoonish with their creative facial hair and drainpipe jeans, the girls deceptively fragile, all thin wrists and dark roots. Many of them are wearing vintage leather jackets against the first chill of September. They surreptitiously check one another out, which only confirms what they already knew: the same people show up at all these things.

Inside, the B.A.N.K gallery is fuggy and loud. A silver-haired man in a dapper dark-blue blazer stands out like a kingfisher among starlings. He is Jean-Charles de Castelbajac, fashion designer and artist. This is the opening night of his exhibition, The Tyranny of Beauty.

Castelbajac revels in his own contradictions: a genuine aristocrat whose clothes are adored by rappers; the fiancé of a former Miss France (Mareva Galanter, 1999) who has chosen to satirize the beauty industry. He has done so by selecting paintings from the 18th and 19th centuries and sending photographs of them to China, where artists have copied them. He has then defaced them with the symbols of branding. A portrait of a lovely young noblewoman is obscured by lettering proclaiming 'New Formula! Concentrated shower cream for dry skin'. The Delacroix painting *Liberty Leading the People* is emblazoned with a Nike swoosh. Castelbajac also commissioned medieval-style tapestries of Snow White in a sly reference to the canons of beauty imposed by popular culture.

But the standout exhibit is a series of three busts of Marie Antoinette – the original is in the ancestral home – which Castelbajac sent to aesthetic surgeons in France, the United States and Russia. The French surgeon was the kindest, fixing the French queen's double chin and giving her a subtle lift to enhance her cheekbones. The American intervention was more dramatic, plumping up her lips with collagen and straightening her nose. The Russian surgeon was the most radical, turning her lips into cushions and her cheekbones into razors: from pastry-loving Austrian duchess to catwalk queen.

With a twinkle in his eye, Castelbajac says that the show is not intended to be political – merely thought-provoking. 'Who is to say that today's ideals of beauty are better than those of the past?' he asks. 'In her day, Marie Antoinette was considered an icon of fashion. If she lived now, as you see, her features would have been altered to conform to an impossible ideal. Why do we give in to this relentless desire for self-improvement, this insatiable need to please?'

JC, I couldn't have put it better myself.

I don't work in the beauty industry, although you could say I operate on the fringes of it, writing about fashion and advertising. And just lately I'd had the feeling that the subject of beauty was becoming more aggressively present in the media. Several trends were pulling in different directions. On the one hand, I was reading more reports about Botox and similar procedures, in a language that was increasingly offhand, as if these interventions were becoming routine. On the other, rising alarm over chemical ingredients was creating a demand for natural and organic beauty products – a new organic brand seemed to blossom every 10 minutes. Hovering above all this were the global beauty giants, hungrily fixing their gaze on China and other emerging markets as the West struggled to lift itself out of a slump.

What started as the germ of an idea quickly grew out of proportion. The more I dug into the cosmetic and personal care sector, the more intrigued I became. For a start there was the sheer size of the thing: estimates varied, but one figure that often surfaced, from Euromonitor International, suggested that the global industry was worth US$350 billion a year, of which the largest portion was generated by skincare products. Then there were the personalities behind the brands: dipping into the biographies of Max Factor and Helena Rubinstein made me yearn to find out more about their colourful, incident-packed lives.

It also struck me that there were alternative concepts of beauty to explore, which is how I ended up talking to tattoo artists in Brooklyn.

Above all, I was fixated on the question that had inspired Castelbajac's show: how did we get to this point? What drives us to spend so much money tampering with our looks?

A survey conducted among 8,600 women by the French website aufeminin. com in 2010 provided additional impetus. A quarter of respondents from across Europe admitted being 'addicted' to beauty, rarely leaving their homes without applying some form of make-up. They considered mascara particularly 'indispensable'.

Analysing this data, sociologist Jean-François Amadieu wrote:

> While people claim that they take up diets, sport, cosmetic surgery, make-up or fashionable clothes for themselves, to feel good in their skin or in front of a mirror... in reality, they are more than ever influenced by the norms of society, fashion and advertising... The efforts that they go to with their make-up and clothing are evidently linked with being 'outside', that is to say, in front of others. The fact that they wish to feel free and autonomous and do not want to admit their conformism does not change the fact that the norms of physical appearance are globalized, known to all, and restrictive.
>
> ('La beauté aujourd'hui, c'est quoi?',
> www.influencia.net, 8 September 2010)

But while there are trends in beauty, some of our ideas about it have not changed a great deal over the centuries. John Armstrong, in his (2005) book *The Secret Power of Beauty*, notes that 'there is a remarkable consistency across history when it comes to what are regarded as the most attractive human forms. Greek statues still embody ideals of male beauty; the women in Titian's paintings still look lovely today.'

It is often proposed that beauty is linked to proportion: 'the love of outline, of balance, of symmetry, of gentle curves'. This theory takes us back to the 6th century BC, and Pythagoras, who discovered that two different lengths of string, if one was exactly half the length of the other, emitted harmonious musical notes when plucked. This exercise could be repeated ad infinitum, as long as the lengths of the strings remained proportional. Pythagoras expanded on this theory to suggest that harmony in all things was governed by symmetry. Writes Armstrong: 'The Pythagorean term for beauty was "cosmos" – a meaning still resonant in the aims of cosmetic surgery and the application of lipstick.'

Another trait that appears not to have changed is our attraction to light and colour. Umberto Eco, in his (2004) book *On Beauty*, observes that, while the medieval period is often referred to as 'the Dark Ages', it was in fact filled with colour and clarity, from illuminated manuscripts to 'clothing dyed with the most precious colours, like purple'. There was also the little matter of status. 'Artificial colours derived from minerals or vegetables thus represented wealth, while the poor wore only fabrics in drab and modest colours… The richness of colours and the splendour of gems were marks of power, and thus objects of desire and marvel.'

It is not hard to make the leap to the jewel-like colours of make-up, often achieved with minerals.

Similarly, it has been stated many times that we are instinctively attracted to those who might help us propagate the human race: in a potential partner we look for a youthful, unblemished complexion, strong white teeth, bright eyes, healthy limbs. Status comes into play here, too, writes Armstrong, as it is 'an important indicator of one's future security. Therefore it is unsurprising that we develop an in-built attraction to objects and features that indicate status.'

'Youth', 'vitality', 'radiance' – these are the words used in advertising copy by beauty brands, which also offer a promise of status with their glossy packaging, exorbitant prices and sleek spas.

Talking to the brands about all this took some doing. Beauty is a highly competitive industry – and an oft-criticized one – and it has a natural aversion to outsiders. My attempts to interview somebody at Clinique, owned by Estée Lauder Companies, were typical of the contortions I went through. First I sent a mail to the US PR department attaching the synopsis of the book, which was finally answered with a mail requesting… a synopsis of the book. Some time after that, I was put in touch with the company's French PR department (as you may have gathered, I live in Paris). A very friendly woman there told me that, as the book would be published in English, I should probably deal with the US PR department. 'But be warned,' she added, 'you are an unknown. The beauty industry is based on relationships. They tend not to talk to people they don't know.'

Sure enough, about a month after my original mail, I received a short message politely thanking me for my interest in Clinique, but adding that, 'due to corporate policy, we do not allow our ads to be printed in text books', which is not what I had asked for in the first place. I understood, however, that this was more about mystique than Clinique: beauty companies construct fantasy worlds, and they do not want their customers to peek behind the screen. I ended up relying on friends of friends, former students who worked in the industry, executive 'insiders' who wished to remain anonymous. At times it felt more as though I was engaged in industrial espionage than writing a book.

I do not pretend that this is a definitive work, nor is it an encyclopaedia: it is a personal project, and I covered the brands and subjects that interested me, hoping along the way to answer the question implicit in the book's subtitle.

Marketing has changed us. It has made us more aware of our non-conformity, of our inability to match up to an increasingly exacting template of beauty. How it did that is the central – but not the only – preoccupation of this book.

First, though, I wanted to travel back in time, to meet the figures who formed our ideals of beauty.

It was a longer journey than I had anticipated.

CHASING

CLEOPATRA

'She who doesn't blush by blood blushes by art.'

I finally caught up with Cleopatra at the Louvre. I had stalked her from the Musée Gustave Moreau, where I had hoped she might be hiding. But although the overcrowded walls of the artist's former home were testament to his passion for wilful women – his brush had erotically evoked Bathsheba, Salome and Delilah – his portrait of Cleo was nowhere to be seen.

'We've got the poster,' said the lady at the ticket desk apologetically. 'But the original is at the Louvre.'

A quick call to the museum revealed that the painting was not on show. Almost as if the archivist could see my crestfallen expression at the other end of the line, she added, 'If you like, you can make an appointment to come and see it.'

There are many other representations of Cleopatra in the Louvre, including a François Barois sculpture of the queen writhing voluptuously on a divan after being bitten by the infamous asp. In another wing, we can see Claude Lorrain's *The Disembarkation of Cleopatra at Tarsus* (1643), an event that preceded her seduction of the Roman general Mark Antony. But the Cleopatra in that painting is a diminutive figure, dwarfed by the flotilla of ships heaving at the quayside, the magnificent buildings that tower above her retinue, and the blazing sunset that draws the eye to the horizon.

In Moreau's late-19th-century watercolour, Cleo is the star of the show. And the palatial viewing room at the Prints and Drawings department of the Louvre was an ideal place to make her acquaintance. Marble columns strode into the distance. A fresco swarmed across the distant ceiling. Statues gazed from niches; cherubs smirked from bas-reliefs.

None of them were going to distract me from my rendezvous with the Egyptian monarch.

She was released from a rectangular black box, one of many lining the room's infinity of shelves. For a moment I felt sorry that she was incarcerated here, prisoner number 27900, instead of taking her rightful place alongside Moreau's other femmes fatales. But then, of course, I wouldn't have been granted the privilege of a private audience.

The archivist gingerly placed the watercolour on an easel. Then she wandered off into the hush, allowing me to contemplate it at my leisure.

The Louvre's description of the painting is thus: 'Cleopatra seated, partially nude, in profile on a very high throne.'

Well, yes – but that hardly does the work justice. This is Cleopatra as we've always pictured her: the seductress of legend. She is framed by a brocaded curtain, as if on stage. She half-reclines on the throne, one bare leg coquettishly crooked, the other decorated with a tracery of henna. Her nakedness is emphasized by the sole garment she wears: a wisp of silk secured below her breasts by a jewelled clasp. She also wears a crown and a pearl earring; the queen, as we know, liked to dissolve pearls in wine. Her skin glows white under a full moon. Her expression is melancholy as she gazes towards the distant Sphinx (which was actually buried beneath the sand during her lifetime) and the pyramids. The fact that she is captured in profile allows us to admire her aquiline nose. 'Cleopatra's nose,' wrote Blaise Pascal, of the looks that sapped Antony of strength and competence, 'had it been shorter, the whole face of the world would have been changed.'

In her right hand she holds a lily, although a rapier is well within reach. Her left hand lingers dangerously close to the small serpent that slides insidiously towards it. In the background there are silhouettes of buildings: an obelisk and a ruined temple. The queen looks radiant, but darkness lurks over her shoulder.

Cleopatra has fascinated for centuries. She is perhaps the earliest example of an icon of beauty, a precursor of the smooth-browed goddesses who gaze at us from advertising posters today. Yet despite all the legends about her, only one thing is certain: she existed. Cleopatra VII – the last and most notorious of the line – was born into the Ptolemaic dynasty in 69 BC. They styled themselves pharaohs, but in reality they were Greek; the first Ptolemy had served as a general under Alexander the Great. Cleopatra was more integrated than her forebears, who disdained even to speak Egyptian. A stone tablet in the Louvre, from 51 BC, shows her presenting an offering to the goddess Isis, of whom she claimed to be a reincarnation. Ironically, as was the tradition of the day, the Queen of Egypt is dressed as a man.

This tomboyish avatar raises interesting questions. There is little evidence to suggest that Cleopatra was a great beauty. There is even a vague suspicion that she might have been plain: Roman coins depict her with a hooked nose and a jutting jaw. In her (2010) book *Cleopatra: A Life*, Stacy Schiff adds to the portrait 'full lips, a sharp, prominent chin, a high brow' and 'wide and sunken' eyes. In his *Life of Antony* (AD 75), the Greek historian Plutarch hints that charisma was the true key to her success. 'For her beauty, as we are told, was in itself not altogether incomparable, nor such as to strike those who saw her; but to converse with her had an irresistible charm, and her presence... had something stimulating about it.'

Nor is there any proof that she bathed in ass's milk, even if the beauty industry has been delighted to take that image and run with it. In the 1980s there was a French brand of soap called Cleopatra. An expensive TV commercial showed the queen sweeping into her private baths, accompanied as usual by an entourage of slave girls, musicians and bodyguards with oiled biceps.

Having said that, it is more than likely that Cleopatra had an extensive beauty regime, as did many Egyptian rulers before her.

ANCIENT BEAUTY

First, of course, there was the kohl. This was in fact galena – lead sulphite – ground into a fine powder and mixed with animal fat to give it an adherent quality. 'The fat [was] applied to the face with a small twig or stick, or a stylus of wood, bone, or ivory. In ancient times the stylus had its little case, and stylus and case together made a dainty little "compact",' recounts *Beauty Treatment in Ancient Egypt*, a vintage pamphlet published by the Egyptian State Tourist Department. The treatment was said to ward off flies, protect the eyes from the sun and stimulate the lachrymal gland, promoting constant cleansing. But the way it was applied, elongating the line of the eye, is thought to have been a reference to Horus, the falcon-headed sky god, bringer of light.

The ancient Egyptians believed that not only cleanliness, but also beauty, was next to godliness. According to Dominique Paquet, author of the (1997) book *Miroir, Mon Beau Miroir: Une histoire de la beauté*, the Egyptian ruling classes felt that their ritual cleansing practices brought them closer to the pantheon of the gods and distinguished them from everyday citizens, who carried out far more limited beauty regimes 'separated from any esoteric significance'. Skin tone took on a class connotation, as a woman with fair skin clearly led a very different life to that of the bronzed labourer. This distinction was to remain in place for centuries to come.

When an Egyptian lady of leisure rose in the morning, a languorous routine lay ahead of her. First she took a bath, washing herself with the multi-purpose cleaning agent *netjeri* – or natron, a mineral sourced from dry lake beds – blended with oil to form soap. The Egyptians also used natron in various dilutions to clean their teeth, antisepticize wounds and aid in the mummification process, owing to its antibacterial qualities (it is a mixture of sodium carbonate, sodium bicarbonate and salt).

The bath culminated in an exfoliating treatment using a paste called *souabou*, which contained clay and ash. Next came a massage with perfumed oil.

Egyptians kept themselves fragrant in the heavy summer heat by applying an ointment of turpentine and incense. They also possessed various remedies for pimples, blemishes and even wrinkles. 'For smoothing wrinkles... a compound of powdered alabaster, powdered natron, salt from the north and honey was employed,' writes Pierre Montet in his (1980) guide to *Everyday Life in Egypt in the Days of Ramesses the Great*.

Egyptian women dusted their skin with ochre to give it a lighter, golden hue. As well as lining their eyes with kohl, they painted their eyelids with malachite, turquoise, terra cotta or charcoal. Their eyebrows were plucked and elongated, their lashes darkened. Their lips were reddened with carmine.

Hairstyles varied according to era and occasion. We know that women used metallic headbands and pins of ivory to control their locks. Pierre Montet insists that, in the time of Ramses, hair was cut short and tied into tiny plaits. Other sources suggest that women of the same period shaved their hair and wore perfumed wigs of silk, horsehair or indeed human hair. These hung in tresses or tight curls, augmented with strands of gold. The wealthy affected coronets and diadems of gold, malachite, turquoise, garnet and other precious substances. Jewellery in general was abundant, both for purely decorative purposes and in the form of amulets to ward off evil spirits.

Hands and feet were meticulously cared for: nails were polished or coloured with henna; the latter was probably also used to decorate skin. Wealthy households were equipped with a sophisticated array of grooming tools: combs and tweezers; hooked blades and knives for manicures and pedicures; razors that had evolved from sharpened stones into slivers of bronze. Circular discs of bronze were used as mirrors; copper, silver and gold mirrors have also been found.

Egypt became the hub of a veritable beauty trade. The highly successful ruler Hatshepsut ('Foremost of Noble Ladies'), who reigned from 1479 to 1458 BC, was certainly aware of the importance of fragrances and cosmetics. In the 19th year of her reign, the pharaoh organized a trade mission to the semi-mythical Land of Punt. Already the subject of a folk tale in Hatshepsut's day – a shipwrecked sailor had told of a fertile island ruled by a serpent god – its location has since faded into obscurity: scholars are now at odds about whether it was located in modern Somalia or in Saudi Arabia.

Nevertheless, Hatshepsut's five-ship delegation made it across the Red Sea to Punt and was warmly welcomed. The boats returned laden with myrrh trees, fabled for their pleasing fragrance. Punt became a key trading post on a network set up by Hatshepsut. 'Until the first century, Egypt held a quasi-monopoly on the transformation of raw ingredients,' writes Dominique Paquet.

Like Cleopatra, Hatshepsut would not have viewed fragrances and cosmetics as mere tools of seduction. Beauty was an expression of divinity; perfume and powder were signifiers of status.

GREEK GYMNASIA AND ROMAN BATHS

While the Egyptians had a demonstrable weakness for bling, the Ancient Greeks had a more… Spartan attitude to beauty. There is some irony here, given that the word 'cosmetics' derives from the Greek *kosmetike tekhne*, meaning 'the art of dress and adornment'.

The Greeks believed that beauty lay in natural harmony rather than the application of face paint. Indeed, make-up was banned in Sparta due to its association with courtesans. Tellingly, newly married women were permitted to wear a touch of make-up on their wedding night. This moment of shared pleasure was brief: Ancient Greece was a male-dominated society and from childhood women were exiled to the gynaeceum, a wing of the house reserved specifically for them. Grandmothers, married women, their daughters and female slaves all lived here, outside the mainstream of public life.

But if Greek society had a primitive attitude to sexual equality, it also had a highly developed body consciousness. Beauty, for the Ancient Greeks, was a matter of proportion. Men rigorously sculpted their bodies in gymnasia, even if they allowed themselves the luxury of a massage with perfumed oil afterwards. To judge from representations of Aphrodite, the goddess of love and beauty, the ideal woman had an oval face and an aquiline nose, a rounded yet youthfully firm body and prominent breasts. Her skin was expected to be of a uniform tone and – surprise, surprise – of surpassing pallor.

From the beginning of the 6th century before Christ, make-up techniques from the Orient began to filter into Athens. Women whitened their skin with ceruse – white lead – or powdered chalk, adding blusher in the form of crushed fig or mulberry. Eyelids were painted with saffron; eyebrows were plucked and blackened with kohl. Beauty preparations were passed down from mother to daughter.

Weakened by internal strife, Greece slowly ceded power to Rome. In the declining years of this great civilization, ordinary women felt able to leave their homes and move freely about the streets, so that others might appreciate their beauty.

The Romans themselves were no less stringent in their demands of women. The poet Ovid encouraged ladies to make the best of themselves in the last section of his *Ars Amatoria* (The Art of Love). 'Taking pains brings beauty: beauty neglected dies.' However, he warned women to use make-up discreetly, as any hint of deception might cool a lover's ardour. 'You know how to acquire whiteness with a layer of powder: she who doesn't blush by blood, indeed, blushes by art... It's no shame to highlight your eyes with thinned ashes, or saffron... Still, don't let your lover find cosmetic bottles on your dressing table: art delights in its hidden face.'

Some believe that Ovid's words were aimed at courtesans, but it is no secret that Romans took great pride in their appearance. Though the baths played a social function, they responded to a desire to be not only clean but also attractive. Fashionable Roman women were scrubbed, plucked and strapped into sylph-like visions of loveliness. Like the Greeks, they whitened their skin with ceruse, despite the knowledge that long-term use damaged the skin, blackened the teeth and played havoc with the nervous system, leading quite literally to a deathly pallor.

DARKNESS INTO LIGHT

Women of the Dark Ages did not lose this desire to lighten their skin, no matter what the cost. Paintings depict the futility of vanity – skin that was once pale and youthful dissolving like a movie special effect into a hideous vision of cratered flesh and sparse hair – but the seeming metaphor is a realistic depiction of the ravages of lead poisoning.

Neither did the rise of Christianity ease the pressure on women to conform to a certain vision of beauty. Now they were exhorted to appear pure and virginal, forever young. This new woman had small high breasts, long hair and a prominent belly – a symbol of fertility. She was torn between puritanical demands that she appear 'natural' and the knowledge that beauty treatments from the Orient would enable her to live up to unrealistic interpretations of that ideal.

In the medieval allegory *The Romance of the Rose*, begun around 1230 by Guillaume de Lorris, a 'lovely and beautiful maiden' is described. 'Her hair shone fair as a burnished bowl, her flesh was more tender than a young chick's, her forehead radiant and her brows arched… her eyes as bright as a falcon's.' To these advantages are added 'a pink and white face', a 'full-lipped mouth' and a 'dimpled chin'. Lorris informs us twice that her neck is long, soft and pale, while her skin is happily 'free from spots or sores'. And in case we still haven't got the picture, he concludes that 'her throat was as white as snow freshly fallen on the branch, her body well formed and slender'. As if to sum up the moral tug of war that such fantasies provoked in medieval men, Lorris then informs us that the name of the rose is 'Idleness'.

This suggests that beauty treatments were the preserve of the wealthy and indolent. Nevertheless, a canon emerged. Eyebrows were plucked and dyed. A high forehead was a sign of breeding and intellect, so it became an unlikely erogenous zone. Women plucked and shaved their hairlines to achieve the effect. They used orpiment (arsenic trisulphide) to keep unwanted hair at bay. Sheer headscarves or decorative headbands drew attention to this desirable feature. Remaining hair was worn long and occasionally braided, ornamented with strands of gold and pearls. Yet the demands of modesty meant that married women covered their hair with scarves or bonnets: medieval beauty was a mass of contradictions.

As Dominique Paquet observes, the invention of the printing press in the 15th century enabled the wider diffusion of beauty remedies. One of the most influential documenters of such knowledge was Caterina Sforza, Countess of Forlì, a powerful Renaissance noblewoman who dabbled in alchemy. Between 1492 and 1509 she wrote *Gli Experimenti*, a veritable beauty manual for Renaissance women. They were urged to boil snakeskin in wine to regenerate their complexions, while an infusion of snails and mallow was said to aid hair growth. To lighten the hair, ingredients such as saffron, sulphur and cinnabar were mixed into a dye. Volume 2 of *The Greenwood Encyclopaedia of Clothing through World History* (edited by Jill Condra in 2008) adds that she 'concocted several different "beauty waters" to brighten the complexion and remove freckles'. Sforza may have felt that dispensing this wisdom consolidated her image as a woman to be reckoned with, a conservator of arcane practices that were close to witchcraft.

The same source notes the existence of several similar manuscripts, such as the *Secreti* by Isabella Cortese, published in Venice in 1584. This proposes recipes 'using ingredients that nowadays appear mysterious, if not scary'. For example, Cortese claimed to have discovered, during her travels in Eastern Europe, a concoction that could remove facial spots and provide the complexion of a 15-year-old. 'To whiten the face, it was recommended that a woman mix rosewater, rock salt, cinnamon, powdered lily bulbs, egg white and milk'; alternatively, she could try 'lemon juice, white wine, breadcrumbs and nutmeg'.

Light, clarity, the life-giving rays of the sun: as in many previous cultures, these were associated with the light of God. Thanks to its associations with youth and divinity – as well as its rarity – blonde hair was deeply desirable. To achieve it, Venetian women would soak their locks in a mixture of lemon juice, ammonia and urine, and then sit on their terraces with their hair arrayed over the wide brims of crownless straw hats (which also prevented their skins from becoming tanned). Such is the doubtful provenance of the Venetian blonde.

From the writings of Sforza and Cortese, it becomes clear that Renaissance beauty was a dangerous blend of science and sorcery.

CORSETS AND CRINOLINES

Death by lead poisoning was the ultimate price to pay for beauty, but discomfort was the very least women could expect to suffer. This was heightened from the 16th century by the adoption of the corset, which enhanced the bust and suppressed the waist. Even before adolescence, girls were fastened into contraptions of iron or whalebone, which squeezed their ribs to such an extent that deformity and organ damage were not uncommon. Freakishly exaggerated busts and tiny waists were combined with increasingly voluminous skirts that entirely concealed the lower part of the body.

For Georges Vigarello, author of *Histoire de la Beauté* (2004), this development reflected the fact that aesthetic ideals of beauty derived from the contemplation of sculptures and portraits. The face, shoulders and bust were exalted, while everything below the waist was hidden, as if the skirts formed a decorative pedestal on which the bust rested. In addition, the hierarchy of the body conformed to the order of the universe: the head was closer to heaven; the feet rested on earth.

The application of make-up also acknowledged the influence of art: white cheeks lightly daubed with rouge gave the angelic appearance of a cherub in a Renaissance fresco. The fashionable – and here we are also talking about men – wanted to ensure that they remained elevated from the filth and savagery of nature; hence artifice was pushed to extremes. White lead now powdered the faces of both sexes, and was accompanied by powdered wigs. Women who strolled in the Jardin des Tuileries in 17th-century Paris protected their complexions from the sun with Venetian-style masks. Blemishes were concealed with false beauty spots – known as 'mouches', or 'flies' – that became popular fashion accessories across Europe.

In the 18th century the passion for paleness momentarily declined, only to be replaced by a rage for rouge among the aristocracy of France and Regency England. This masked the weariness provoked by endless balls and nights at the gaming tables, as well as mimicking a state of sexual excitement. According to figures unearthed by Dominique Paquet, more than two million pots of rouge were sold in France in 1781, including the version used by Marie Antoinette, which was made by 'Sieur Dubuisson' of the rue des Ciseaux.

The French Revolution robbed the aristocrats of their wigs – and more besides – and provoked a return to 'natural' beauty. Clothing regained an almost Grecian simplicity. This inevitably put paleness back on the agenda; but now it evolved into a moody and Romantic pallor, as if fashionable women had been struck simultaneously by a mysterious malady. In order to achieve the effect, writes Paquet, 'Women drank but vinegar, ate but lemons and read late into the night to provoke dark circles under their eyes.' They were the heroines of Gothic novels – Ann Radcliffe's *Mysteries of Udolpho*, or *The Monk* by Matthew Gregory Lewis.

Towards the middle of the 19th century, however, another type of woman emerged – one who began to infringe on the territory of men for the first time. In Paris she was known as 'La Lionne'. She rode and fenced, swam and read the newspapers. She was a forerunner of the Gibson Girl, an American archetype created in the 1890s by the illustrator Charles Dana Gibson: tall, slender, athletic, yet a paragon of beauty, with eyes glowing from beneath sensuous lashes and masses of hair piled with artful nonchalance on her head.

Like Gibson's creation, La Lionne was a largely fictional figure. In reality, women were expected to be more decorative than ever: their curves exaggerated by the corsets that crushed their waists, their legs invisible under swirling crinolines. Tomorrow was still another day.

THE KINGDOM OF ROUGE

Rouge was deployed with more subtlety than it had been a century earlier, but once again it was highly fashionable. In 1894, the English satirist Max Beerbohm wrote an essay called 'A defence of cosmetics', in which he hints at a growing democratization of beauty. '[T]he use of pigments is becoming general, and most women are not so young as they are painted,' he reports, cruelly. Earlier in the piece he notes:

> No longer is a lady of fashion to be blamed if, to escape the outrageous persecution of time, she fly for sanctuary to the toilet table... [It is] no wonder that within the last five years the trade of the makers of cosmetics has increased immoderately – twenty-fold, so one of these makers has told me. We need but walk down any modish street and peer into the little broughams that flit pass or... under the bonnet of any woman we meet, to see over how wide a kingdom rouge reigns.

Back in Paris, too, the democratization of beauty had progressed apace. In 1830, according to Vigarello, the pots of rouge offered by the Reine des

Fleurs boutique in rue Saint Martin ranged in price from 5 francs to 85 francs, while the average workman earned less than 3 francs a day. By 1851, however, an advertisement by a cosmetics company named A Schoelcher promised products for 'every class of society', including pink or white powder at 1 franc a pot (or 60 centimes for a half-pot).

Skin creams were also more widely available. In his (2010) book *Beauty Imagined: A history of the global beauty industry*, Geoffrey Jones writes:

> There was a small luxury trade for most of the 19th century. This market consisted largely of two types of products sold by perfumers: 'milks', or emulsions intended to freshen and clean the face, made by crushing the seeds of plants, such as roses, and mixing with water; and 'cold creams', made from mixing fats with water and used to smooth skin.

These competed, of course, with domestic creams 'whose ingredients were passed down from generation to generation like kitchen recipes'.

By the turn of the century, the fabrication of 'beauty products' was evolving into an industry. One young woman, in particular, symbolized this transition. Chaja, to use her original name, had been born in 1870 in Krakow, Poland, where her father was a shopkeeper. Although she initially wished to study medicine, she came under increasing pressure from her parents to marry a wealthy local widower. To escape this fate she travelled to Australia, where her uncle Bernhard kept a store in the remote outpost of Coleraine, Western Victoria.

The local ladies, whose skins had been reddened by sun and roughened by dust, were entranced by Chaja's pale, unblemished complexion. She ascribed it to a Polish face cream made by a certain Dr Jacob Lykusky and promised to write home for supplies. She soon began selling the product under the brand name Crème Valaze. In no time, she had a thriving business and a small salon in Melbourne.

By then she had Westernized her first name, creating what was to become a global brand: Helena Rubinstein.

BEAUTY TIPS

* Ancient Egyptian beauty regimes derived from religious rituals.

* The use of cosmetics became an expression of status.

* Pale skin has been associated with beauty for millennia.

* Thanks to the printing press, texts written by powerful Renaissance women became early beauty manuals.

* Beauty began to democratize in the late 19th century, driven by advertising and the widening circulation of magazines.

* Once home-made or artisanal, industrially manufactured beauty products began appearing in boutiques and salons.

* The scene was set for the creation of the first global beauty brands.

THE GLAMOUR
PROFESSIONALS

'Some women won't buy anything unless they can pay a lot.'

When Helena Rubinstein stepped off a cruise ship in New York in the winter of 1914, she saw opportunity all around her. 'It was a cold day,' she recalled. 'All the American women had purple noses and grey lips, and their faces were chalk white from terrible powder. I recognized that the US could be my life's work.'

The quote resurfaced in *Time* magazine's obituary of 'Madame' Rubinstein, as she styled herself, on 9 April 1965. She had died nine days earlier, leaving behind a US$60 million beauty empire. It was founded not just on pots of cream, but also on brilliant, ground-breaking marketing.

Back in Australia, Rubinstein had given her first product, Crème Valaze, a name that evoked Paris, the eternal symbol of luxury and sophistication. But she had also wound her Central European origins into the tale, advertising that the cream's recipe included 'rare herbs from the Carpathian mountains'.

Along with her assertion that the lotion had been invented by Doctor Lykusky in Krakow, recent probes into her life – notably Lindy Woodhead's excellent 2003 book *War Paint* – have cast serious doubt on this claim. While she may have arrived in Coleraine clutching a few pots of cream, these would not have lasted long, and in the early years she did not have enough capital to ship crates of product from her homeland. Similarly, research has failed to turn up any trace of a Dr Jacob Lykusky operating in Krakow at the time. It is far more likely that Rubinstein created the cream herself. A key ingredient lay close at hand: lanolin, or wool grease, a natural moisturizer secreted by the sebaceous glands of sheep. Helena devised her own formula, disguising the unpleasant odour with lavender.

One might ask where a young woman from Krakow acquired such skills. But Rubinstein was a natural networker, and she met a number of influential figures thanks to the childminding posts she was obliged to take up when she fled Coleraine for the more desirable Melbourne. One of her acquaintances was a Mr Frederick Sheppard Grimwade, of pharmaceutical manufacturers and distributors Felton, Grimwade & Co.

Lindy Woodhead proposes Grimwade as the mentor who showed Rubinstein how to formulate her cream, and specifically how to distil a crucial ingredient from Australian pine bark. Often sold under the brand name Pycnogenol, pine bark extract is a flavonoid – an antioxidant. Writes Woodhead: 'Flavonoids work to repair the connective tissue and boost the immune system – thus to slow the ageing process visible in the face by "plumping out" collagen and improving the overall appearance of the skin.'

Crème Valaze, then, was lanolin, soft paraffin, distilled water and pine bark extract. Here's how Rubinstein advertised it in 1903: 'VALAZE BY DR LYKUSKY, the most celebrated European Skin Specialist, is the best nourisher of the skin. VALAZE will improve the worst of skin in one month… Available from Helena Rubinstein & Company, 138 Elizabeth Street.'

It's amusing to note that Dr Lykusky later mysteriously disappeared from ads for Valaze. Rubinstein herself assumed his role, positioning herself as beauty scientist forever toiling to invent products that would help women hold back the years.

Rubinstein's real life was so tangled in mythology that it's often difficult to separate the two. For example, she once claimed that her first backers were a wealthy couple she met on a cruise ship, and that they provided the funding that enabled her to open a salon. But other sources suggest that her starting capital came from a successful tea merchant named John T Thompson, an 'admirer' she'd met while waitressing at the Winter Garden tea room in Melbourne.

Thompson was a brilliant salesman, whose Robur Tea Company had a hefty advertising budget. He helped Rubinstein perfect her advertising copy and promotional tricks, at which she became an absolute expert. For example, she quickly understood that, if she spent heavily on advertising, she could expect – or demand – reciprocal editorial coverage. Hence, glowing press reports about Helena and her cream began to appear almost as soon as her salon opened its doors.

Most beauty specialists agree that they are in the anti-ageing game, but Helena was one of the first to bluntly – some might say cynically – exploit this paranoia. *War Paint* cites a 1904 ad headlined 'BEAUTY IS POWER'. It promises that 'Dr Lykusky's celebrated Valaze Skin Food makes a poor complexion good and good skin beautiful... Valaze gives the skin the soft, clear, transparent appearance of a little child.'

Woodhead writes: 'Helena was always one step ahead in offering something new. She was the first beauty specialist to classify skin as "dry", "normal" and "oily"... The single pot of Valaze was the first of a whole raft of treatment creams the beauty-conscious – and presumably now terrified – consumer had to purchase.' Almost for the first time, women began to feel that their skin conditions – wrinkles, blemishes or shininess – were an indication that something was wrong 'and that buying creams would put it right'.

Within two years, the success of Crème Valaze had enabled Rubinstein to move from her small salon in Melbourne's Elizabeth Street to swanky new premises in the more fashionable Collins Street. One of her customers was an opera singer named Nellie Melba, who apparently liked to belt out *Aida* in the salon. The diminutive Helena – who was only 4 feet 10 inches tall – had to stand on a stool in order to scrutinize the statuesque diva's complexion.

Later, after an inspiring trip to Europe, Rubinstein kitted out her salon with little gilt chairs in the manner of a Paris couture house. Donning a white lab coat, she renamed her establishment the 'Institute Valaze' and offered an 'operating theatre' that treated dry skin, wrinkles, blemishes and unwanted hair. Facials, depilation and massages were all available. The treatments were conducted by 'two Viennese specialists'. These were, in fact, Helena's sister Ceska and her cousin Lola, whom she had brought over from Poland to join her flourishing business. Thus, Rubinstein combined the key ingredients of modern beauty marketing: glossy packaging, celebrity endorsement and pseudo-science.

But she never made the mistake of believing her own publicity. 'I am a merchant,' she stated. And she kept prices high. 'Some women won't buy anything unless they can pay a lot.'

Even Australia was too small for an ambition like Rubinstein's, and in 1908 she set sail for Europe. She established 'Helena Rubinstein's Salon de Beauté Valaze' in London's Mayfair. A Paris branch soon followed. Around this time, she married a Polish-American journalist named Edward William Titus, who further polished her advertising copy as well as encouraging her interest in art and the theatre. Now she added another ingredient to the marketing mix: culture. The decor of her salons began to resemble sets for Diaghilev's Ballets Russes, ensuring that her well-heeled clients felt at ease. Over the following years she became a prominent art collector. So began her transformation from Australian upstart to the Madame Rubinstein of legend.

It was probably Titus who suggested to Helena that, when she opened her European salons, she should offer free treatments to a selected number of aristocrats and socialites. This would stimulate word of mouth while creating the required upmarket image for her establishment.

An enthusiastic womanizer, Titus later separated from Helena, but he remained a consultant to her company and a valuable link to the bohemian fringe of Parisian society, which he had entered thanks to his growing publishing business. Rubinstein and her estranged husband were well aware of the influence of art on trends in fashion and beauty.

The war in Europe persuaded Rubinstein to expand her operations to North America. A New York salon in 1915 was followed by outlets in San Francisco, Boston, Philadelphia, Chicago and Toronto. She became one of the first cosmetics manufacturers to place her brand in department stores; but she insisted on training her own sales staff and advising on the setting in which her products would be sold.

'The hawk-eyed Helena personally vetted each store, insisting that each one carrying her line not only put up the cash for a hefty minimum order, but sent sales staff back to New York for intensive training,' writes Woodhead. 'She also insisted on prominent, branded counter-space, provided smart uniforms for sales staff, and backed each store with initial local advertising.'

'Face painting' was looked down upon in the early years of the 20th century, as it had once again become associated with women of dubious morals. This began to change with the rise of Hollywood, which successfully translated sex appeal into glamour. Rubinstein soon added make-up to her range of creams, starting with tinted face powders and then expanding into lipsticks and the first waterproof mascara. But skincare remained her primary concern. Throughout her life she warned her customers about the dangers of sunshine, and promoted sunscreen even when tans were at their most fashionable.

Rubinstein seemed invincible. She beat the Wall Street Crash by briefly selling the American arm of her business to Lehman Brothers in 1928 and then buying it back when the share price fell from 60 dollars to just 3. Following her divorce from Titus, in 1937 she married the Russian émigré Prince Artchil Gourielli-Tchkonia. As if to support her claims that a woman over the age of 35 could still be seductive, he was 20 years her junior. Madame outlived him by 10 years.

Even when her health declined, Rubinstein continued running her business from her bed. She died in New York City at the age of 94, perhaps comforted at the end by the knowledge that sales of her products had increased by 500 per cent since the Second World War.

Yet her work in the United States had been marked by an intense rivalry with another brand: Elizabeth Arden.

BEAUTY TRANSFORMED

In just over two decades, from the turn of the century to the years after the Great War, the image of women changed dramatically. Although the Gibson Girl was a fantasy figure, women genuinely became more active. Sea bathing had been rising in popularity since 1753, when Dr Charles Russell published

The Uses of Sea Water, insisting that it could be as salubrious as taking spa waters. Swimming costumes evolved from cumbersome all-concealing garments to svelte one-pieces, which were considered acceptable by the end of the 1900s. Georges Vigarello notes that gymnastics classes became obligatory in schools in many European countries and several American states from 1880.

The revelation and acceptance of the body were encouraged by the industrial fabrication of full-length mirrors, which were produced in ever-greater numbers throughout the late 19th century, becoming a fixture of fashionable bedrooms. In addition, corsets and crinolines began to feel distinctly cage-like at a time when women in many countries were demanding the right to vote. Couturiers, always skilled at spotting trends, refined the female silhouette: dresses designed by Paul Poiret followed the natural line of the body; under Gabrielle 'Coco' Chanel they became short and definitively liberating.

Chanel had started out as a milliner, establishing a small Paris hat shop in 1909 with the backing of her wealthy lover, a rakish Englishman named Boy Capel. The pair vacationed in Deauville and Biarritz, where Chanel found inspiration as well as a target market. Soon she had opened a boutique in Deauville selling resort wear inspired by Boy's polo outfits and yachting apparel. This unfussy clothing took on a new utility during the war years, when women required freedom of movement as they adopted roles previously held by men, now at the front. Cheap material like jersey, which would have fallen from the contemptuous fingers of more snobbish designers, worked perfectly for Chanel's pared-down designs. By the time the Great War was over, she had practically rewritten women's dress codes.

The Chanel-clad woman of the 1920s was long-limbed, bob-haired and toned from swimming, riding and tennis. She was also, for the first time, sun-tanned. Leisure was no longer equated with domesticity: the wealthy flocked to the coast. Women's bodies were out in the open.

The emergence of a more liberated form of femininity coincided with a media revolution akin to the rise of the internet in the early 21st century. Magazines and newspapers were becoming ever cheaper and more plentiful. In fashion publications and advertising, illustration was making way for photography, transforming hairdressers and make-up artists into stars. Commercial radio broadcasts began in the United States in 1922, adding to the clamour of voices that were calling out to consumers.

Creams that had begun life as pharmaceutical products were now the vectors of a new language of self-improvement and aspiration. A classic example was that of Theron T Pond, a New York pharmacist who had developed a range of creams, soaps and balms containing witch hazel, which soothed irritated skin. He began working with the great New York advertising agency J Walter Thompson at the end of the 19th century. In 1916, when the agency's founder – known as 'The Commodore' thanks to his naval background and trim beard – retired owing to ill-health, it was taken over by his protégé, Stanley Resor. Working closely with Resor was his wife, Helen Lansdowne Resor, a brilliant copywriter who brought her sharp wordplay and consumer insights to many beauty products.

When she was handed the accounts for Pond's Vanishing Cream and Pond's Cold Cream, she sought endorsements from celebrities, socialites, even the Queen of Romania. Skin creams emerged from the chemist and took on the allure of luxury goods.

This was the period in which Elizabeth Arden carved out her name.

THE ARDEN TOUCH

In fact it was more of a brand than a name: she was born Florence Nightingale Graham in 1881 and grew up on a farm not far from Toronto. As with the biography of Helena Rubinstein, the dissembling and misdirection begin from that moment on: both women retrofitted their lives with elegant features that sat better with the images they had created for themselves. For instance, it has been suggested that Florence's father, William Graham, was a British jockey. But he met and married her mother, Susan, in Canada. And whatever he'd done before, at that time he was a door-to-door salesman.

Florence certainly came from a rural background and maintained a lifelong love of horses, as well as a somewhat outdoorsy image that contrasted with Helena Rubinstein's jewel-heavy cosmopolitanism. But her childhood sounds awful: her mother died of TB when she was very young, and her father struggled to support the large family of four girls and a boy. Florence shivered in the cold, fretted about her health and escaped into romantic novels, gossip magazines and 'nickelodeons': early cinemas showing short films accompanied by a tinny piano or melodramatic organ. Primitive these entertainments might have been, but they set her dreaming of better things. It's notable that many people in the glamour profession come from modest backgrounds. They dream – and they sell their dreams to us.

A college education was not on the cards given the parlous state of the family's finances. Like Rubinstein, and perhaps inspired by her namesake, Florence initially tried her hand at nursing – but she appears not to have had the stomach for it. Her ears still ringing with the piano of the nickelodeon, she was inevitably drawn to New York, with its notionally gold-paved streets. Finally, in 1907, we find her sitting behind the cash register at Eleanor Adair's beauty salon on Fifth Avenue.

Mrs Adair specialized not so much in skincare as in skin manipulation. She was an advocate of 'strapping', a technique that involved artificially lifting the skin with rubber straps or braces, attached under the chin and across the forehead, which if left in place for a certain period would smooth out wrinkles – until it was time for the next treatment, of course. Adair's advertisements from the mid-1900s promised to 'restore youthful beauty' with chin straps that 'remove double chin and restore lost contour' and forehead straps that cure 'deep lines between brows, corners of eyes and over forehead'. The salon also offered electrolysis for 'superfluous hair' and facial massages that restored 'lined, withered skins to velvety smoothness'.

Supporting all this was a range of creams and oils marketed under the brand name Ganesh: Adair attributed their efficacy to Indian beauty secrets that she'd picked up on her travels. One product, Ganesh Diable Skin Tonic, appears to have had the dual aim of evoking Eastern exoticism *and* French sophistication.

Florence Graham learned a great deal from Adair: we see traces of her apprenticeship in her enthusiasm for massage, her early adoption of yoga and her gift for the emotionally charged language of beauty advertising.

The next rung on the ladder was a partnership with one Elizabeth Hubbard, who had created a small range of skincare creams. Possibly they met at Adair's salon. In any case, Florence set to work deploying some of the strategies she had picked up from her previous employer. The creams had an exotic name – Grecian – attractive packaging and advertising aimed squarely at the premium market, as was the pair's salon on Fifth Avenue. For unknown reasons, the partnership fell apart after six months, but Florence kept the salon. ('The landlord preferred me,' she explained cheekily.

The scene was now set for her transformation. She took the name Elizabeth – still visible in gold lettering outside the salon – and completed it with Arden. This is sometimes held to be a reference to Tennyson's poem *Enoch Arden*, but it is more likely to have been inspired by an article about the recent death of a prominent railroad baron and racehorse owner, who called his country estate 'Arden'. That kind of scene was very much to the newly minted Elizabeth Arden's taste.

Her name would soon join that of Helena Rubinstein on the list of the earliest global beauty brands.

Tinkering with the line she'd created with Hubbard, she launched a new product range called Venetian, paying particular attention to the gold, white and pink packaging. Over the years packaging proved to be her particular forte – she was more skilled at it than Helena Rubinstein – although she could also turn a beguiling phrase. She renamed her salon the 'Salon d'Oro', which lent it the requisite European touch, and advertised that its 'spirit of youth is so all-pervading that you cannot leave without catching some of it'. The salon featured a lustrous red door that was to become an integral part of the brand's identity.

Arden entered the beauty business at exactly the right moment. The idea that cosmetics were somehow 'sinful' was beginning to seem outmoded – or, worse, oppressive. Elizabeth noted that, during a suffrage march in New York on 6 May 1912, the women wore bright red lipstick as a symbol of liberty. That same year, during a fact-finding tour of Europe, she saw beautifully made-up women on the streets of Paris. Very soon, the former devotee of the nickelodeon was drawn to the silvery light of the cinema screen, where actresses in full make-up were the new embodiments of sophistication. 'Face paint' was becoming desirable again. Like Rubinstein, Arden used her socially acceptable skin creams as outriders for a full range of beauty products.

Three men aided her ascension. The first was A Fabian Swanson, who worked at the pharmaceutical supplier Stillwell & Gladding – until Arden lured him away to become her personal product formulator. Swanson devised the formula for one of her first hits, a light and fluffy face cream called Venetian Cream Amoretta. To this faintly risible name was added the patently false advertising claim that the product had been devised 'from a famous French formula'.

Arden began to suspect that consumers would buy into almost any hokum in the quest for beauty. Lindy Woodhead points out that Mr Swanson's next concoction – a gentle astringent called Ardena Skin Tonic – sold at 85 cents a bottle when it cost only 5 cents to make, including the bottle and the label.

The biggest cost centre for the Arden organization was, of course, advertising. In the early 1920s the Elizabeth Arden account was awarded to the Blaker Agency, run by the appropriately named Henry Sell, a former journalist who had edited *Harper's Bazaar*. Copywriters, art directors and even agencies came and went, but over the years Sell remained Arden's favourite adman. The 1938 Food, Drug, and Cosmetic Act put a break on some of their most outrageous claims; but mostly they worked around it, with luxurious product pamphlets sent by request to loyal customers, and lifestyle advertising that evoked a world of privilege and romance.

Arden's husband, Tommy Lewis, a former salesman she'd met on a cruise ship during one of her voyages to Europe, was a third and vital pillar of her growing empire. He ran the firm's wholesale division, recruiting agents around the world and deciding which department stores were in line with the brand's premium image. Elizabeth herself did her bit, travelling to stores with a posse of pink ribbon-adorned 'treatment girls' for week-long promotional appearances.

Meanwhile, the unmistakable red doors of her salons had begun opening all over the world: by the late 1930s the Elizabeth Arden brand was as global as Coca-Cola. Keeping prices high and refusing to dilute her luxury positioning enabled her to ride out the Depression. Mr Swanson helped by devising one of her most successful products, still popular today – a skin-repairing emollient called Eight Hour Cream. Despite the legend, it is unlikely that Arden ever rubbed the cream into the bruised legs of the racehorses she had begun to invest in.

Arden's wealth enabled her to fulfil her youthful dreams by acquiring several countryside properties, including a horse ranch in Kentucky and a beautiful summer home in Maine. In 1934, the latter was opened to the public in the new guise of a health resort called Maine Chance. It combined beauty and massage treatments with diet and exercise regimes – fencing, riding and tennis were among the activities available. Naturally, formal dress was required at dinner.

This unusual mixture of the sporty and the sophisticated stood Elizabeth in good stead throughout her career. She loved the world of horses and racing, but was equally drawn to the urban sophistication of Hollywood. She provided cosmetics to movie studios and ran a 20-minute cinema advertisement, called 'Young and beautiful', in 1940. She was a perceptive manipulator of the media and did not hesitate to send free gifts to beauty journalists. She also knew exactly how to expand her brand, launching a 'couture lingerie' collection that was not quite a line of underwear, but rather a range of vaporous garments, metaphorically located somewhere between boudoir and dressing room, that women could waft around in looking divine.

By the 1950s, the use of make-up was free of any lingering suggestion of impropriety – indeed, the world of cosmetics had grown into a vast, international and highly competitive industry. Accusations of copying, industrial espionage and even wire-tapping began to surface. Right up until their deaths in 1966, a few months apart from one another, Helena Rubinstein and Elizabeth Arden remained fierce rivals, despite the fact that they never actually met.

Between them, Rubinstein and Arden unquestionably laid the foundations of the modern beauty business. As personalities they are hard to like: snobbish, vain and manipulative, regularly stooping to barefaced lies to sell their products, the proceeds of which made them two of the richest businesswomen the world has ever seen. On the one hand, their products pleased, pampered and, yes, beautified millions of women. On the other, their advertising copy contrived to persuade their customers that ageing was not only undesirable, but somehow shameful. They were both admirable and detestable in equal measure.

Like many sworn enemies, they had much in common. For example, they loathed Charles Revson, the creator of Revlon.

BEAUTY TIPS

✳ Helena Rubinstein created the first global beauty brand.

✳ She used extravagant storytelling to convince women that signs of ageing were shameful – but could be slowed.

✳ Her advertising and her clinics potently combined science with well-being and aspiration.

✳ Founded in Australia, her business was built on local materials and an idealized 'European' sophistication.

✳ A dreamer from a humble background, Elizabeth Arden cast a spell of luxury and romance with her packaging, salons and advertising.

✳ Like Rubinstein, she carefully monitored which department stores stocked her goods and the way they were displayed and sold.

✳ Both women found that high prices did not deter consumers – merely convinced them that the products were worth having.

✳ They forged relationships with fashion and beauty journalists that bordered on bribery.

✳ Their talent for making millions by exacerbating women's fear of ageing laid the foundations of today's beauty business.

OUT COME

THE TALONS

'A little immoral support.'

In the early 1930s, a young salesman began doing the rounds of New York beauty salons. He was fairly good-looking, but would have been otherwise unremarkable were it not for one thing: he wore nail varnish. Not only that, but he wore a different colour on each nail. It became his greatest sales gimmick: he would walk into a salon, nails aglitter with a rainbow of colours, and proceed to charm everyone around him, particularly the ladies.

While Helena Rubinstein and Elizabeth Arden made their fortunes from women's faces, Charles Revson started lower down. He founded Revlon Nail Enamel in 1932 with his brother Joseph and the chemist Charles Lachman, the L in the company name. They'd developed a new manufacturing process that used pigments instead of dyes, allowing for opacity, staying power and a wide range of vivid colours.

Revson had not produced this expertise out of thin air. He'd been working as a salesman for a cosmetics company called Elka, where he had hoped to rise to position of national distributor. When this promotion was denied him, he went into business on his own, bringing with him a chemist and the germ of an idea.

Toughness and determination had been bred into Revson. The website of the Charles H Revson Foundation states that he was born in Boston in 1906 and raised in New Hampshire. Once again, it seems likely that the story was varnished. Several online sources suggest that Revson was born in Montreal, Quebec, and that his family emigrated to the United States a little later. But this is a detail: in the lively (1976) book *Fire and Ice: The story of Charles Revson, the man who built the Revlon empire*, author Andrew Tobias writes that Revson grew up with his two brothers in a cold-water tenement in Manchester, New Hampshire. His father was a cigar roller and his mother a saleswoman – later a 'supervisor' – in a local dry goods store. 'They virtually never entertained, virtually never went out to eat… and had no telephone. (Or radio or gramophone.)' The boys trudged two miles to school every morning.

Revson's mother urged him – pushed him, even – to do better than his parents. He grew up streetwise, a natural talker. The family wanted him to be a lawyer, but he had a gift for sales. When he moved to New York, he got a job at the Pickwick Dress Company, run by a cousin. And there he began to display another, less expected talent – for colour. Writes Tobias: 'By the time he left Pickwick he had worked his way up to being a piece-goods buyer, a job he preferred because it gave him the opportunity to work with materials and colours. He supposedly became proficient in differentiating between shades of black, which demands a sensitive eye.'

After a couple of unfortunate adventures – including a short-lived marriage to a showgirl – Revson ended up at Elka. So here he was, this fast-talking character from a poor background making his way in the business of beauty. Although Elka was a small firm in Newark that 'did not have a great deal of class', Revson noted that its opaque cream enamel was superior to other varnishes on the market, which were transparent. As he delivered Elka varnishes to beauty salons around the city, he paid attention to what customers said – their likes and dislikes, their needs and desires. And he would try the varnish on his own nails. He said so himself, in a 1949 interview: 'I learned how to put it on for demonstration – still can. To this day, I try colours on myself. When you gotta learn, you gotta learn.'

When Elka refused to hand Revson the national distribution post, he got in touch with a business contact, Charles Lachman, who had married into a large chemical company called Dresden. Revson needed financial backing as well as Lachman's technical expertise. Lachman came on board, bringing with him a nail enamel formula developed at Dresden. Revlon Nail Enamels set up shop in 'a few feet of space in a cousin's lamp factory at 38 West 21 Street'.

Revson was only 25. With nail varnish, he painted a future brighter than his mother's most spectacular dreams.

Revlon Nail Enamel began selling its tough, colourful varnishes to beauty salon distributors, department stores and upmarket drugstores. Revson was particularly keen on department store beauty salons: if a woman had her nails painted with Revlon during a beauty treatment, she'd buy the same shade before she left. He was also careful to position Revlon as a premium brand. This was partly because – at least once the company had grown – the consumer was paying for Revlon's sophisticated advertising campaigns. On average, the cost of making a Revlon product – including packaging and overheads – was about 33 per cent of what the consumer actually paid for it. But, like Rubinstein and Arden, Revson understood that women did not associate glamour with low prices. The hefty price tag, the lush advertising, the glossy packaging – these were all part of the beauty experience.

According to Geoffrey Jones, the company had secured 80 per cent of the American nail varnish market by 1940. At that point Elizabeth Arden had not even entered the category, which she still considered morally dubious, suitable only for temptresses and worse. Revlon now offered a full manicure range and swiftly moved into selling lipstick.

How did Revlon get so far so fast? One of the keys, purely and simply, was the hard sell. Revson was the consummate deal closer. Tobias quotes a former associate:

Charles personally went out and did the selling... personally got the distribution, personally slept with half the girls around the country to get counter space for Revlon. He was very human, very charming, very witty, smoked three packs of cigarettes a day, and drank bourbon neat. His charisma is what built Revlon – and the rest of the industry as well.

While this makes Revson sound like one of the cast of *Mad Men*, it at least demonstrates the benefit of the personal touch. He criss-crossed the country, visiting salons and beauty shows. In a 1950 article in the advertising journal *Printer's Ink*, Revson recalled an incident at the Midwest Beauty Show in 1934, held at the Sherman Hotel in Chicago:

> I started my sales talk by showing the prospect how to apply our cream nail polish, then a new type. Before the week was out, I was teaching beauty shop operators and clerks how to demonstrate and use the polish. That group grew so big I had to rent the booth next to ours, and that additional space made my exhibit larger than our entire plant.

The incident resulted in a huge order from the Chicago department store Marshall Field's. The company barely had enough stock to cover it.

Revson's younger brother Martin joined the company as its sales manager in 1935. While he proved an equally gifted salesman, his greatest contribution was the recruitment of a nationwide sales force. They were driven hard. One of Martin's innovations was what he called 'Psycho-Revlons': role-playing sessions in which his salesmen would demonstrate their techniques, only to have their performance taken apart by their boss. Tobias confirms: 'It was an aggressive sales force; slackers were not tolerated. The pressure from the top came right down through the ranks to the salesman. One district sales manager required a lagging salesman to call in every two hours to report on his progress until his performance improved.'

Revlon was built not just on aggressive sales, but on after-sales too. Charles Revson bowed down to nobody – except his customers. 'They are the real boss,' he would say. In the early days he would wear nail varnish and lipstick to bed to see how it looked the next morning; later he set up sophisticated quality-control facilities.

He prided himself on being available for customers. According to Tobias in *Fire and Ice*, an advertising agency once tested this claim by getting a secretary to ring Revlon and complain about a lipstick she had bought – it was too soft.

> [I]n a minute [Revson] was on the line. 'You got the lipstick with you?... Turn it around and there's a batch number. Give me the number... What kind of dress were you wearing with that lipstick?' She shouldn't wear *Fifth Avenue Red*, he told her, she should wear *Pink Lightning*... She

got a nice lecture about what she should wear with what, her name was put on the list with the consumer relations department, and they sent her samples and questionnaires and everything else.

Revson understood what women wanted. His early background in the garment trade meant that he positioned his varnish as a fashion accessory, with colours to suit every ensemble, ambience and occasion. He abhorred research and test marketing – the Procter & Gamble approach – because he felt fashion moved too fast. He was the first to introduce the fashion industry concept of seasonality into the beauty market. Revlon launched new colours every winter and spring season.

As the company grew, Revlon was able to target different consumer segments: for example, it launched a hypoallergenic line called Etherea and a premium collection named Ultima. Like many marketing geniuses, Revson excelled at storytelling – which he referred to as 'honest fiction'. As Tobias points out: 'It didn't cost any more to make dark red polish called *Berry Bon Bon* than to make plain dark red polish, and the one could be sold for six times the price of the other.'

The idea of colour themes proved particularly advantageous when Revlon introduced lipsticks in the 1940s. Now women could match their lips to their fingertips, as the brand's advertising suggested. The concept also allowed Revlon to embark on flamboyant integrated marketing campaigns. The launch of a shade called Fatal Apple in 1945 comprised colour spreads in fashion magazines, complementary department store window displays, and a launch party featuring genuine apple trees, a snake charmer and a golden apple from Cartier.

It was inevitable that somebody as obsessive as Charles Revson should bring his perfectionist streak to the brand's advertising – which was, after all, just a glorified version of his slick salesmanship. He would send print ads back for adjustments if a single colour in the lower right-hand corner displeased him. Marketing meetings could go on for days. (As one woman who worked in the packaging and design department in the 1950s observed, this was not unreasonable given that the then US$55 million company had been built almost entirely on marketing.)

Two classic campaigns put Revlon in the advertising history books. In those days, Revlon's all-purpose advertising guru was a man called Norman B

Norman, co-founder of the agency Norman, Craig & Kummel. But it's generally acknowledged that agency copywriter Kay Daly did all the heavy lifting, with input from Revlon's in-house marketing executive Bea Castle. Indeed, Daly eventually joined Revlon in 1961 as its creative director.

The first blockbuster ad appeared in the *New York Times* in 1950. It was minimalist in the extreme, bearing the headline WHERE'S THE FIRE? above a smoking hole, as if the paper's pages had been charred. And that was all. There was no hint of a brand name or any explanatory text. It was a teaser ad – the kind of stunt media buyers still boast about today when they're evoking 'creativity' in their profession. Revlon launched its new red lipstick, Where's the Fire?, a few days later.

The brand struck again in 1952 with a product called 'Fire and Ice'. The ad was created by Kay Daly, who recruited photographer Richard Avedon and supermodel Dorian Leigh. Daly and Avedon put Leigh in a skin-tight sparkling silver sheath dress, a scarlet cape falling insouciantly from her shoulders. Her red talons caressed her cheek, drawing attention to her bright red lips. The other hand rested suggestively on her hip, the nails angled downwards like arrows.

This time the text was all-important. It read: 'For you who love to flirt with fire... who dare to skate on thin ice... for lips and matching fingertips... a lush and passionate scarlet... like flaming diamonds dancing on the moon!'

As if this breathless prose was not enough, the double-page spread came with a list of questions headed: 'Are you made for Fire and Ice?' These included: 'Have you ever danced with your shoes off? Did you ever wish on a new moon? Do you blush when you find yourself flirting? Do you sometimes feel that other women resent you? Have you ever wanted to wear an ankle bracelet? Do sables excite you, even on other women? Do you think any man really understands you? Do you close your eyes when you're kissed?'

Daly later said she enjoyed giving women 'a little immoral support'. It's perhaps this more than anything that distinguishes Revlon from Rubinstein and Arden. Charles Revson did not sell the promise of eternal youth. He sold sex, pure and simple. He understood, as Hollywood did, that glamour came with a naughtiness quotient.

Norman B Norman claimed that Revlon's ads were read more closely than the magazine editorial around them. 'All Revlon advertising had to do with emotions... how women thought, how they lived, how they loved... and we wove in our products. That's quite different from what most companies do, where they describe their products, the benefits of them.'

Initially, Charles Revson steered clear of TV advertising, for one very obvious reason: in the 1950s, TV was still broadcast in black and white. Other beauty companies were not as shy of this infinitely promising medium. Hazel Bishop swept in from nowhere to take sales of her 'No Smear' lipstick to a quarter of the US market simply by being one of the first beauty entrepreneurs to advertise on TV. Her success was short-lived, as more powerful players stepped in and refined her formula. Among them was Max Factor, who developed make-up specifically for television performers and began sponsoring televised beauty pageants (see Chapter 7, 'The stardust factor'). If Hollywood transformed making up from a sin into a glamorous luxury, TV turned it into a daily habit, an essential component of womanhood.

Norman B Norman persuaded Revson to try sponsorship in the form of a CBS quiz show called *The $64,000 Question*. At first Revson was uneasy about the deal – he wasn't sure that it was the right environment for his trendy, 'premium' products – but he soon changed his mind. Four weeks after the first broadcast, on 7 June 1955, the show was at the top of the ratings and Revlon products were selling out.

Writes Andrew Tobias:

> *The Question* raised Revlon sales, profits, and consumer awareness so dramatically as to put it miles ahead of its competitors... Sales... suddenly shot up 54 percent in 1955... The next year, sales were up yet another 66 percent, to $85 million, and profits better than doubled... Helena Rubinstein, Max Factor, Coty, and Hazel Bishop, which had all been at least within striking distance of Revlon before *The Question* went on the air, were left bitterly in the dust.

Revlon was allowed three one-minute commercials per week – and it made the most of them. They were staged live, which added to the drama for the viewing public. This also enabled them to overrun considerably, ensuring maximum publicity for the brand. The problem of expressing colour on a black-and-white screen meant that each ad had to be as spectacular as a Hollywood musical: dry ice, waterfalls, willow trees and even live ducklings – which predictably ran amok – were some of the features of these mini-epics.

The quiz show rollercoaster ride did not last long. In 1959 *The $64,000 Question* was derailed by the discovery that another popular show, *Twenty One*, was rigged – the contestants knew the answers from the outset, their reactions stage-managed. (The scandal is captured perfectly by Robert Redford's 1994 film *Quiz Show*.) During the Congressional hearings that followed, it became clear that, although *The Question* was not rigged in quite so obvious a way, the questions were written to play to contestants' strengths. It also emerged that Revlon had voiced its opinion – quite forcibly – about which contestants it liked and which it didn't. But, no, of course it didn't try to have unattractive contestants thrown off the show: how could you suggest such a thing?

Revlon escaped relatively unscathed, and the scandal turned out to be the merest dip in the company's rapidly ascending fortunes. By now it had begun to expand abroad, launching its products in France, Italy, Argentina, Mexico and Asia. In Japan, Revson took a gamble. Instead of taking a local approach – with specially formulated products and ads featuring Japanese models – he sold a racy American lifestyle, with the same sexy models who'd worked so well back home. The approach paid off: Japan became one of the brand's most successful markets.

Meanwhile, Revson diversified. Initial acquisitions in the areas of shoe polish, electric shavers and women's sportswear were quickly abandoned – but he did far better in the pharmaceutical market, acquiring a company that made a best-selling diabetes drug. He later sold this to Ciba-Geigy in exchange for a portfolio of other pharmaceutical products. Revson was aware that the world of skincare and pharmaceuticals would soon overlap: in 1968 he introduced Eterna 27, a moisturizing cream containing Progenitin (pregnenolone acetate), which can affect levels of oestrogen when taken orally, and is said to create a 'lifting effect' when used on the skin.

Revson was now stepping firmly on territory that had previously been dominated by his competitors. In 1973 he launched a fragrance called Charlie. The advertising aimed the brand squarely at modern young women: spirited, independent, sexually liberated. Flick-haired model Shelley Hack twirled through the TV ad in a Ralph Lauren outfit, including trousers. This was a perfume advertising first; women got the message that the Charlie girl wore the pants. Hack went on to play a similarly empowered young woman in the TV show *Charlie's Angels*. 'It was a time when women were changing,' she told Oprah Winfrey in a 2008 interview. 'Women looked at [the ad] and said, "I want to be like that."' Geoffrey Jones describes Charlie as 'the first modern lifestyle fragrance'. By 1980, it was outselling Chanel No. 5.

But Charles Revson was no longer around to savour the success of his creation. He died of pancreatic cancer in 1975. His way with beautiful women stayed with him almost until the end. The same year that he launched Charlie, he signed up Lauren Hutton – with her unmistakable gap-toothed smile – as the exclusive model for the Ultima line of cosmetics. The fee was US$400,000, the highest ever paid to a model at the time. Richard Avedon came on board as exclusive photographer. The story was so big that Hutton made the cover of *Time* magazine.

Revson had ensured his company's future by hiring sharp businessman Michel Bergerac (born in France, he'd taken US citizenship in 1963) as his successor. Revson had launched a headhunt to find the best businessman in the world, and he'd decided that Bergerac fitted the bill. The son of a Biarritz electrical company executive, Bergerac had studied law and political science at the Sorbonne before earning a Master's in business administration at Stanford. He was working at the Canon Electrical Company in Los Angeles when it was acquired by ITT. By the time Revson found him, he was running the company's European operations and tipped to become its chairman. Revson offered him an unprecedented US$1.5 million 'signing fee' to come and run Revlon ('Michel Bergerac: a 1.5 million dollar man takes charge at Revlon', *People* magazine, 8 December 1975).

Revson had tacked up a quotation in the company's corporate dining room: 'O, Lord, give me a bastard with talent.' But while Bergerac had plenty of talent, he did not appear to possess a mean streak. His 'soft-talking, insouciant' style was in complete contrast to that of the abrasive Revson. In other words, he was the perfect choice for running what had become a corporate machine. He expanded the company's healthcare division, making acquisitions in dental care, optical equipment and contact lens manufacturing, as well as in the pharmaceuticals sector. This helped turn Revlon into a US$1.7 billion corporation by 1979.

It also meant that the company became rather colourless. It was a beauty giant, but it was no longer a trendsetter. Revson had feared as much. In the years before his death, he had become aware of a third threat to his market share beyond that of Helena Rubinstein and Elizabeth Arden. The name had been cropping up since the late 1950s, and now it was one to be reckoned with.

BEAUTY TIPS

* Charles Revson forged ahead in the nail enamel and make-up business because he did not care that they were still seen as vulgar.

* Pushy and charismatic, he went on the road to sell his products to salons – and then trained an aggressive sales team.

* He marketed nail varnish and lipsticks as luxury goods, but added the new element of sexiness.

* He innovated with integrated marketing campaigns that combined colour spreads in fashion magazines, department store window displays and media-magnet launch parties.

* In the 1950s Revlon was the first beauty brand to fully embrace TV, massively increasing sales.

* Rather than adapting to overseas markets, it sold the idea of a racy American lifestyle abroad.

* Revlon's breezy Charlie perfume ads of the 1970s astutely targeted the new, free-spirited, liberated woman.

THE BEAUTY
QUEEN OF CORONA

'Some day I will have whatever I want.'

For a while, in the early 1960s, Estée Lauder and Charles Revson worked in the same building at 666 Fifth Avenue. Estée was both contemptuous and wary of the nail giant, commenting: 'I don't want to get started with him… Right now Charles Revson is my friend. He doesn't take me seriously… He thinks I'm a cute blonde lady… The moment I put something on the market that competes with him, he's going to get *upset*. He's going to get difficult. And we're not big enough to fight him.'

Lauder later upset Revson by launching Clinique, forcing him to play 'me too' with Etherea in order to catch up with the hypoallergenic trend. This put her on a more even – if hardly equal – footing with him. And she had other ways of irritating him. His company was far larger, but Estée made it clear that she was more sophisticated, more at home in the upper echelons of society.

It was all a show, as Revson well knew. If anything, Lauder's beginnings were even more humble than his own.

To judge from the facts uncovered by Lee Israel, author of the (1985) book *Estée Lauder: Beyond the magic*, the beauty queen grew up in a neighbourhood for which the term 'dump' was entirely appropriate. It was called Corona and it was in Queens, New York City.

In 1907, a speculator named Michael Degnon had bought a large tract of land there and begun encouraging neighbouring boroughs to use it as a refuse tip, creating a hellish landscape of ashes and garbage. His plan was to level these mountains of trash and use them as the foundation for a new port complex. But the First World War scuppered the project and the area 'remained an eyesore until 1937', according to the website Forgotten New York (www.forgotten-ny.com). 'All this did for Corona was to make the town stink like garbage,' the site adds. 'When the residents looked east, all they saw were ugly gray mounds on the horizon.' Indeed, F Scott Fitzgerald describes this 'valley of ashes' in his book *The Great Gatsby*.

Corona cleaned up its act when the dumps were turned into a park shortly before the 1939–40 World's Fair. The area was home to many immigrant communities – first European, then Hispanic and Asian – and even experienced a brief flutter of fame thanks to a line in a Paul Simon song: 'Goodbye Rosie, Queen of Corona. See me and Julio, down by the schoolyard.'

Estée Lauder was not the Queen of Corona. At least, not at first. Josephine Esther Mentzer was born on 1 July 1908 to Rose and Max Mentzer. Rose already had five children from a previous marriage; Estée (Esty, as she was known then) also had a full sister called Grace, two years her senior. They lived in 'an almost entirely Italian neighbourhood', writes Lee Israel. 'When Estée was growing up, the streets were unpaved; most of the Italians settled there had factory jobs; and the place smelled horrifically.'

Estée's mother was Hungarian, her father Czech. Rose arrived in New York in 1898, at the age of 29, aboard the SS *Palatia*. Max became a US citizen in 1902. Profession: tailor. By the time Estée was a little girl, he was running a hardware store; the family lived above it.

Little Esther's early interest in beauty seems to have compensated for the earthiness of her surroundings. In an interview cited by Israel, she says,

'I loved to make everyone up when I was young. My mother would say, "You brushed my hair twice today." I was always interested in people being beautiful – the hair, the face... I love to see people just walking or playing tennis, who look like they have a cared-for face.'

Her obituary in the *New York Times* put it slightly differently. 'Perfection in the face of a woman consumed Mrs Lauder, and so did a desire to make a lot of money and leave the conditions of her childhood behind her. "Some day I will have whatever I want," she is said to have predicted many years ago.' The paper concedes that she was 'a petite blonde... known for her lovely skin and for her determination to always look good' ('Estée Lauder, pioneer of beauty and cosmetics titan, dies at 97', 26 April 2004).

Her evolution into a purveyor of skin care products comes in both fairytale and prosaic versions. The fairytale was told by Estée herself to the *Palm Beach Daily News* in April 1965. 'An uncle of mine... who was a very famous skin specialist in Vienna came to New York because of the World's Fair... Then the war broke out and he couldn't go home. So he took a stable – it was an elegant stable – lined it with linoleum and began making skin creams there. I used to help him every chance I had.'

His name was John Schotz. He was Hungarian – the younger brother of Estée's mother – and he had arrived in New York in 1900. He was not a dermatologist, but rather a chemist who had set up a small business called New Way Laboratories in 1924. Here he formulated products like 'Six-in-One Cold Cream', 'Dr Schotz Viennese Cream' and even 'Hungarian Mustache Wax'. (He also made poultry lice killer, a cure for mange, suppositories, a cream that was supposed to build muscles, and embalming fluid.) He became Estée's mentor, and she built up her business selling his creams to beauty salons.

Around the time that she was setting out on this path, Estée met a 'sweet-looking, curly-haired young man' called Joseph Lauter (note the 't'), supposedly on a golf course. He was a salesman: silk and buttons. They began dating when she was 19 and married three years later. Mrs Lauter gave birth to a boy, Leonard, in 1933. In 1937, the name 'Estée Lauder' appeared in the New York telephone directory for the first time. By the end of 1939, the couple were already divorced. Estée wanted more, her biographers imply. She wanted to be richer.

Meanwhile, her confidence was growing. She travelled to Miami, setting up a concession selling her uncle's products in the Roney Plaza Hotel on Collins Avenue. She worked resorts and beach clubs, where she offered facial massages and creams to the ageing rich. But the real turning point in Estée's career came when she met her second mentor, a man who became a lifelong friend, Arnold Lewis van Ameringen, a Dutch-born industrialist who would go on to head International Flavors & Fragrances, a formulator of scents for perfume houses (see Chapter 8).

Impressed by Estée's drive, van Ameringen provided support for her nascent business and, it's thought, some of the formulas for the products that bore her name. The pair may or may not have been lovers for a time, but the fact was that Estée missed Joe, who was still assiduously courting her. 'Joe's a nice man. I don't know why I broke off with him,' she confided to a friend. In 1942, they remarried.

Over the next few years, the Estée Lauder brand began to outshine that of Dr Schotz, although many of her creams were still based on his formulas. Her network of concessions grew; she also sold her products to salons nationwide via 'jobbers', or agents. A great deal of her success was based on the fact that she would spend time at concessions herself, tirelessly promoting her products to customers. A friend recalled, 'She stood there in stocking feet and sold... She was a good salesgirl.'

She was warm and beautiful; she would put a dab of cream on the wrist of a potential customer and gently rub it in, so that the customer could admire the silky effect. 'Touch your customer and you're halfway there,' she told her sales people. Although Dr Schotz's products were undoubtedly effective, Estée's charisma was the magic ingredient. By now she was also selling lipstick, which probably came from a different supplier. Lee Israel recounts that Estée had managed to get herself on to the public speaking circuit in New York, giving women beauty tips. At the start of one such charity luncheon at the Waldorf-Astoria Hotel, every female guest found an Estée Lauder lipstick with a silvery metallic tube at her place setting – this during wartime when metal cases were rare and expensive. That afternoon, women streamed into Saks department store asking for Lauder lipsticks. The problem was that Estée did not have a concession at Saks. Very soon afterwards, she did.

Estée Lauder officially became a company in 1947. It is not known how she compensated John Schotz; her *New York Times* obituary merely observes that 'he died in the 1960s in modest circumstances'. No matter: Estée was finally on her way to becoming a beauty queen, leaving Corona far behind.

One of Estée's pivotal innovations – which influenced the development of beauty marketing in general – was born of necessity. In the early days, she could not afford to advertise. When she asked the agency BBD&O if they could come up with a campaign for US$50,000, almost her entire capital at the time, she was politely shown the door. And so she decided to approach potential customers directly, by mail. Fortunately, she had an excellent database to hand in the form of the Saks Fifth Avenue mailing list, which the direct mail manager obligingly let her have. (Being a petite blonde had its advantages, Estée often found.) Customers would receive an elegant letter telling them that an additional free gift awaited them at the store if they bought one of her products: the 'gift with purchase' strategy now practised by beauty retailers far and wide. As the earlier experiment with the free lipsticks had shown, generosity paid off. 'If you give, you get,' she said.

Yet the Lauder brand might have remained an also-ran were it not for an unexpected turn of events in 1953. The company suddenly found itself with a huge hit on its hands – a landmark product that would utterly transform its fortunes. It was not a skin cream, but a bath oil called Youth-Dew. And it probably came about thanks to Estée's friendship with AL van Ameringen of International Flavors & Fragrances.

According to Lee Israel, Estée had approached IFF with a fragrance in mind. The result was an essence that Estée, true to form, initially gave away in department stores as a sampler. It was, writes Israel, 'a try-it-you'll-like-it kind of thing. And they tried it, and they loved it, and they bought it.' She describes Youth-Dew as 'something you dumped in the tub and that adhered to the skin because of the high concentration of essential oils'. It answered a market demand for 'an assertive, tenacious and unsubtle essence'.

Israel also cites one of Lauder's colleagues, who analyses the product's success. 'The fragrance had a lot of punch. It was long-lasting. She gave the American woman a bath oil that substituted for a perfume. They could buy it for US$8.50 and have a perfume that lasted for twenty-four hours. It was a whole new direction, and it was affordable. Middle America felt it was getting its money's worth.'

Youth-Dew became Estée Lauder's flagship product. It appeared in many different variations, including as a perfume. Flipping her original strategy on its head, she would give away samples of her skincare products when customers bought the fragrance. Crucially, she did almost no advertising. Instead, she did what might be called 'sensory branding' today. 'Estée... wore her new fragrance everywhere, and spritzed it on friends... Saks was totally suffused with it. She sprayed it in the elevators; the entire area carried the message of Youth-Dew.'

With the success of Youth-Dew, the entire Lauder operation moved up several gears. While the family moved into a large townhouse and Estée began mixing with the fashionable set at Palm Beach – the start of her inexorable ascension of the social ladder – the company's marketing techniques grew in sophistication. As Revlon had begun to realize (and, to be fair, as Helena Rubinstein had understood years before), skincare products could be sold more effectively if their benefits were explained in the language of science. The advertising copy had to be sly, as the Food and Drug Administration (FDA) was quick to crack down on false claims, but with the right wording purchasers could be convinced that there were scientific reasons why a cream might slow or even reverse the ageing process.

This was the thinking behind Lauder's Re-Nutriv, 'a name that said nothing and everything'. It was extremely expensive. To justify its price, Estée accompanied the launch with her very first advertising campaign, in *Harper's Bazaar*. A picture of a frostily beautiful blonde – which became the defining Lauder alter ego – was accompanied by copy that combined all the best (or worst) attributes of beauty marketing: snobbery, emotional blackmail, the cult of celebrity, *faux* continental sophistication and pseudo-science.

'WHAT MAKES A CREAM WORTH $115?' read the headline. 'Re-Nutriv by Estée Lauder. Rare ingredients. Rare formula. But above all the perception of a woman like Estée Lauder who knows almost better than anyone how to keep you looking younger, fresher, lovelier than you ever dreamed possible. She has created what she likes to think of as "a goldmine of beauty" – her Crème of Creams Re-Nutriv.' Among the list of ingredients were 'youth-giving agents [that] help rebuild and firm the skin, reflecting the freshness and radiance of a years-younger complexion'.

One of Lauder's colleagues commented that Estée was 'ahead of her time for... the vagueness of her claims'.

But the pictures were as important as the words. Lauder used a Chicago-born photographer called Victor Skrebneski, who had been influenced by French movies in his youth and inhabited the same elegant dream world as Estée. His photos were the purest black and white – which made them cheaper to run in magazines – but their content was opulent. As Lee Israel observes, they showed 'not only the woman but the way she lived, among Ming vases, chinoiseries, pre-Columbian art, oriental rugs or Picasso ceramics'. Copywriter June Leaman, who worked alongside Skrebneski on the campaigns, added that people who saw the Lauder woman somehow knew that 'her closets were impeccable, her children well-behaved, her husband devoted and her guests pampered'.

The model who came to define the Estée Lauder look was Karen Graham. Svelte and graceful, with cool clear eyes, she first appeared in one of the company's ads in 1970, but captured its image so effectively that she became its exclusive model from 1973 until the early 1980s. Her name was never publicized, and many people thought she was Estée Lauder. This was quite deliberate. In fact she was a projection – Estée's avatar. (Ironically, for a woman who became the symbol of urban sophistication, Mississippi-born Graham turns out to be an earthy, outdoorsy type, with a passion for fly fishing and horse-riding.)

By 1965, Estée Lauder was making US$14 million. The company was still nowhere within firing range of Revlon – which at that point was in 15,000 stores as opposed to Lauder's 1,200 – but it was beginning to get noticed. And then it launched the Clinique range, a concoction of pure branding genius.

CLINIQUE AND BEYOND

In image and conception, Clinique seemed diametrically opposed to Estée Lauder. But that was the secret of its success, and proof of the company's clarity of vision. Leonard Lauder – who was by now deeply involved in his mother's business – later explained: 'The most formidable competition you can conjure up is yourselves and something you dream up yourself... The reason we launched Clinique is that I felt that if we were going to go into business against Estée Lauder this is exactly how I would do it.'

The genesis of Clinique dates back to a 1967 article in the US edition of *Vogue* headlined 'Can great skin be created?' It was written by beauty editor Carol Phillips and based on an interview with the dermatologist Dr Norman Orentreich. The answer was 'yes'. The doctor felt that cleaning with soap and water was a good start, but this needed to be followed by an astringent for exfoliation, and then a moisturizing lotion. His theory was that, while the upper layer of skin thins, it might be induced to retain water with the application of moisturizing cream. This would in turn prevent the lower layer from losing moisture, providing better support and 'plumping up skin'. According to Clinique, 'Orentreich was tapped by the Estée Lauder Company to work with Carol Phillips to create Clinique, the first dermatology-tested, fragrance-free cosmetic brand.' Orentreich remains associated with the brand as its 'guiding dermatologist' along with his son David and daughter Catherine (www.cliniquetv.com.au/heritage).

Inspired by the original article, Clinique was based on a three-step process: wash, exfoliate, moisturize.

With its minimalist pale green packaging – the kind of colour you might find in a hospital ward – and neutral positioning, Clinique answered a growing need for a pragmatic, 'scientific' solution to skincare. The number of articles about allergens in cosmetics had been increasing, along with awareness that the chemical content of beauty products might not have been entirely healthy. Clinique looked clean, antiseptic and reassuringly... well, clinical.

But some interesting decisions lay behind its key claims 'allergy tested and 100% fragrance free'. The more familiar term is 'hypoallergenic', a word that the US Food and Drug Administration dislikes and has been trying to ban for years. It nearly managed in 1975, when it proposed regulations insisting that products could carry the term only if they had been scientifically tested on human subjects. But the proposal was overruled in 1978 after being challenged in court by Almay... and Clinique.

The current situation is this, as stated on the FDA website (www.fda.gov):

> There are no Federal standards or definitions that govern the use of the term 'hypoallergenic.' The term means whatever a particular company wants it to mean. Manufacturers of cosmetics labeled as hypoallergenic are not required to submit substantiation of their hypoallergenicity claims to the FDA. The term 'hypoallergenic' may have considerable

market value in promoting cosmetic products to consumers on a retail basis, but dermatologists say it has very little meaning.

With all the controversy around 'hypoallergenic', it's perhaps not surprising that Clinique went with the safer 'allergy tested'. On its website, it states that its products are formulated 'without allergens' and 'tested 12 times on 600 people'.

So what about 'fragrance free'? That is a semantic minefield too. Clinique declined to comment on the matter, but as far as the FDA is concerned the term is almost as meaningless as 'hypoallergenic'. In fact, a neutral odour is generally achieved by using a chemical masking agent to keep odours at bay.

Clinique established some smart visual triggers too. As Lee Israel explains: 'The FDA was… able to prevent Clinique from making medical-*sounding* claims. But there was no law on earth that prevented them from *looking* as medical as they bloody well pleased. The salespeople… are referred to as "consultants". They are done up in white lab coats.' The consultants would ask customers leading questions about their skin type and submit the answers to a 'Clinique computer', which would then spew out a list of recommended products. This was all very new and science-fictional, perfect for an era forged in the white heat of technology.

The print advertising was new, too. In fact, it is widely regarded as among the best beauty advertising of all time. It owed much to the artistry of Irving Penn, a photographer so skilled at composition and the manipulation of light that he was able to give objects personalities. And that's all the ads showed: objects. The first still life, which ran in the *New York Times* in 1974, simply showed a toothbrush in a glass and the words 'Twice a day', the pristine image emphasizing the necessity of the Clinique regime. Later versions featured Clinique products, all imbued with a severe elegance thanks to Penn's lens. More than skincare potions and cosmetics, they were streamlined fashion accessories.

When Irving Penn died, in October 2009, Clinique ran an ad in *Vogue* in homage to him. It read: 'Irving Penn gave us the truth and made it so inviting that we never needed the fantasy. He transformed beauty for us, and for the world.'

Nobody knows quite how the partnership came about – it seems likely that Penn worked with Carol Phillips at *Vogue* – but it was the perfect fusion of brand image and advertising creativity. The campaign is still running and remains unique.

Clinique was such a ground-breaking product that it lost money at first, but Estée Lauder persisted and by the 1980s fashion had caught up with the company's foresight. This happened several times. In the early 1970s, Lauder had tentatively introduced a men's fragrance, Aramis, in the form of after-shave and cologne. By 1978, Aramis was one of the most successful men's lines around, encapsulating a whole range of grooming products, from scented soap to hairspray. This expertise encouraged the company to launch Clinique Skin Supplies for Men in 1976, the first time a women's beauty brand had been extended into a second line for men (see Chapter 17, 'The new male order').

As we've seen, the creation of successful beauty products is as much about copywriting as it is about formulation and packaging. Take Estée Lauder's successful Night Repair, launched in 1983. This was, as its name suggests, a cream that worked only at night. Think about that for a moment. In fact, don't think about it – read the advertising copy:

> Night Repair is a biological breakthrough that uses the night, the time your body is resting, to help speed up the natural repair of cells that have been damaged during the day by the ultraviolet light all around us (which incidentally occurs all year long, winter as well as summer). Night Repair also greatly increases the skin's ability to hold moisture.

Like Helena Rubinstein and Elizabeth Arden, Estée Lauder was skilled at the art of using poetic language spiced with science to suggest that the hands of time could be stilled.

She was equally adept at creating the perfect frame for her products, fighting for every inch of branded space in department stores. She opened her first beauty spa in Bloomingdale's as early as 1965, personally planning the counters and decreeing that each would be 'a tiny shining spa'. The colour she chose was 'in between a blue and a green' that 'whispered elegance, aristocracy and complemented bathroom wallpapers'. Throughout her career, she kept a hawk-like watch on these spaces, often insisting on training her own sales staff to work in them. She knew that, however fancy your advertising language might be, sales came down to the interaction between the customer, the sales assistant and the product.

When Estée Lauder Companies went public in 1995, it was worth about US$5 billion. Estée was given the title of founding chairwoman. She had outlived all her rivals. She'd even shown up at Elizabeth Arden's funeral. One report has it that she was noticed by Monica Smythe, Arden's British press secretary, who told her: 'Thank you so much for coming today.' Estée shot back: 'She wouldn't have said that if she knew I was here.'

She had been dismissive about Helena Rubinstein ('the skin on her neck was less than perfect') and, as for Charles Revson, he had remained her 'arch and implacable enemy' until his passing.

Now Estée was the ruling monarch of beauty. Her skilled networking in Palm Springs and beyond, the glittering soirées she had attended and organized, had reaped friendships that included Princess Grace of Monaco, the Begum Aga Khan, Nancy Reagan and Douglas Fairbanks Jr. She actually lived in the world that her early advertisements had fabricated.

By the time of Estée's death, in 2004, the value of the company had soared to US$10 billion. It had 21,500 employees and was present in more than 130 countries. At the time of writing, it owns a total of 27 brands and is still majority-owned by the Lauder family.

No matter what one might think of the strategies that led to her success, Estée seems to have genuinely believed in the utility of her products. 'The pursuit of beauty is honourable,' she stated. Right from those early days in Corona, she felt she had a purpose in life. The company's website quotes her advice to staff: 'I didn't get there by wishing for it or hoping for it, but by working for it.'

BEAUTY TIPS

* Like her predecessors, Estée Lauder developed storytelling skills to plot her way out of a humble upbringing.

* She promoted her early products by holding lectures about skincare and offering free samples.

* She pioneered the direct mail and 'gift with purchase' strategies.

* Her advertising was peppered with vague but emotive words like 'rare', 'youth-giving', 'natural' and 'radiance'.

* It was also highly aspirational, with pictures of wealthy women in opulent surroundings.

* Yet Lauder built her empire on Youth-Dew, a cheap, tenacious fragrance that was seen as offering great value for money.

* Estée Lauder also launched an 'allergy tested' product, Clinique, along with the innovative three-step skincare process.

* Clinique Skin Supplies for Men was the first women's beauty brand to be extended into a line for men.

* Lauder trained her own sales staff because she felt that no amount of advertising was as valuable as the personal touch.

THE FRENCH
BEAUTY FACTORY

'I no longer age – I dye with L'Oréal.'

Shortly after I began researching this book, I started looking for a new place to live in Paris. As prices in the centre of town had climbed to dizzying heights over the previous decade, my wife and I began to look on the fringes of the city, for gentrifying areas where we might find an old-fashioned yet affordable apartment. We found the perfect place in Clichy, a cosmopolitan suburb – about 10 minutes by metro from Montmartre – made famous by the writer Henry Miller, who lived here in the 1930s and wrote a book about it called *Quiet Days in Clichy*.

For many Parisians, however, Clichy has an entirely different significance. It is home to the global headquarters of L'Oréal, the world's largest cosmetics and beauty company, with sales of close to €18 billion a year. L'Oréal has facilities dotted all over the neighbourhood, but its main base is a glowering steel-clad building whose façade varies in shade from raven to brunette depending on the weather and the time of day. It is located on the ancient road to Montmartre, about five minutes away from where I'm writing this sentence.

Fate had led me almost to the front door of L'Oréal, but that did not mean I was going to get inside. The company guards its secrets closely. Its traditional wariness of the press – particularly the non-beauty press – was exacerbated in 2009 by a scandal that brought the personal life of its founder's daughter, the fabulously wealthy octogenarian Liliane Bettencourt, directly into the glare of the media.

This was not the first time the less attractive side of the company had been exposed. Bettencourt's father, Eugène Schueller, the man who created the French beauty factory, was by no means an uncontroversial figure. In the 1930s, he summed up his approach to marketing: 'Tell people they're disgusting, they don't smell good and they're not attractive' (Bruno Abescat, *La Saga des Bettencourt*, quoted by *Le Monde Diplomatique* in June 2009).

THE ROOTS OF L'ORÉAL

Schueller's work ethic developed early. The son of *boulangers-pâtissiers* who had relocated to Paris from Alsace in 1871, he realized by the age of 10 that he needed to work hard at school, that he wanted to get a good job and that 'the customer is always right'. As noted in Jacques Marseille's centenary history of the company, *L'Oréal 1909–2009*, young Eugène's greatest fear was that his hard-working parents would say of him, 'He's a lazy-bones!'

Little danger of that: Schueller worked part time at his parents' patisserie right through school and his subsequent studies in chemistry, which took him to the Sorbonne. It was here that a hairdresser appeared one day with a problem for the students: how to dye greying hair in a long-lasting and convincing way? Challenged by his professor to find a solution, Schueller bent to the task. Although his first efforts were unsuccessful, he worked feverishly until he got the formula right. Finally he became so confident in his product that he applied for a patent and went into business.

His 1907 patent application stated that existing lead-based products, 'aside from their toxicity, which has led to them being banned in several countries', failed to deliver a consistent and enduring tint. Schueller insisted that his product was harmless and enabled the user to obtain a satisfactory colour, from blonde to black, via a single flacon. This transformation could be achieved instantaneously, in a matter of moments, or progressively over a few hours.

In other words, Schueller was convinced that he had invented the perfect synthetic hair dye.

Most accounts claim that he initially called it L'Auréale – inspired by a hairstyle that was itself a corruption of the word *auréole*, or 'halo' – but the company's advertising archives show that by 1910 it was already being advertised as L'Oréal, 'the best product currently known', available for 2 francs 50.

Another ad depicts a young woman standing before the sinister 'clock of time'. The copy reads: 'I no longer age – I dye with L'Oréal.'

Like most beauty pioneers, Schueller got used to late nights and raw knuckles, fabricating his product in his small laboratory in the evening and slogging it around hairdressing salons during the day. Backed by an acquaintance – an accountant named Georges Spery, who so admired Schueller's dynamism that he pumped the best part of his inheritance into the company – the young chemist hired a salesman and a demonstrator. The latter was said to have been 'hairdresser to the Imperial court of Russia', hinting at a talent for marketing bombast.

History was on Schueller's side. In the early 1900s, France was hit by a wave of industrial and technical innovation that would bring with it automobiles, cinema, the popular press and – both driving and profiting from all these – mass advertising. The celebrity hairdresser Antoine noted in 1912 that, with the coming of the motor car, fashionable women were wearing their hair shorter. But as Jacques Marseille points out, even factory girls who cycled to work wanted to look as pretty as the women in the illustrated magazines. And Eugène Schueller, the son of humble bakers, who regularly pounded the streets in search of new clients, saw no reason why they should not.

Schueller's success depended on a two-pronged strategy: a close relationship with salon owners and hairdressers, and marketing that posited hair styling as a vital component of fashion. As early as 1909, Schueller had a column in the newly launched trade magazine *La Coiffure de Paris*, in which he promised to respond to all questions concerning hair-tinting techniques. In 1923 he went a step further by launching his own trade magazine, *L'Oréal Bulletin*, which kept salons up to date with the company's latest products. On the consumer front, he launched *L'Oréal Humoristique* in 1925 – designed to be distributed and read in salons – followed by a fully fledged women's magazine called *Votre Beauté* in 1933.

For his advertisements, Schueller worked with fashionable illustrators and photographers such as Herbert Libiszewski and Harry Meerson, whose work emphasized the artistry of the perfect hairstyle. As is often the case in the beauty industry, Hollywood lent a helping hand: when Jean Harlow appeared in the 1931 film *Platinum Blonde*, the demand for bottled glamour hit an all-time high. Fortunately, L'Oréal had launched an even faster-acting product, Imédia, a couple of years earlier.

The company was sensitive to fashion in other ways, too. It had already begun diversifying in 1928 with the acquisition of the soap company Monsavon. Now it was ready for a more radical innovation. Noting that sun-tanned skin had become all the rage, Schueller set his small research team to work devising a lotion that would enable its users to tan evenly without burning. Ambre Solaire was launched, as Geoffrey Jones observes, 'just in time for the summer vacations' in 1935.

Gradually, L'Oréal had begun to modify the grooming habits and appearance of its customers. Another revolution came with the launch of a mass-market shampoo named Dop in 1934. This may not seem particularly ground-breaking, but in Eugène Schueller's time hairdressers made up their own shampoo by mixing soap and soda crystals in hot water. The result was a white liquid in which tiny fragments of soap drifted like snowflakes. Schueller had noticed that, when he emerged from the hairdresser, his hair was 'practically as dirty as it was before the shampooing'. In Germany, chemist and perfumer Hans Schwarzkopf had begun experimenting with powder shampoos in 1908, but these were still based on soap, and the result was the same matt effect. Although Schwarzkopf is credited with popularizing the word 'shampoo' – it derives from the Hindi *champo*, meaning 'to massage' – he did not launch a successful non-alkaline product until 1933.

Dop sprang from Schueller's theory that washing hair was like washing any other kind of fibre. He sought advice from a chemist who specialized in treating textiles. The result was a cleaning solution based on alcohol sulphates, which did not leave a soapy residue: in fact, it left hair shiny and soft. Schueller patented the product under the name Dopal, which he put on the market as Dop. By 1938, L'Oréal was selling three formulas of Dop: for normal hair, for greying hair and for children. This was extremely avant-garde in a period when it was still considered unnecessary to wash one's hair more than once a week.

Schueller himself explained the problem to his sales people. 'There are 43 million people in France. Let's imagine that those 43 million people washed their hair once a week. We would sell 20 times the number of units that we sell at the moment.'

In order to reach this dream target, Schueller advertised his product aggressively. Alongside traditional print media, billboards and bus-sides, he turned to the emerging medium of radio, saturating the airwaves with jingles. He also organized hair-washing competitions for children at circuses. Dop was everywhere.

As a businessman, Eugène Schueller was building an empire of hair dye, soap suds and shampoo.

Politically, however, he was far from squeaky clean.

A DIRTY WAR

In the economic turmoil and mounting political tension of the late 1930s, a number of French politicians and businessmen felt that appeasing Hitler might be the only way of saving their country from ruin, as well as securing their own financial futures.

While the full extent of his involvement has never been established, Schueller hovered on the fringes of an extreme right-wing group known as *La Cagoule* (or 'The Cowl'). Founded by former artillery officer Eugène Deloncle, the Secret Committee of Revolutionary Action, to give it its official name, vowed to fight for 'the national and economic recovery of the country' against all those who opposed its aims. Ideally, this meant overthrowing the government.

It may have sounded like a conspiracy from one of the pulp paperbacks that were popular at the time, but *La Cagoule* was both real and lethal. Towards the end of the 1930s it carried out a number of assassinations, including that of the Soviet banker and freemason Dimitri Navachine and the anti-Fascist Italian journalist Carlo Rosselli and his brother Sabatino (in return for a cache of 100 Beretta machine pistols from the Italian secret service). The group also bombed two buildings in Paris owned by a metalworkers' union in a bid to frame the French Communist party. Organized more like a private army than a political organization, it possessed a formidable arsenal ('La Cagoule tombe le masque', *Historia* magazine, 1 June 2007). In October 1941, its members blew up seven synagogues.

According to Jacques Marseille in his history of L'Oréal, Eugène Schueller was familiar with a number of 'Cagoulards'. Following the fall of France in 1940, he helped to finance Deloncle's next group, Le Mouvement Social-Révolutionnaire (The Social Revolutionary Movement), whose aim was to 'construct a new Europe with the cooperation of Germany and all other nations free, like her, of liberal capitalism, Judaism, Bolshevism and Freemasonry'. This time Schueller's name appeared for all to see on the group's posters and political tracts – alongside that of Jacques Corrèze, Deloncle's secretary, who would later become chairman of L'Oréal's American operations ('Jacques Corrèze, L'Oréal official and Nazi collaborator, dies at 79', *New York Times*, 28 June 1991).

After the war, Schueller was called before a committee set up to identify collaborators. During the inquiry, a different view of his wartime activities was proposed. It appeared that, in the fog and ambiguity of the years before and immediately after the Occupation, Schueller had allied himself with those he felt best placed to help him advance his economic theories – notably the 'proportional salary', in which workers would be paid according to their contribution to the bottom line. By 1942, he had distanced himself from Deloncle. He was later active in the Resistance, helping people escape Nazi work camps and assisting Jews in their flight to the unoccupied zone.

The committee also found that products sold to the occupier between July 1940 and August 1944 represented only 2.5 per cent of L'Oréal's total sales, and 12.5 per cent of Monsavon's.

In 1947, the committee cleared Schueller's name. He had behaved imprudently, the record stated, but his later acts of patriotism showed that he was no collaborator. The stain on his reputation had been scrubbed away – almost. Its dark traces were to resurface long after his death.

AFTER SCHUELLER – FROM LANCÔME TO NESTLÉ

In 1952, Eugène Schueller accepted 'the Oscar for Advertising' from a French advertising industry association. The following year, a group of cinema advertising sales houses would launch another awards scheme, the Lions, which has since become the international reference in creative advertising circles. But for the time being, this odd Gallic Oscar was the greatest accolade a French marketer could hope for.

Schueller himself knew that the French were ambivalent about advertising. The general consensus, he admitted, was that advertising enabled companies 'to sell cheap products at higher prices'. He believed the opposite was true. Advertising, he argued, kept consumers informed about life-improving innovations and boosted the income that drove research into even more effective products. It stood to reason that L'Oréal's advertising balanced images of beauty with explanations of the science behind the glamour.

When Schueller died at the age of 76 in 1957, his seat at the head of L'Oréal was filled by François Dalle, who had joined the accounts department of Monsavon in 1942 and risen through the ranks to become managing director. Dalle himself had a somewhat ambiguous relationship with advertising. 'I would consider it very dangerous if the perception of a company was driven more by its advertising than by its products,' he commented. Like Schueller, he believed L'Oréal's core mission was one of research and innovation, the results of which would fuel its marketing initiatives.

Dalle's theory was seemingly corroborated in 1962 with the launch of the hairspray Elnett. Thanks once again to the cinema – especially the artfully tousled locks of Brigitte Bardot – French women's hairdos were becoming harder to manage without the help of an on-set stylist. Something was needed to fix them in place, and Elnett did the job splendidly. This was the first time women had access to a product that held their hair without, as Jacques Marseille puts it, 'giving it the aspect of cardboard'. Advertising was minimal, but word of mouth more than made up for it: soon Elnett had grabbed 28 per cent of the French hair lacquer market. The fact that L'Oréal's researchers had distributed the product to colleagues, friends and family for testing no doubt contributed to this phenomenon.

Thus Dalle began what was to be an almost 30-year run at the top of L'Oréal. He was aided behind the scenes by Eugène Schueller's daughter, Liliane, who had married the politician André Bettencourt (a friend of her father's, with a similarly ambiguous political past) in 1950. Dalle was responsible for many of the initiatives that laid the foundations for L'Oréal's evolution into a global titan. Take, for example, the acquisition of Lancôme.

Armand Petitjean had created the brand in 1935, its name inspired by the wild roses he'd seen growing around the Château de Lancosme in the Indre region of France. Petitjean had lived at least three lives before then: as an exporter of European products to Latin America, as an adviser on Latin America to the Foreign Ministry during the First World War, and as an executive of the fragrance company Coty. These experiences had bred within Petitjean a desire to share French elegance with the rest of the world. To help him he handpicked a crack team from Coty, including the d'Ornano brothers – skilled salesmen – and the bottle designer Georges Delhomme.

He launched his first five fragrances (Tendre Nuit, Bocages, Conquête, Kypre and Tropiques) at that year's Universal Exhibition in Brussels, where he was awarded a prize for innovation. Meanwhile, this aspiring ambassador of luxury established a small factory in a space previously devoted, appropriately enough, to the manufacture of artificial pearls. He also opened a boutique in the prestigious rue du Faubourg Saint Honoré.

Working with a horse veterinarian, Petitjean developed a skin cream containing a 4 per cent solution of horse serum, an antitoxin derived from the blood of horses and commonly used in vaccinations. An advertisement from the 1950s described Nutrix as 'a miracle cream… the guardian angel of your skin'. It's said that the British Ministry of Defence even recommended it as a potential defence against the effects of exposure to nuclear radiation ('Il était une fois Lancôme', www.joyce.fr, 2008).

Instinctively, Petitjean preferred word-of-mouth marketing to traditional advertising – a considerable irony given that Lancôme is now one of the world's most aggressive cosmetics advertisers, having recruited celebrity endorsers such as Isabella Rossellini, Juliette Binoche, Uma Thurman, Kate Winslet and Julia Roberts, among many others.

Petitjean's rigid perfectionism was to determine the company's future. In 1937 he had launched a soft, luxurious and highly successful lipstick called Rose de France, which made 'lips shine like those of a child'. Lancôme's lipstick tubes were works of art, plated with silver or gold. But by the 1960s, fashion was veering toward cheap disposable plastic lipstick cases. Petitjean recoiled at them in horror, unable to believe women would want to carry such monstrosities in their handbags. Drifting out of touch with consumer trends, Lancôme experienced a dramatic sales slump.

In 1964, a white knight appeared in the form of L'Oréal and François Dalle. Petitjean agreed to the acquisition offer – provided L'Oréal did not betray the luxury heritage of his brand. L'Oréal had no intention of doing so. In fact, it used Lancôme to reposition itself as a purveyor of luxury beauty products. As if to mark the dawn of an upmarket new era, it sold off Monsavon that same year.

The sixties obsession with youth was bound to be helpful to a company like L'Oréal. Taking advantage of a flourishing market for beauty products, it opened an enlarged research and production facility. Alongside Lancôme, it added the luxury brands Jacques Fath and André Courrèges to its roster, as well as the hair care company Garnier. It stepped up its international expansion, creating distribution arms in Algeria, Canada, Mexico, Peru and Uruguay.

Although L'Oréal had gone public in 1963, Liliane Bettencourt was still its majority shareholder. But L'Oréal was too ambitious to remain a family firm. In order to fund future growth, it needed a partner with deep pockets. In 1974, Liliane Bettencourt signed an agreement that effectively gave almost half the company to Nestlé.

The advantages of such a deal could be seen in L'Oréal's diversification into pharmaceuticals, with the acquisition of 53.4 per cent of Synthélabo, and into glossy magazines with stakes in the French publishers of *Marie Claire* and *Cosmopolitan*. L'Oréal also took full control of skincare brand Vichy

Laboratories, which had been a research partner since the 1950s. Expansion continued into Australia, New Zealand, Hong Kong and Japan. In 1984, Dalle could relinquish the leadership of L'Oréal safe in the knowledge that the group had already far exceeded Eugène Schueller's ambitions for it.

SCIENCE AND SCANDAL

Dalle was succeeded at the head of L'Oréal by Charles Zviak, whose reign was short but decisive. Now aged 62, Zviak had worked at L'Oréal since 1942, when he had joined Monsavon as a laboratory technician. He helped to pioneer methods that transformed the way women styled their hair, including the 'cold permanent wave'. Over the years he had risen to the post of research director, then vice-president. Zviak well understood the connection between beauty and science. In fact, as Jacques Marseille states, Zviak believed that successful beauty brands were built on a 'golden triangle' of research, marketing and quality.

Zviak steered L'Oréal further in the direction of dermatological research. In the 1980s, the group acquired Galderma, Goupil and La Roche-Posay – all laboratories specialized in skincare. The chemist and researcher also ensured that L'Oréal could compete in the expanding market for anti-ageing creams, thanks to a product called Niosôme (based on a new form of liposome) launched in 1986 by Lancôme.

But François Dalle was by no means out of the picture at L'Oréal. In fact, he'd managed to get the group into the movie business.

Dalle had teamed up with a TV and film producer named Jean Frydman to create a production company called Paravision, in which L'Oréal took a 75 per cent stake. Frydman was a Jewish concentration camp survivor and former Resistance hero who lived part time in Israel, where he had interests in satellite television. The significance of this will become clear in a moment.

In 1989, the pair fell out over Paravision's future direction. Through the press, Frydman claimed L'Oréal was trying to force him out because the group had acquired the Helena Rubinstein brand and was being threatened with a boycott by Arab countries. The articles suggested that L'Oréal knew the League of Arab States was assessing the extent of its connections with Israel, which made Frydman a liability. This would have been distasteful in any circumstances, but a 1977 French law meant that it was illegal for companies to cooperate with the boycott. Frydman evoked L'Oréal's dark past, notably the links between its founder, Eugène Schueller, and its former American CEO, Jacques Corrèze, with La Cagoule. The grime that the post-war court case was supposed to have washed clean became abruptly apparent again, shocking a new generation.

In the midst of the scandal, Jacques Corrèze was forced to resign as chairman of Cosmair, the American marketing arm of L'Oréal. Already suffering from cancer, he died that same night. Dalle and Frydman later settled their dispute out of court. The bitterness and scandal dissipated as the media turned their attention to other matters.

But 'the Frydman affair', as the French press called it, was no doubt an instructive experience for the L'Oréal group's new boss, Lindsay Owen-Jones.

MAYBE HE WAS BORN WITH IT

The appointment of Owen-Jones as president and CEO in 1988 was a symbol of L'Oréal's desire to become a global player. He certainly had little truck with the idea – still ingrained in the company's culture – that L'Oréal was primarily a hair care business. On his watch, it was to become one of the first Western businesses to enter Eastern Europe after the fall of the Berlin Wall. It expanded throughout Asia, setting its sights on China well before many of its competitors. Above all, it conquered the United States, taking full control of Cosmair and acquiring iconic American brands, which it then marketed around the world. In the history of L'Oréal, there is definitely a before and after Lindsay Owen-Jones.

A Welshman, Owen-Jones joined L'Oréal in 1962 after studying literature at Oxford and management at INSEAD, a respected business school outside Paris. Initially he'd considered a career as a diplomat, but he had come to the conclusion that international business might be an alternative way of experiencing different cultures. The multicultural aspect of his personality was the key to his success and the motor that utterly transformed L'Oréal.

As you may have gathered, L'Oréal prefers its leaders to have worked their way to the top within the group. Owen-Jones was no exception. He quickly discovered that joining L'Oréal amounted to an old-fashioned apprenticeship. There were stints at the factory, the laboratory (where he learned to perm and dye hair) and on the road as a salesman in Normandy before he became a product manager for Elnett. As he once told an interviewer from *Barron's* magazine, Owen-Jones had an affinity for beauty. 'I had already discovered that I really loved women, and having been brought up with sisters I was less awe-inspired and more aware of the day-to-day. I was far less lost looking at a lipstick than most of my men friends were' (cited in the *Encyclopaedia of World Biography*, online edition, 2004).

It helped that Owen-Jones believed in what he was doing. Beauty products were no mere commodities: these tubes, creams and lotions made people feel better about themselves and eased their rapport with others. By working at L'Oréal, Owen-Jones was making a positive contribution to society.

His ascension of the ladder continued: product manager in Belgium, marketing director of the consumer division, CEO in Italy and finally chairman and CEO of the US marketing division. Here he transformed the performance of the Lancôme brand.

The key was the department store Macy's, which had refused to give the French interloper the same amount of space as the all-American Estée Lauder. As Geoffrey Jones relates, Owen-Jones successfully argued that 'the spread of European clothes and cars like BMW into affluent suburbs suggested that their customers were "ripe for some European sophistication"'. Even more persuasively, he observed that the overall cut for Macy's would be greater if the rival brands were given equal billing. Macy's bought the argument. To improve his firepower, Owen-Jones took on actress and model Isabella Rossellini as the face of the brand and tripled its advertising budget. The result: Lancôme's annual US sales grew by 30 per cent between 1983 and 1988, by which time US sales accounted for 35 per cent of the brand's global revenues.

It was more than enough to make Paris sit up and notice. But Jacques Marseille writes that Owen-Jones was appreciated by L'Oréal not so much for his ability to make money for the group as for his fit within its culture. 'In other words, having ideas – successful ones – working without excessive fatigue because the métier is gratifying, and anticipating the market in order to create products that will work.'

When Owen-Jones became CEO of L'Oréal, he was one of the first foreigners ever to occupy such a position at a French company. His trick was to keep L'Oréal entirely French, while turning it into a truly international concern. 'I've tried to be a hyphen between France and English-speaking countries,' he told *Businessweek* ('L'Oréal: the beauty of global branding', 26 June 1999). Rather than homogenizing brands into blandness, he emphasized their cultural roots. The acquisition of the Maybelline brand in the United States is an example of this approach.

A chemist named TL Williams had founded Maybelline in New York in 1915. He named it after his sister Mabel, whose habit of thickening her eyelashes with Vaseline and coal dust had inspired him to develop an eyelash darkening product. In 1917, he launched one of the world's first modern mascaras. Until the 1960s, Maybelline concentrated on eye make-up. In 1969 the company was acquired by Plough, Inc (later Schering-Plough), which moved its base to Memphis, Tennessee and expanded its cosmetics range. In 1991 it adopted the well-known advertising slogan 'Maybe she's born with it, maybe it's Maybelline'.

At Owen-Jones's instigation, L'Oréal acquired Maybelline for US$758 million in 1996. He took it back to its birthplace, tacking the evocative words 'New York' on to its brand name and positioning it as synonymous with 'the size, style, colour and success that give the city its captivating flavour' (Maybelline.com).

Convinced (as Revlon had been several years earlier) that Manhattan cool travelled well, Owen-Jones then set about selling this image to the rest of the world. 'I had what may have been an unrealistic ambition,' he told *Time* magazine, 'to put a Maybelline lipstick into the hand of every Chinese woman.' Not so unrealistic, apparently: launched in China in 1998, by 2004 the Maybelline brand name was recognized by 98 per cent of Chinese women. In fact, it was soon reaping more than half of its US$1 billion in sales from markets outside the United States. In Japan alone, Maybelline became the top-selling mass-market cosmetics brand in 2000 ('Dreams of beauty', *Time* magazine, 26 April 2004).

Other triumphs followed. L'Oréal acquired the US brands Soft Sheen and Carson, which made hair care products for African American consumers, merged them into Soft Sheen/Carson and exported the brand to South Africa and Senegal. Soon, it was deriving 30 per cent of its revenues from these new markets.

In 2004, L'Oréal acquired Japanese cosmetics brand Shu Uemura. Named for its creator, a make-up artist who'd found fame in Hollywood after transforming the actress Shirley MacLaine into the titular character of the 1962 film *My Geisha*, the company had exactly the right multicultural profile. It gave L'Oréal a stronger foothold in Japan, but could also be flipped on its head to sell the idea of avant-garde beauty from Tokyo to sophisticated Western consumers. Its brand positioning focuses on 'the art of beauty'.

Another savvy acquisition was the cult New York skin and hair care brand Kiehl's. Founded in 1851 by a homeopathic pharmacist named John Kiehl, the company was still run from its original store – which looked as if it had barely changed – in the East Village. This was the only retail outlet it owned; the rest of the distribution was through selected department stores. The brand's no-nonsense image and utilitarian packaging made it popular with male consumers – an elusive target group for beauty companies. Marketing was resolutely word-of-mouth, relying on generous samples and customer endorsements. When L'Oréal snapped up the brand in 2000, it began opening Kiehl's outlets all over the world. Ironically, it risked destroying the down-to-earth quality that had attracted customers in the first place. Long-term fans began to complain that the brand had lost its authenticity, but its low-key marketing strategy remained intact.

Similar criticism greeted the acquisition in 2006 of Body Shop, the British 'natural' beauty brand created in 1976 by the late Dame Anita Roddick and her husband Gordon. Although it was occasionally accused of exaggerating its Green credentials for marketing purposes, the brand was closely associated with issues such as fair trade, sustainable development and an abhorrence of animal testing. The purchase allowed L'Oréal to exploit growing consumer interest in these areas.

Behind the scenes, Owen-Jones streamlined L'Oréal's structure. He strengthened and expanded the range of cosmetics sold under the L'Oréal Paris brand name, ultimately transforming it into a global mid-market beauty brand. He slashed brands that were underperforming or had little global potential, retaining a core of international 'mega-brands'. To aid this process, he established an international team of brand managers who could maintain a coherent global identity for each brand while responding to local trends. (An example of this was the launch in Japan of Maybelline's Water Shine lipstick, which responded to a local desire for moist, sparkling lips. The product was highly successful and later rolled out worldwide.)

In accordance with Eugène Schueller's theory that successful brands are built on research and innovation, Owen-Jones multiplied the company's research staff eightfold (there are now more than 3,000 of them) and oversaw the establishment of 14 research centres around the world. Research into tissue engineering was aided by the acquisition of a company called SkinEthic, which specializes in lab-grown skin that eradicates the need for animal testing. A partnership with Nestlé's nutritional research arm resulted in Innéov, a range of beauty pills.

Meanwhile, Owen-Jones returned the lustre to some of L'Oréal's fustier brands, establishing Lancôme as an international watchword for sophisticated beauty 'with a touch of French charm' (lancome.com) and repackaging Helena Rubinstein's 'scientific beauty' for a new generation.

Sir Lindsay Owen-Jones (he was knighted in 2005) stepped down as CEO of L'Oréal in 2006, although he remained chairman until early 2011. With him at the helm, the company had achieved decades of double-digit growth and transmogrified from a successful French hair care company with luxury aspirations into a corporate behemoth with more than 64,000 employees and a presence in 130 countries. And it had done all this with a portfolio of 23 core international brands.

The unenviable task of stepping into Owen-Jones's shoes fell to a Frenchman, Jean-Paul Agon. Described by the group as having 'an affinity for marketing', Agon was Owen-Jones's point man during the great Asian expansion. Later, he headed L'Oréal in the United States during the period when Garnier stormed that market with its Fructis range. He also helped to devise the Body Shop deal.

Like his predecessor, Agon had joined L'Oréal straight out of business school. What kind of corporate culture breeds employees who never seem to want to leave?

BECAUSE YOU'RE WORTH IT

We met on the terrace of a restaurant in the Montparnasse district of Paris. I'd managed to persuade a former L'Oréal employee to talk to me about how the group instils extreme loyalty within its staff. He told me many things, but one in particular sticks in my mind. 'They always tell you that you have talent,' said my contact, whom we'll call Alex. 'Never that you have "potential". Always "talent". Think about what a difference that makes.'

Actually, I was thinking of L'Oréal's famous tagline, 'Because you're worth it'. It's the perfect pitch for a beauty company with a luxury positioning. In fact the slogan has been through several iterations, starting in 1973 with 'Because I'm worth it'. The line was penned by 23-year-old copywriter Ilon Specht, who worked for the advertising agency McCann Erickson. First uttered by the actress Cybill Shepherd, it was the ideal sentiment for a period when women were demanding greater equality. And it endured – at least until 2004. By then, the feminist message had been diluted and the line seemed arrogant and narcissistic, especially on the lips of an actress earning millions of dollars in endorsement fees. So it became the more inclusive 'Because *you're* worth it'. Later still, in 2009, the line was changed to 'Because *we're* worth it', with the aim of reinforcing the connection between consumers and the brand.

The line is occasionally used by the group's human resources department to federate its staff. But it does not feel lame or silly when you work there – L'Oréal goes out of its way to make its employees feel valued. In fact, the process of inducting you into the family can work a little too well.

'Every intern follows more or less the same path, over about a six-month period,' Alex explained. 'First you get the full tour behind the scenes – R&D, distribution, marketing and so forth – to such an extent that you already feel as if you're on the management fast track. Then you go on the road as a sales person. That sounds tough – but it isn't. You're staying in great hotels; you're treated with maximum respect. It's actually a very enriching experience. When you get back, you're rewarded with a product manager post.'

In parallel, these young trainees are encouraged to bond with one another. 'L'Oréal organizes many social events for its interns, so you make a lot of friends. And because you're all on the same track, throughout your career at L'Oréal, you keep bumping into one another. This gives you an amazing network within the company. Soon you find that you're socializing outside of work. A great deal of the conversation revolves around L'Oréal and your colleagues.'

This is fine – until you leave. 'During my time at L'Oréal I never saw anyone get fired. And very few people quit, because by the time you've finished your internship you're more or less convinced that you won't find a better post elsewhere.'

Research carried out by Béatrice Collin and Daniel Rouach for their (2009) book *Le Modèle L'Oréal* suggests that people work at L'Oréal for an average of 13 years. The annual turnover worldwide is 5.9 per cent for executives and 4.5 per cent for the entire workforce. But one should not infer from this that L'Oréal is an easy ride. Lindsay Owen-Jones was famous for fostering a spirit of competition within the company. He often launched rival brands into the same market, thus pitching their teams against one another. Employees were constantly challenged to defend their decisions. To a certain extent, L'Oréal employees are brothers in arms, united in battle against their own demanding hierarchy.

'There's a cult of perfection at L'Oréal,' confirmed Alex. 'Nothing is ever right the first time. No matter if you've followed your superior's instructions to the letter, they'll still find a way of making you start over, even if it means changing the parameters or contradicting themselves. You learn quite quickly that you should always have a back-up plan.'

Early mornings and late nights are de rigueur, as young executives strive to impress their bosses. Yet Alex still considers L'Oréal a positive experience. 'Few companies are as diverse or give as many chances to young people. You're given a lot of autonomy very early on, because L'Oréal wants you to develop decision-making skills and a sense of responsibility. At the same time, mistakes are usually forgiven, because they are a natural part of a culture that encourages innovation.'

The company's international profile is another attraction: prospects for travel or a post abroad are strong. There seems little doubt that Alex would have stayed longer at L'Oréal if he had been given the chance. But sometimes people slip through the net. 'I was filling in for somebody who was on sick leave, and when he returned they couldn't find a full-time position for me,' he told me.

With L'Oréal on his CV he quickly found another job. But one evening was enough to remind him that at L'Oréal, once you're out – you're out. 'Soon after I'd left, I invited some friends round. As luck would have it, a few people were out of town and the bulk of the crowd were former colleagues from L'Oréal. Sure enough, all they talked about was a place I no longer worked and people I no longer knew. I felt excluded at my own dinner party. When I worked there, I hadn't realized how deeply immersed in the company we all were. That's when I had to accept that L'Oréal is a sort of sect.'

Sects, of course, are known for their secrecy. And the *L'Oréaliens* have a reputation for keeping their ranks tightly closed. 'If they don't know you, or you aren't introduced to them by somebody they trust, you won't get a word out of them,' a press attaché from a rival company warned me. Her prediction turned out to be entirely accurate. My e-mails and calls were met with a wall of silence.

This was not paranoia. As Collin and Rouach put it, 'L'Oréal is both highly accessible thanks to its advertising and its corporate communications, and difficult to penetrate because it is concerned about revealing its strategic advantages in a particularly competitive industry... The taste for secrecy within the group has become an art practised by a number of its managers.'

The authors add that people who work at L'Oréal feel as though they have signed a confidentiality agreement. Even after they have left the company, sharing its secrets would seem like a betrayal.

This 'taste for secrecy' made the scandal that reached its peak in the summer of 2010 seem particularly succulent. The story revolved around a feud between Liliane Bettencourt and her daughter, Françoise Bettencourt-Meyers. Françoise disapproved of a friendship between Liliane and a society photographer named François-Marie Banier, who had grown close to the elderly heiress after photographing her for a magazine. Taking the matter to court, Françoise claimed that Banier had exploited her mother's 'fragile mental state' in order to obtain gifts and donations worth almost €1 billion. She urged the court to hand control of her mother's estate over to her.

The matter was finally settled with a surprise reconciliation between the women. Bettencourt-Meyers dropped legal proceedings after her mother promised to sever all ties with Banier, including cutting him out of life insurance policies that named him as a beneficiary. The future of France's largest fortune was secured – but not before the media had gorged themselves on tales of illicit tape recordings, secret donations to France's ruling party, tax evasion on a jaw-dropping scale and the sort of largesse that considers an island in the Seychelles an appropriate gratuity.

A line was drawn under the affair when Liliane Bettencourt and her daughter were seen together in public for the first time since settling their differences. They attended the Paris fashion show of Armani, for which L'Oréal makes perfume.

In the world of beauty, even a scandal ends on a glamorous note.

BEAUTY TIPS

* Eugène Schueller sold his hair dyes using a two-pronged strategy: a close relationship with salon owners and hairdressers, and consumer marketing that linked hair styling with high fashion.

* He also evoked the need to look younger as a reason for purchase.

* Later he innovated in the fields of mass-market shampoos and suntan lotions.

* Schueller's successors moved L'Oréal into the luxury and skincare sectors – through acquisitions such as Lancôme and Vichy – and greatly expanded its research department.

* Charles Zviak believed that successful beauty brands are built on a 'golden triangle' of research, marketing and quality.

* Lindsay Owen-Jones, appointed CEO in 1988, is credited with having turned L'Oréal into a global giant.

* He specialized in emphasizing the heritage of a brand – such as the vibrant atmosphere of New York for Maybelline or the sophistication of Paris for Lancôme – to give it worldwide appeal.

* International brand managers ensured that L'Oréal's global 'mega-brands' maintained consistent values and identities worldwide but responded to local trends.

* Owen-Jones encouraged a spirit of internal competition between brands and employees to make the company more dynamic.

* L'Oréal's recruitment and training policies breed highly loyal and competitive employees.

GIANTS IN
THE BATHROOM

'Find out what consumers want
and then give it to them.'

William Procter may have had a spring in his step as he walked through the London streets that morning in 1832. Certainly, the prospect of a hard day's work held no fears for him. As a boy he'd been an apprentice in a general store, where he'd learned to make candles, a process known as 'dipping' from the way the wick was plunged into the wax. Now he was in his early 30s, and the future seemed brighter than a thousand candles. Just a day earlier, Procter had opened his own store selling woollen textiles and clothing. It was his first entrepreneurial venture and he had no reason to doubt that it would be a success.

Approaching the store, Procter noticed something wrong. The door appeared to be ajar, and there was a crack in the pane. A few moments later, his worst fears were confirmed: thieves had broken in. The shelves were empty. The burglary left Procter £8,000 in debt – a vast sum at the time. He had been ruined overnight.

Driven by either shame or undimmed optimism, Procter decided to start again in the New World. He and his wife left for the United States. When they arrived, they followed the example of many pioneers before them – and headed West. But bad luck hadn't quite finished with William Procter. As they journeyed down the Ohio River, his wife became ill, forcing him to seek medical attention in Cincinnati. She died a few months later.

Seemingly unable to move on, Procter got a job in a Cincinnati bank. Labouring to pay off his debts, he turned to candle-making in his spare time. This was a logical step, given the ready availability of oil and fat as a by-product of the city's most prominent trade: meat-packing. Soon Procter had abandoned the bank and was running a profitable one-man business.

Although he never left the town where his first wife had died, he recovered enough to court and marry a young woman named Olivia Norris, the daughter of prominent candle-maker Alexander Norris. Olivia's sister, Elizabeth Ann, was married to an Irishman, a soap-maker whose family had emigrated to the United States in 1819. By coincidence, this young man's illness had originally delayed his family in Cincinnati. When he recovered, they decided to stay. By the time William Procter met him, his soap and candle manufacturing business was doing passably well. His name was James Gamble.

PROCTER & GAMBLE: UNITED BY FATE

Alexander Norris was clearly a shrewd man. One imagines him sitting with his sons-in-law around the fire, perhaps smoking an after-dinner pipe. In any event, he had good advice for them. He observed that they were competing for the same raw materials. Why didn't they go into business together? Procter & Gamble was founded on 31 October 1837. Total assets: $7,192.24. (The story is recounted in a different form in the group's 2006 publication *P&G, A Company History: 1837 – today*.)

It was not, strictly speaking, a beauty company. Its success was built largely on soap, especially after the light bulb put candles in the shade. But like the beauty pioneers, Procter and Gamble were experts at branding – both instinctively and out of necessity.

The concept of branding emerged during the industrial revolution, when shopkeepers who had previously sold their products over the counter began shipping them far and wide, thanks to the age of steam. With access to both the railroad and the Ohio River, Procter and Gamble were ideally placed to profit from this new era. In common with other manufacturers, they were obliged to mark their crates with a symbol that would enable the often illiterate stevedores and freight handlers to identify them. The original P&G trademark was an encircled star. Eventually, William Procter added the moon and 13 stars, for the 13 first US colonies. The logo was to remain largely unchanged until the 1930s. And the company that it symbolized was already a million-dollar business by the end of the 1850s.

P&G proved skilled at spotting opportunities. Soap manufacturing depended on a substance called rosin, a solid resin extracted from pine sap. Amid rumours of an impending civil war, the sons of the founders – James Norris Gamble and William Alexander Proctor – travelled south to procure a huge supply of rosin, negotiating a bulk discount into the bargain. Meanwhile, the company began building a new plant to keep pace with increased sales. Sure enough, in 1862, while other manufacturers were forced to stand by helplessly as rosin supplies dwindled away, Procter & Gamble won contracts to supply soap and candles to the Union army.

This new generation also came up with one of the company's most enduring brand names. Ivory soap was developed by James Norris Gamble and another of Procter's sons, Harley. A happy accident in the mixing process had whisked more air into the product than usual, with the result that the bars of soap floated. The name was inspired by a line from the Bible that Harley Procter had spotted while in church: 'out of the ivory palaces'. It also had psychological power: in those days, the use of soap was often associated not only with cleanliness, but with fair skin.

Advertising at that time had a dismal reputation in the United States. It was thought of as glorified 'snake oil' salesmanship – fancy language designed to fool naïve consumers into purchasing dubious goods, the modern equivalent of the medicine man stepping off a stagecoach with a chinking bagful of ineffective potions. But Harley Procter felt that Ivory's unique properties would lend themselves well to an advertising campaign. He persuaded the partners to set aside an impressive budget of US$11,000. The miraculous soap, 'so pure it floats', was advertised in the *Independent* newspaper nationwide in 1882. It was destined for immense popularity. P&G later took advantage of the emergence of women's illustrated magazines, placing its first full-colour ad in *Cosmopolitan* in 1896.

As P&G raced toward the 20th century, it began to take on some of the shape of the company we know today. In 1886 it constructed a vast, ultra-modern factory called Ivorydale a few miles north of downtown Cincinnati. Four years later, this became home to one of the first product research labs in the United States, dedicated to devising better soap formulas and manufacturing methods. But a breakthrough in 1911 took P&G out of the bathroom altogether. The company had been experimenting with hydrogenated cotton seed oil, which stays solid at room temperature, as a raw material for soap. Along the way, it invented an alternative to conventional cooking fat. It marketed the product as Crisco, the healthier shortening. P&G boosted sales in 1912 by producing a cookbook containing recipes that required the use of Crisco.

Needless to say, the First World War barely troubled the company, which had once again prepared itself for tougher times. As the United States entered the consumer boom of the Roaring Twenties, P&G was in excellent shape to invest in a powerful new medium: radio. Crisco sponsored cooking shows, while Oxydol washing powder later attached its name to a serial called *Ma Perkins*. The sponsorship was so successful that P&G repeated the tactic with other brands. You certainly don't need me to tell you that this was the birth of the soap opera.

REDEFINING BEAUTIFUL

The desire to understand how consumers responded to its advertising led Procter & Gamble to innovate in another way. In 1924, it set up one of the first market research departments. Until that time, product development had been a largely instinctive, seat-of-the-pants affair. But P&G was determined to meet the quotidian needs of its customers – and to do that it needed more information about their lives.

The department was led by an economist named Paul 'Doc' Smelser. The (2000) book *American Business, 1920–2000: How it worked,* by Thomas K McGraw, portrays Doc as 'a small, feisty, serious man' whose dapper sports jackets and ties clashed with the sombre attire of most P&G executives. He would further provoke them by walking up to them and 'asking them, out of the blue, questions such as "What percentage of Ivory soap is used for face and hands and what percentage for dishwashing?" Often, nobody knew the answer.'

Doc ran the market research department for 34 years, building it into 'perhaps the most sophisticated unit of its kind in the world'. His staff of researchers swelled to hundreds. He recruited thousands of door-to-door interviewers, many of them women who were required to wear 'a conservative dress, high heels and a hat'. They gently quizzed interviewees about their cooking, laundry and housework habits. During this process 'they were to carry no lists, forms, or writing materials' in order not to intimidate their subjects. This meant that they had to dash back to their cars to write down what they'd heard.

From the swathes of intelligence coming into his department, Doc discovered 'almost everything that could be learned about how the company's products and competing items were being used, how they might be used, and what consumers liked or disliked about them'. In addition, he concerned himself with media research. 'He liked to surprise managers of radio stations by giving them precise statistics about the size of their audience, statistics they themselves did not possess.'

With Doc's help, P&G could fulfil its mission: 'Find out what consumers want and then give it to them.' But that particular phrase was coined by another pioneer within the group. His name was Neil McElroy – and he was the inventor of brand management.

McElroy had joined P&G straight from Harvard in 1925. Six years later, he was working on an advertising campaign for Camay soap when it occurred to him that there might be a more effective way of running the marketing department. He fired off a three-page memo suggesting that, rather than having its marketing people work across several different brands, the company should establish dedicated teams for each brand. These would be run as separate businesses, with a small group of employees reporting to a brand manager. As well as marketing, they would be responsible for sales, product development and all other tasks related to ensuring the success of the brand. Each brand would compete with all the others within P&G, as well as with those outside. This would drive innovation and force brands to discover new niches.

Procter & Gamble adopted McElroy's proposal. It was a forerunner of the technique that Lindsay Owen-Jones would use many years later to create internal competition at L'Oréal. 'Brand management as a business technique was one of the signal innovations in American marketing during the twentieth century,' confirms McGraw.

By the end of the Second World War, P&G was a true leviathan. Its competitiveness had created a tough corporate culture. McGraw sees it as 'tightly knit, secretive, ambitious [and] marketing-obsessed'. Through a series of new launches and acquisitions, it seemed to insinuate itself into every aspect of consumers' daily lives. The roster of brands launched in the second half of the 20th century reads like a weekly shopping list: Tide detergent (1946), Crest toothpaste (1955), Charmin toilet paper (1957), Pampers diapers (1961), Head & Shoulders shampoo (1961), Ariel detergent (1967), Pringle's potato chips (1968), Bounce fabric softener (1972) and Always sanitary pads (1983).

It extended its reach into the beauty sector with the acquisition of Richardson-Vicks (Oil of Olay, Pantene and Vidal Sassoon) in 1985, Noxell (maker of CoverGirl and Noxzema) in 1989, Old Spice a year later and Max Factor and Ellen Betrix cosmetics the year after that.

These purchases encouraged it to develop its fragrance business with the launch of Giorgio Beverly Hills; eventually it would produce scents for Dolce & Gabbana, Dunhill, Escada, Gucci, Hugo Boss, Lacoste and Puma, among others.

The company's market research and brand management techniques made it a formidable machine. One of its goals, according to Tom McGraw, was to double its sales every 10 years. To do this, it set billions aside for advertising, mostly on television. By 1993 its sales exceeded US$30 billion – more than half of those outside the United States.

But despite its interests in the beauty sector, P&G was still a mass consumer goods company dabbling in the beauty business. As Geoffrey Jones describes in *Beauty Imagined*, all that changed in the early 1990s. In 1992, P&G chief executive Ed Artzt gave a speech called 'Redefining beautiful', in which he opined that beauty was 'the most dynamic sector' that the company operated in, as well as the one 'with the most potential for growth'. Explaining why a '155-year-old soap and detergent company would want to venture into the world of fashion and glamour', he pointed out that the beauty business was increasingly driven by research and technology, which made it 'our kind of business'.

Less than a decade later, P&G was headed by AG Lafley, who had previously run the company's beauty management group. He understood that the high margins of beauty products delivered impressive returns on investment. Beauty also chimed, writes Jones, 'with P&G's strengths in branding and innovation, and the company's deep knowledge of the discount, drug and grocery store channels'. It began to pile advertising money behind the dormant Oil of Olay brand and expand its hair care business, buying hair colorant maker Clairol.

Then, in 2005, it acquired Gillette for US$57 billion, creating at a stroke the world's largest consumer goods group. The move gave it access not only to Gillette's shaving products, but also to Braun electrical appliances, Right Guard deodorant and Duracell batteries. And the deal gave P&G strength in an area where it had been somewhat lacking: the male grooming market ('P&G to buy Gillette for US$57 billion', Associated Press, 28 January 2005).

By the end of the decade, Procter & Gamble had shape-shifted from 'a soap and detergent company' to one that owed half of its total sales to beauty, personal care and health.

UNILEVER: CONTRIBUTING TO PERSONAL ATTRACTIVENESS

P&G has other competitors in the household goods and personal care categories. You'll be familiar with Colgate-Palmolive, Reckitt Benckiser and Johnson & Johnson, all of which are present in our bathrooms in one form or another, from toothpaste and headache tablets to shampoo and baby powder. But let's take a closer look at Unilever, which has a handful of major brands in Dove, Lux, Pond's, Lifebuoy, Sunsilk, TIGI, Vaseline and the cheeky men's fragrance brand Axe (known as Lynx in the United Kingdom).

It also had a major impact on the history of personal hygiene. In the late 19th century, one of the founders of the company that became Unilever, an Englishman named William Hesketh Lever, had an idea that was to revolutionize the way people bought and used soap.

Born in Bolton in 1851, Lever was the son of a grocer, and as was the way of things he naturally followed his father into that trade. In those days, soap was sold to grocers in large blocks, which the shopkeeper cut into smaller chunks for each customer. Young William Lever began wondering if it wouldn't be possible to sell soap in individual bars. He started his own business, initially marketing soap from other manufacturers.

Convinced that the quality of soap could be improved, he began reinvesting his profits into research. With his brother James, he leased a factory in Warrington in the name of Lever Brothers. (James never played a role in the business – Adam Macqueen's 2005 book *The King of Sunlight: How William Lever cleaned up the world*, suggests that he had diabetes, a poorly understood illness at the time, which may have led to him being regarded as mentally unstable.)

At Warrington, Lever experimented with various formulas before arriving at a blend of palm kernel oil, cotton seed oil, resin and tallow. He marketed it as Sunlight soap, wrapping each bar in colourful, eye-catching packaging. This was affordable, unfussy, mass-produced cleanliness. Sales rose so rapidly that Lever was obliged to open a larger factory beside the River Mersey in Cheshire. In an echo of Procter & Gamble's Ivorydale, he called the new premises Port Sunlight. By 1895, it was producing 40,000 tons of soap a year.

Lever saw himself as more than a mere entrepreneur. He aimed to improve the lives of everyday Victorians, 'to make cleanliness commonplace; to lessen work for women; to foster health and contribute to personal attractiveness, that life would be more enjoyable and rewarding for the people who use our products' (www.unilever.com).

He also strove to ensure that his workers led happy, comfortable lives. Port Sunlight was not just a factory – it was a village, with housing and amenities for all those who worked there. This had the built-in disadvantage that, if you lost your job, you also lost your home.

Adam Macqueen writes that Lever's workers

> lived in great style, their spacious houses an extraordinary mishmash of architectural details and chocolate-box tweeness built according to Lever's peculiar tastes, but every aspect of their lifestyle was strictly prescribed. They ate together in vast, segregated dining halls under the gaze of Pre-Raphaelite masterpieces, the overflow of Lever's personal art collection. They exercised together in the village gymnasium or swam in the open-air swimming pool next to the village green. They worshipped at the fake medieval church, drank at the Temperance Inn and sat together through 'absolutely compulsory' lessons in history, languages and literature.
>
> ('The king of sunlight', *Times*, 13 May 2004)

This paternalist approach extended to their social lives. In their spare time they were expected to engage in one of the activities laid on by the village, from a philharmonic orchestra to an amateur dramatic society 'complete with its own 1000-seater auditorium'. Women had to ask permission from the 'social department' if they wished to attend the weekly dance at the town hall with a male colleague. Rule-breakers or those who did not fit in could be fired. Lever was by no means the first to equate physical cleanliness with enlightenment and probity, but few took the idea to such extremes.

At work, Lever kept a beady eye on proceedings, peering out over the factory floor from his glassed-in office. Nevertheless – like their homes and their works canteen – the eight-hour day, pension schemes, and unemployment and sickness benefits enjoyed by his employees were practically unheard of elsewhere. Writes Macqueen:

> In 1888, the year Port Sunlight was founded, more than 1,000 workers at the Bryant & May match factory in East London went on strike over being forced to work unbroken 14-hour shifts handling yellow phosphorous, a carcinogen that literally rotted away the faces of those exposed to it. Most factory staff were expected to pay for their own

overalls and tools out of their meagre wages, and even to stump up for the cost of heating the factory.

(Ibid)

Not all of Lever's innovations attracted universal praise. In 1906 he joined forces with other soap manufacturers to form a monopoly 'soap trust', with the idea that consumers as well as manufacturers would benefit from economies of scale in terms of raw materials, production and advertising. But such monopolies had already come under attack in the United States, and Lever's move was harshly criticized by the British press. A newspaper cartoon in the *Daily Mirror* parodied his empire as 'Port Moonshine' and depicted a greedy soap tycoon telling a cowed customer: 'I'm boss of the situation, nobody else can make soap but me and I can raise the price to what I like.' Similar accusations by the *Daily Mail* prompted Lever to sue. He won to the tune of £50,000, but the monopoly was dismantled before the year was out.

This setback did not prevent Lever from expanding his company. In 1910 he acquired Pears soap. The popular brand had been launched in London at the end of the 18th century by a Soho barber named Andrew Pears. Many of Pears's customers complained about the effects of harsh soap on their skin, so he began experimenting with natural, gentler ingredients, finally creating a product based on glycerine. The soap's transparency and floral aroma proved highly appealing, although it was only at the instigation of Andrew's grandson, Francis Pears, that it became the basis of a business under the name A & F Pears Limited.

Francis Pears was aided by an early marketing genius in the form of his son-in-law, Thomas J Barrett. In a famous moment from advertising history, Barrett convinced the pre-Raphaelite artist Sir John Everett Millais to sell him a sentimental painting of an angelic young boy gazing at rising soap bubbles. He even persuaded Millais to add a bar of Pears soap to the image. 'Bubbles' became an icon – the kind of advertisement that people hung on their walls at home. In addition, Barrett secured one of the first celebrity endorsements – from Lillie Langtry, actress, courtesan and mistress of the Prince of Wales.

When Lever got his hands on Pears, he moved production to Port Sunlight. He also took a leaf out of Barrett's book, acquiring paintings and transforming them into advertisements for his goods. Unlike Barrett, he did not always ask permission.

Lever took a unique approach to advertising by creating what was effectively an internal agency: Lever International Advertising Services, better known as Lintas. Though it later broke away from its parent to become an independent agency, it remained heavily dependent on its creator for decades, until its name eventually dissolved in the advertising industry's endless churn of acquisitions and consolidations.

The altruistic approach that William Lever had adopted in Great Britain did not extend to his palm oil operation in the Belgian Congo, where he took advantage of a horrifying forced labour system introduced by the colonizers. The atmosphere was more *Heart of Darkness* than Port Sunlight. Today such practices would provoke consumer outrage and a boycott, but the colonial era operated under different moral rules, and Lever maintained his reputation as a philanthropist. He was made Baron Leverhulme in 1917, and Viscount Leverhulme in 1922. He died of pneumonia in 1925.

Five years later, palm oil formed the slippery foundations of a new entity. Lever Brothers joined forces with Dutch margarine producer Margarine Unie, which also depended on palm oil to make its product. Together, they could import bulk quantities more efficiently and economically. The merged company was named Unilever.

The company weathered the Great Depression of the 1930s, partly by riding a trend away from the use of 'hard soap' in household cleaning towards flakes and powders. Additionally, it ran campaigns vaunting the merits of vitamin-enriched margarine, driving sales to an all-time high. In 1941, during the Blitz in London, Unilever's Lifebuoy soap sponsored a free emergency washing service. Lifebuoy-branded vans equipped with hot showers, soap and towels sped to areas whose water supply had been knocked out by the bombing.

From 1950 onwards, Unilever's progress closely resembled that of Procter & Gamble. At Port Sunlight, there was an increased focus on research, as laboratories were set up to analyse consumer trends and technological advances in the fields of hygiene and nutrition. The same decade saw the launch of two of Unilever's most successful brands: Sunsilk shampoo and Dove soap.

When Sunsilk first began advertising on TV in 1955, the message was that – unlike rival brands – it required just one application, washing out fewer natural oils. But the brand's advertising really got into its stride in 1967, thanks to Bond movie soundtrack composer John Barry, who provided a melody called 'The girl with the sun in her hair'. The ads themselves were evocative enough. In one, a fresh-faced young woman is rowed across a lake by her boyfriend: 'A face without make-up proves it – a girl's most important cosmetic is her shampoo… it's part of the art of beauty.' But true classiness was bestowed on them by Barry's haunting theme, which proved so popular that it became a hit single.

Stricken by the oil crisis, the 1970s were tough for everyone, but for Unilever the general ambience of struggle was exacerbated by the rise of the supermarket chains, whose buying clout sapped it of its negotiating power. Unilever struck back: pushing into the United States with the purchase of National Starch and becoming one of the world's biggest providers of tea by adding Lipton International. The deodorant brand Impulse ('Men can't help acting on impulse') was also launched during this period. Like P&G at the time, though, Unilever was still a consumer goods company with some beauty interests.

That situation changed, for a time, in the 1980s, when Unilever sold off non-core activities – such as transport and packaging – and went shopping for the kind of businesses it liked best: detergents, food and toiletries. Amidst this spree it snapped up Chesebrough-Pond's in the United States, owner of Vaseline Intensive Care, Pond's Cold Cream and, somewhat incongruously, Ragú spaghetti sauce.

A trio of acquisitions in 1989 made Unilever a major player in the perfume and cosmetics sector. In swift succession it bought Schering-Plough's European fragrance business, Calvin Klein and Fabergé Inc, which included the Elizabeth Arden brand and the fragrances of Chloé, Lagerfeld and Fendi. Like P&G, Unilever reasoned that beauty was a high-margins business, and one that it needed to be big in. Seven years later it added Helen Curtis Industries, the Chicago-based company whose body and hair care brands included Suave, Finesse and Salon Selectives.

By 2000 it had merged all its beauty interests into a separate company called Unilever Cosmetics International. Ironically, that move marked the beginning of the end of its flirtation with prestige beauty.

REAL BEAUTY

In 2005, Unilever once again decided to rationalize its brand portfolio. Throughout the 1980s and 1990s the company's volume growth had averaged a lacklustre 2.5 per cent. At the turn of the millennium it had implemented a strategy called 'Path to Growth', but while this delivered efficiencies in areas like the buying of raw materials it failed to move the needle on sales growth.

This was because Unilever had not changed with the times. Historically it had 'acted local' rather than global, with largely autonomous companies managing their own brand portfolios in each market. As the world became smaller, a more focused top-down strategy was needed. Unilever would become a global business with a single global message and strong global brands.

As part of the new approach, Unilever would make a clear-eyed assessment of its strengths and weaknesses and sell off underperforming brands. Its analysis showed that fast-growing areas in the personal care sector were deodorants, skincare and hair. Note here the absence of the word 'fragrances'. In the end, Unilever was more at home with the likes of Sunsilk and Dove than with high-end fashion brands like Vera Wang and Cerruti. So Unilever Cosmetics International had to go – sold to the giant US fragrance company Coty for US$800 million ('Unilever parts with perfume names', news.bbc.co.uk, 20 May 2005).

At around the same time, Unilever launched a new mission, announcing that its goal was to 'meet everyday needs for nutrition, hygiene and personal care with brands that help people look good, feel good and get more out of life'. This policy of 'bringing vitality to life' would influence everything it did.

It certainly had a dramatic effect on one particular brand: Dove.

As we've established in the preceding chapters, the oldest marketing tactic in the book for beauty brands is to make consumers paranoid about their looks. Something is wrong with you – acne, dry skin, oily skin, signs of ageing, *especially* signs of ageing – and they can fix it. But what if Dove positioned itself as the skincare range for people who refused to buy into this emotional blackmail? What if Dove made you feel good about being you?

The Dove Campaign for Real Beauty was launched in 2004, with creative work from the advertising agency Ogilvy & Mather and PR support from Edelman Public Relations. Its flagship was a press and poster campaign shot by the fashion photographer Rankin. The images showed ordinary women – some of them recruited via newspaper advertisements – posing self-confidently in their underwear in all their imperfect glory. Though they were perfectly lit and displayed to their best advantage, they were clearly not supermodels. For a start, they had breasts and thighs – and even tummies. The campaign stood out so strongly in a sector populated by digitally enhanced naiads that it immediately attracted a slew of press coverage.

Another successful element of the campaign was a 2007 online video called 'Evolution'. This showed an ordinary, rather spotty teenage girl facing the camera. A time-lapse sequence demonstrates how make-up, hair styling and – crucially – Photoshop alterations transform her from the girl next door into the kind of goddess we're used to seeing in beauty ads. 'No wonder our perception of beauty is distorted' comments the end-line, before providing a link to Dove's 'Self-Esteem Fund'. This was created by Unilever 'to support different initiatives that help educate and inspire girls on a wider definition of beauty'. For example, it has partnered with the Butterfly Association, an Australian organization helping people with eating disorders.

'Evolution' won two Grand Prix at the Cannes Lions – the ad industry's equivalent of the Oscars – but it also prompted some observers to look harder at the ethics behind the Dove campaign. There were suggestions that the print ads themselves were not entirely free of Photoshop tampering. It was also pointed out that Unilever makes skin lightening cream Fair & Lovely for the Asian market – and that its ads for male personal care brand Axe (Lynx in the UK) are based on the premise that the smell of the product is irresistible to the impossibly sexy babes who queue up to get it on with the hero.

The journalist Alicia Clegg had considered the ethical dilemma of the campaign in an earlier piece for Interbrand's Brand Channel website. 'The campaign... has an implied moral purpose,' she wrote, 'one that takes on the ethical issues of consumerism: the psychology of self-esteem, the supposed link between the pressure to conform and eating disorders and the various stigmas attaching to old age and disfigurement.' And yet, she opined, 'Dove's marketing is the reality of reality TV, not of everyday life. The models – though not glamorous – have all been given the glamour treatment... Just as a reality TV turns ordinary Joes into stars for a day, so

Dove's campaign elevates ordinary women into honorary beauties' ('Dove gets real', brandchannel.com, 18 April 2005).

The clincher, of course, was that the entire purpose of the campaign was to sell beauty products. The original ads shot by Rankin were for 'skin firming creams' designed to 'visibly reduce the appearance of cellulite'. If the ethical approach was not hypocritical, it was at least disingenuous.

But it worked. It gave Dove a purpose that demarcated it from competing brands, it significantly increased sales (by as much as 700 per cent in some markets) and it reaped millions of dollars' worth of free media coverage.

After the initial spike, however, sales began to flatten out. A new debate began about whether women really wanted to look at 'realistic' portrayals of themselves. Perhaps what they actually wanted to hear was that 'fabulous' women – the actresses and the supermodels – shared some of their problems and insecurities? And that beauty products helped them be the best they could be?

A French advertising professional told me: 'The problem with the Dove campaign is that it does not offer hope, which is what beauty advertising is all about. People buy beauty products because they haven't given up on themselves. They don't want to look 'ordinary'. They want to look extraordinary. They want something transformative. Morally and intellectually, women approve of Dove's message. But when they're in the store, their heart tells them something else. So they reach for the product that promises to make them more beautiful.'

THE WORLD'S BIGGEST SKINCARE BRAND

Another brand in our bathroom cabinets has long occupied the 'healthy and natural' territory partly encroached upon by Dove. According to the researcher Euromonitor, it is the world's top-selling name in skincare. It comes from Germany and it is, of course, Nivea.

Compared to some of the more upmarket beauty brands, Nivea feels innocuous, friendly, almost innocent. As it reaps more than €5 billion in annual sales, there is every reason to believe that this is the result of a consistent marketing effort.

Nivea was launched in 1911. According to its website, it has always been 'fuelled by... a mixture of research, creativity and business know-how', all of which recall the 'golden triangle' described by L'Oréal's Charles Zviak.

The brand is owned by Beiersdorf, but it was not created by that company's founder, Paul Carl Beiersdorf. Not that Beiersdorf was not innovative in his own right. A pharmacist by trade, he set up shop in Hamburg in 1880 and worked with a researcher named Paul Gerson Unna to develop the first sticking plaster. It was based on gutta-percha natural latex, obtained from the sap of the tropical plant that gave it its name. The invention was patented in 1882.

In 1890, Beiersdorf sold the business to another pharmacist, Dr Oscar Troplowitz. This was the man who would turn Beiersdorf into a global branded goods company. He combined an entrepreneurial spirit with a shrewd understanding of customers and an ability to translate their needs into products.

Paul Beiersdorf's former scientific adviser, Paul Gerson Unna, told Troplowitz about a new emulsifying agent called Eucerit, derived from lanolin, which made it possible to create a stable oil-and-water-based cream and manufacture it in industrial quantities. Swiftly buying the patent for the product, as well as the factory that made it, Troplowitz used it as the basis for Nivea. The name derived from the Latin for 'snow', *nix, nivis*. As well as the Eucerit that bonded oils with water, the cream also included 'glycerine, a little citric acid and, to lend it a delicate scent, oil of rose and lily of the valley'. The recipe has changed little.

The product's pure white colour and subtle fragrance hint at Troplowitz's marketing savvy. He understood that skincare was not just about efficacy, but also about emotion. Early advertisements featured a vulnerable 'femme fragile'. Their style, though, was contemporary and dynamic – the work of Hans Rudi Erdt, one of a new generation of artists specializing in commercial art.

Troplowitz died in 1918, but his successors proved equally visionary. Long before the likes of L'Oréal, P&G and Unilever espoused the 'mega-brand' approach, the Nivea name was stretched to embrace a multiplicity of personal care products: soap, shampoo, powder and shaving cream.

The 'femme fragile' survived until the 1920s, when the emergence of short-haired, athletic, automobile-driving lasses began to make her look distinctly out of date. 'Youth and freshness' were adopted as brand values for changing times. In addition, the cream was positioned as a multi-purpose product for all the family – as good for softening a man's beard as it was a woman's skin. This approach was underlined by a print ad featuring three fresh-faced young boys grinning at the camera. At the same time, the brand launched a competition to find 'the Nivea girls'. The copy exhorted: 'We don't want beauties or belles of the ball… but you should be healthy, clean and fresh and simply gorgeous girls.'

This was also the moment when the brand adopted its iconic blue and white colouring: pure and uncomplicated.

In the late 1930s, responsibility for the brand's advertising was handed to the talented Elly Heuss-Knapp, who became one of the most famous women in the field. She took Nivea outdoors, associating it with blue skies and the sporting life in illustrations of athletic young women who had nothing to envy the Gibson girls. Significantly, she was forced to steer the brand's image through the Nazi era.

Jewish members of Beiersdorf's management – including chairman Willy Jacobsohn – fled soon after the Nazis took power. Control of the company passed to Carl Claussen, who had married one of Troplowitz's nieces. The Nivea brand was further safeguarded by licensing it to manufacturers abroad – a strategy that caused problems after the war, when licensees' differing marketing strategies threatened to dilute the image of the brand. Decades would pass before Beiersdorf was able to bring Nivea back under central control. It patched up the problem by liaising closely with foreign owners to ensure that branding messages were in sync.

In the meantime, writes Geoffrey Jones, Heuss-Knapp's ads performed 'a delicate balancing act'. They might 'be interpreted as aligned with the Nazi ideology about the superiority of blonde and blue-eyed Nordic natural beauty, but they also built on the long-established brand identity, which emphasized health and athleticism for the liberated modern woman'.

Thanks to its diplomatic manoeuvring and the ambiguity of its image, Beiersdorf survived the war intact. It entered the 1950s optimistic that Nivea remained a much-loved brand and that there were still plenty of areas into which it could expand. It did not have to wait long. As economic prosperity returned and international travel grew more common, Beiersdorf responded to the trend for overseas beach holidays with a range of Nivea sun care creams.

As the global skincare market became increasingly competitive, Beiersdorf emphasized Nivea's heritage with claims of unrivalled quality, effectiveness and honesty. 'La crème de la crème', read one of its print ads in 1971, with an unadorned picture of the classic blue tin. No models, no opulent backdrops; rather than trying to compete with luxury brands, the ad seemed to be mocking their pretentiousness – a subtle way of asking: 'Why pay more?'

Beiersdorf owns other brands – notably the luxury brand La Prairie, about which we'll hear more in Chapter 9 – but Nivea is a phenomenon. The unwavering focus that Beiersdorf kept on it, as well as the equity of trust it enjoyed among consumers, enabled it to thrive in a globalized environment. It now embraces some 500 different products for women, men, babies, skin, hair, hand, bath and sun. It offers shaving creams and anti-ageing products, hair styling gels and facial cleansers. Its research department in Hamburg is as advanced as those of its rivals. It is sold in 170 countries, and in Germany it has a brand recognition of 100 per cent. Above all, no matter what the brand extension, its marketing has steadfastly maintained the fresh, optimistic, family-oriented approach that it adopted in the 1920s. Neither promoting the 'ordinariness' of Dove's real women nor the 'extraordinariness' of L'Oréal's glossy superstars, it exists to soothe us, in almost any circumstances.

Nivea exudes a halo of reliability that one would be hard pressed to find among more prestigious brands. Consider whether you would rub a cream labelled Chanel or Yves Saint Laurent into an infant's skin. This is perhaps because Chanel and Yves Saint Laurent are associated first and foremost with perfumes: potent, tangy, faintly sinful, irredeemably adult.

BEAUTY TIPS

✳ In the 19th century, Procter & Gamble in the United States and Unilever in the UK brought hygiene to the masses.

✳ Initially relying on the savvy of their founders, they later developed advanced scientific and marketing research departments.

✳ Their goal was to deliver products that exactly matched the quotidian needs of specific target groups of consumers.

✳ Mainly concerned with fast-moving consumer goods, P&G and Unilever moved into beauty because it offered high margins.

✳ Unilever pulled out of the prestige fragrance sector to concentrate on mass brands that make consumers 'feel good about life'.

✳ One example of this is Dove, which was cunningly repositioned as a brand that promotes 'real beauty'.

✳ Beiersdorf turned Nivea into the world's biggest skincare brand by ruthlessly focusing on its healthy, wholesome, family image.

✳ Consistent branding and a legacy of trust have enabled the 100-year-old Nivea to expand into many areas of skincare and beauty.

✳ Very early on, the 'bathroom giants' realized that selling beauty products is not just about efficacy, but also about expectancy, emotion and experience.

THE STARDUST
FACTOR

'Make-up madness, like movie madness, was here to stay.'

Make-up saved Max Factor's life. At the time, he was still Maximilian Faktorowicz, cosmetician and make-up artist to the Imperial Russian Grand Opera and the court of Czar Nicholas II. He was, writes Fred E Basten in his (2008) book *Max Factor: The man who changed the faces of the world*, 'forever on call, at the whim of the court favourites who wanted him to attend to their beautification, to create a new hairstyle, or to correct cosmetic problems, so that their eyes might sparkle, cheeks glow and hair gleam when the Czar of all Russia looked on them'.

But Max was under surveillance in another way, too. As a Jew, he was considered an interloper, constantly watched by the Czar's secret police. He had witnessed the passing of anti-Semitic laws, and was aware of riots and pogroms in the Pale of Settlement. In strict contravention of the rules of court, he had married in secret and fathered three children. 'I was a slave,' he said. 'All I wanted was to be free.'

Typically of the beauty pioneers, it is impossible to separate embellishment from reality in the early life of Max Factor. But here the story is so ravishing, so full of detail and incident, that one wants to believe. Max had a friend at court – an important general, perhaps a little vain, whom the cosmetician had aided with a tip or two. This man – his hair blacker than it might otherwise have been, his beard more trim and dashing – helped Max to escape. He put it around court that the cosmetician looked ill. A physician was duly dispatched. He found an ailing Max in bed, his skin the yellowish hue of old parchment. Pronouncing jaundice, the doctor recommended a cure of 90 days at Carlsbad, a Bohemian spa.

The jaundice was faked: the sickly skin an undetectable cosmetic preparation.

The guards left Max at Carlsbad railway station. Shortly afterwards, he reunited with his family. They slipped into the forest around the ancient spa town and headed for the coast – and a ship to the United States. It was February 1904.

THE CZAR'S BEAUTICIAN

Max Factor does not seem to have been seduced by glamour. Rather, he created it. He was born in 1877 in Lodz, Poland, and if he had any schooling he never spoke of it. When we meet him as a small boy, he is selling fruit and bonbons in the lobby of the Czarina Theatre, his 'introduction to the world of make-believe'. Soon after that, we find him working as an assistant at a local apothecary. At the age of nine, he is apprenticed to a leading wigmaker and cosmetician. He has talent, and rises quickly: he works with Anton of Berlin, a hairstylist and creator of cosmetics; he travels to Moscow to work under Korpo, wigmaker and cosmetician to the Imperial Russian Grand Opera. By the age of 18, when most of us are still dithering about a direction, Max is skilled in the arts of wig-making and, crucially, stage make-up.

There was no other kind. It was a period of history when face paint was distinctly unfashionable; in fact, it was considered wicked. The ravages caused by lead-based whitening products and other toxic powders that were widely used before the 19th century had led to a demonization of cosmetics. Ordinary women might apply creams to soften their skin, a subtle blush of rouge, perhaps even a dab of lip pomade. Anything more daring was for actresses and their semi-equivalents, prostitutes.

After obligatory military service, Max almost escaped the gravitational pull of the imperial court. He opened his own boutique on the outskirts of Moscow: wigs, rouge and creams of his own making. But news of his talent spread. A theatrical troupe engaged by the imperial family became his largest client. Soon, he was back at the imperial opera, leaving his store in the hands of an assistant, under orders to return only once or twice a week to gather make-up supplies. It is astonishing that he found time to meet and clandestinely court Lizzie, the woman who became his wife.

There is a picture of the Faktorowicz family in Basten's book: three serious young children in matching smocks, Lizzie dark-eyed, her hair pulled back, big hoop earrings giving her a gypsy exoticism but otherwise serious, pale, distinctly unmade up. Max sits beside her, slim and dapper in his sombre suit and wing collar, his wavy black locks brushed back with brilliantine, lustrous and just at the edge of rebelling. His moustache curls jauntily: appearances matter. The picture was taken in 1904, only weeks before they fled to America.

They arrived in New York aboard the *Molka III*. They were not in steerage, or even in third class: Max's slavery had come with gilded chains, and his family was among the more well off on the vessel. They did not see Ellis Island, but passed through immigration on the pier, where the customs official inevitably barbered the family name. From then on, the make-up artist was known as Max Factor.

He hated New York from the first: too rushed, too aggressive. Stopping a man on the street, he asked 'if there was any place in America without so many people, and not going someplace so quick'.

Max himself was going places fast – but not to a language school. He posed his question in Polish. He would never learn to speak English properly: one imagines him with an amiable, movie immigrant patter, like Carl the head waiter from *Casablanca*.

Faintly comic though his accent may have been, Max Factor was a sharply intelligent entrepreneur. On the ship, he'd convinced a young man who spoke English to help him set up a stall at the forthcoming St Louis World's Fair. This enabled him to test his preparations on the US public: 'cosmetics, perfumes, combs and hair products created by the former beautician to Russia's royal family'. The pitch was sound, the seven-month engagement a success. Max stayed in St Louis to open a barber's shop; make-up was not used widely enough to sustain a business, but everyone needed a haircut from time to time.

Tragedy nudged him towards Hollywood. Lizzie died suddenly of a brain haemorrhage on 17 March 1906. In August that year, desperate to find somebody to help him look after his children – there were now five of them – he married a Russian girl, the daughter of a friend. It was a disaster; they were neither in love nor compatible, and divorced within two years. A helpful neighbour, Jennie Cook, offered to mind the children. She became Max's third wife on 21 January 1908.

At around this time, customers in the barber's shop began talking of a new form of entertainment: 'photoplays' – moving pictures, the same nickelodeons that entranced Florence Nightingale Graham, the future Elizabeth Arden. Max paid his nickel and was enchanted too. But, unlike Arden, he did not wish to enter the dream world of movies. He scrutinized the badly applied make-up, the unconvincing wigs, the laughably false beards – and realized that he could work for them.

MAKING UP THE MOVIES

The popularization of make-up in the 20th century was directly linked to the development of cinema and its alluring stars. Max Factor was at the leading edge of this evolution. The word 'visionary' is entirely appropriate: Max was always one step ahead, constantly innovating, unafraid to take risks. His biggest gamble was also his smartest: he opened his first store at 1204 South Central Avenue in Los Angeles on 11 October 1908. In January the following year, Max Factor & Company was officially founded.

The store stocked theatre 'greasepaint' by brands such as Leichner and Minor, alongside Max's own powders, creams and pomades. In his spare time he visited the makeshift movie sets where directors like DW Griffith were forging a new industry. The actors generally used stage make-up, which looked heavy and fake on screen. Writes Basten: 'Stage make-up had to be applied one-eighth of an inch thick, then powdered. When it dried it formed a stiff mask and often cracked, which wasn't a problem in the theatre where audiences were seated far away from the performers, but on-screen, especially in close-ups, it didn't work.'

Some actors were experimenting with their own flesh-coloured concoctions, like ground brick dust mixed with Vaseline. Max gently urged them to drop by his store: his powders were far more comfortable. In the meantime he set up a laboratory out back, where he worked on adapting stage make-up for the screen. As his store became busier, he found himself in demand for his wig-making skills too: he kitted out dozens of Indian braves for Cecil B DeMille's *The Squaw Man*, the first feature-length movie ever made in Hollywood.

The year the movie was released, 1914, Max perfected his 'flexible greasepaint'. This came as a cream in jars, rather than in the old stick form, and was far thinner and easier to apply. It was available in twelve different shades designed to mimic the skin tone of the wearer. Max was already well known thanks to his work with Griffith and DeMille – now stars like Buster Keaton, Charlie Chaplin and Fatty Arbuckle visited his store personally to buy their make-up; many of them also asked him to apply it. For the remainder of his Hollywood career, Max would ensure that his boutiques were equipped with dressing rooms for the stars.

Max Factor & Company expanded as Hollywood grew from a bucolic suburb into the hub of the movie industry. The business moved into larger premises in the Pantages Building in downtown Los Angeles. Max created false eyelashes out of human hair for the actress Phyllis Haver; this started a trend among young women. In 1918 he launched a revised version of his 'flexible greasepaint', which he called the Color Harmony line: he believed that make-up should complement not only skin tone, but also hair and eye colour.

He used dark eye shadow to give Gloria Swanson a languidly sexy gaze, turned her frizzy hairstyle into the sleek cut of a femme fatale – and made her career. Rudolph Valentino may also have owed his stardom to Max, who trimmed the Italian actor's eyebrows, slicked back his hair and subtly lightened his complexion. In the 1920s, Max began using the theatre insiders' term 'make-up' instead of cosmetics in his promotional material, helping the phrase towards wider adoption.

Stung by the cold reception he received at Leichner when he visited the greasepaint manufacturer's headquarters in Germany on a rare vacation – he was kept waiting in reception for an hour – he cut his ties with the company and began marketing his own brand aggressively. Max Factor began selling greasepaint in collapsible tubes in 1922: this time it came in 31 different shades, including 'white, very light pink, sallow, sunburn, dark brown and black'. Visitors to Hollywood began to notice that actresses were still wearing make-up after the day's filming. The seductive 'bee-stung lips' of actresses like Clara Bow were particularly desirable. They were the simple result of a technique Max had developed to rapidly apply lip pomade, before the invention of the lipstick tube. '[H]e dipped his thumb into the pomade and pressed two thumbprints onto the upper lip. Then he turned his thumb upside down and pressed another thumbprint on to the centre of the lower lip. Finally, he used a brush to contour the lip.'

In polite society, the resistance to make-up began to break down. Fred Basten writes: 'As more and more women sat in darkened theatres thinking Clara Bow's bee-stung lips and Theda Bara's daring rouge and shocking mascara looked irresistible, they began testing the limits of old-fashioned respectability. Worse, the immoral word "make-up" had replaced the more refined and acceptable "cosmetics"… Make-up madness, like movie madness, was here to stay.'

Hollywood inevitably had an impact on hairstyles too. Max understood that the luminescence of the silver screen was particularly flattering to blonde hair. After he dyed Jean Harlow's hair an almost white – 'platinum' – blonde, the look became more desirable than it had been since women struggled to bleach their locks in Renaissance Italy.

He adapted to every change the movie industry threw at him. When talking pictures required a new kind of lighting – silent tungsten lamps rather than juddering carbon arc lights – he perfected make-up suited to the softer illumination and the more sensitive panchromatic film that went with it. In 1928, his giant new establishment near the corner of Hollywood Boulevard and Highland Avenue opened.

Up to this point, Max Factor & Company had never done any advertising. Instead, make-up demonstrations were held in the foyers of cinemas: 'Try Max Factor's famous cosmetics of the stars and see how lovely you really can look.' The products inevitably sold out.

Now the company teamed with a sales and distribution operation called Sales Builders, which suggested that national advertising was required. Max Factor & Company struck a celebrity endorsement deal with the studios. It would use the leading ladies of the silver screen in its advertising in return for promoting their latest films. The cost of this arrangement to Max Factor, according to Fred Basten, was one dollar per actress. The grateful stars – all of them genuine users of Max's product – included Mary Astor, Lucille Ball, Madeleine Carroll, Joan Crawford, Paulette Goddard, Betty Grable, Rita Hayworth, Veronica Lake, Myrna Loy, Ida Lupino, Merle Oberon, Maureen O'Hara, Barbara Stanwyck, Lana Turner... the list was endless. 'By the 1950s virtually every major actress and aspiring starlet had signed on to be a Max Factor Girl.'

Meanwhile, Max had unexpected competition on his hands in the form of Helena Rubinstein and Elizabeth Arden, who had made their names in skincare but were now tentatively exploring the territory of make-up. However, their elitist impulses made them wary of a world that, for them, was still tainted with vulgarity. This put them at a disadvantage. As Basten puts it, they 'asked famous society women to endorse their products in advertising, but most women in America were more interested in looking like Greta Garbo than Mrs Vanderbilt'.

Arden, who had the same relationship with cinema that many people have with chocolate, made a bold incursion into Hollywood in 1935, creating a division called Stage and Screen. She was, writes Lindy Woodhead, 'seemingly oblivious that Max Factor was the übermeister in the field'. Indeed, she launched just as Max opened his revamped premises, a US$600,000 Art Deco beauty palace inaugurated with the kind of glittering party that only Hollywood can throw. Searchlights panned the sky and flashbulbs popped as celebrities waved their way down the red carpet before a baying press pack. Inside, ribbons on each dressing room were cut by four movie stars: Jean Harlow, Ginger Rogers, Rita Hayworth and Rochelle Hudson.

In addition to being entirely overshadowed by Max, Arden had distribution problems: stores did not want to make space on their shelves for the Stage and Screen line next to her existing, more premium products. The project was 'ill thought-out, costly, and quietly folded'. Both Arden and Rubinstein remained in their ethereal, luxurious space, leaving the glitzy world of the entertainment industry to others.

With the field clear once again, Max and his sons – Frank and Davis, already closely involved with the business – began to address the latest evolution in the history of cinema. Technicolor had arrived, bringing with it a whole new set of make-up challenges. The solution was a range of make-up named 'Pan-Cake', after its flat containers and cake-like consistency. The tints were even subtler and more flattering than before. When it was used during screen tests for the film *Vogues of 1938*, extras ran off with US$2,000 worth of product in just one week. Even before the film was completed, Pan-Cake was used in another: *The Goldwyn Follies*. And this time there was a screen credit: 'Color Harmony Make-Up by Max Factor'.

The films premiered within months of one another. At the same time, Pan-Cake in a special, lighter formula devised by Frank Factor was released to the general public through stores. It was backed by the brand's first colour advertising campaign, which sparkled with star names and debuted in *Vogue*. The result, according to Basten, was 'the fastest and largest selling single make-up item in the history of cosmetics'. (Elizabeth Arden briefly launched a copycat product called Pat-A-Kake, changed to Pat-A-Crème after a threat of legal action.)

Max Factor's extraordinary life came to an end with an incident as bizarre as any depicted on screen by the Hollywood he had conquered. He was on his way to Rome to investigate the possibilities offered by the new Cinecitta studio there. Breaking his journey in Paris, he received a note threatening him with death unless he came up with the equivalent of US$200. The extortionist proposed a meeting at the foot of the Eiffel Tower. Appropriately, the French police sent a stand-in made up to look like Max, with a false moustache and glasses. Nobody showed, but Max was badly shaken by the incident. Weakened, he returned to America.

He died on 30 August 1938. After all he had lived through, one might imagine that he was in ripe old age. But he was only 61.

FACTOR AFTER MAX

The magazine *Glamour* (cited by Basten) summed up Max's contribution to the world of beauty:

> If you have ever… tried a powder brush, admired a screen star's make-up, harmonized your lipstick with your hair colouring, used a lip brush, sent for a mail-order wig or hairpiece, said 'make-up' instead of 'cosmetics', then your life has been touched by the vital Factor known as Max. For all these things were invented or coined or perfected by Max Factor, who came to symbolize beauty on and off the screen, in this country and a hundred and one others.

Cosmetics would have made their way down from stage and screen without Max, thanks to the sheer hypnotic beauty of the stars and the emancipation of women, who adopted make-up as means of self-expression and a statement of independence. Let's not forget that Elizabeth Arden saw women from the suffrage movement marching in bright red lipstick. Nevertheless, it's hard to overestimate the role Max Factor played in making cosmetics not just acceptable, but desirable.

Following in his father's footsteps, Frank Factor changed his name to Max Jr. Demonstrating a flair for self-publicity, he insured his hands for US$50,000. He set to work devising a new 'indelible lipstick', inventing a hand-cranked 'kissing machine' that smooched two pairs of moulded rubber lips together to test the staying power of the product. Tru-Color lipstick was launched in 1940.

The behaviour of women during the war was testament to the power of beauty: in London, lipsticks were equipped with flashlights to help women see during the blackout; Max Jr was among those who offered tips to women who were forced to paint on stockings. Like other beauty companies, Max Factor's expertise was sought to develop effective camouflage. And the men who decorated their barrack rooms and aircraft with pictures of leggy, scarlet-lipped pin-ups reinforced the idea of Hollywood beauty as a symbol of liberty.

In 1947, Max Factor & Company launched its best-selling Pan-Stik make-up. Even more convenient than its predecessor, it came in lipstick-style tubes. By the 1950s, Max Factor was a global empire, with worldwide distribution and 10,000 employees. It was not left behind by the arrival of television:

Lucille Ball's immensely popular show *I Love Lucy* included the line 'Make-up by Max Factor'. The company was now so powerful that it was able to buy its long-term distributor, Sales Builders. In a pleasing twist to the beauty tale, it acquired a perfume company called Corday. It's one of those moments when worlds intersect: the brand had been created in Paris by Blanche Arvoy as a more aristocratic version of her playful Jovoy range (see Chapter 8, 'The 5 per cent solution').

In 1959, Max Factor & Company celebrated its 50th birthday with a stream of advertising and press releases, as well as a party that had nothing to envy the Golden Age of Hollywood. Yet this was the start of a bumpy, uncertain era for the brand. In the early 1960s, Max Factor became a public company, with a listing on the New York stock exchange. Cosmetics had become a giant industry – it was no longer run by visionaries with odd Central European accents, but by financiers and marketing professionals. The Factor family slowly withdrew from the company. Max Factor Jr retired in the 1970s, but not before witnessing the enormous success of a range of perfumes in the name of the fashion designer Halston – for a while, its worldwide sales were second only to those of Chanel No. 5. (Max Jr died in 1996.)

In 1973 Max Factor merged with Norton Simon – a strangely diversified company that included Hunt Foods and Avis Car Rental, among others. Thanks to successive mergers and acquisitions it passed into the hands of Esmark, then Beatrice Foods – which merged the brand with its Playtex lingerie division – and then investor Ron Perelman, who since 1985 had been the owner of Revlon.

Finally, in 1991, it was sold to Procter & Gamble. At the time of writing it is in a sort of suspended animation in the United States, available only online via the website Drugstore.com, as P&G prefers to focus on its CoverGirl make-up range. But the Max Factor brand remains well known internationally, where it has a young target market and is positioned as 'the make-up of make-up artists'.

MAC AND COMPANY

Max Factor has an unlikely competitor in Great Britain in the form of Rimmel. The brand's origins are intriguing: it started life in London in

1834 as a perfume house founded by a Frenchman named Eugène Rimmel, whose father had also been in the fragrance business. An enterprising marketer, Rimmel operated from prestigious premises in Regent Street and established an upmarket reputation with lavish illustrated mail order catalogues and advertisements in theatre programmes. He commissioned the French illustrator Jules Chéret – famous for his posters for the Folies Bergère cabaret – to design the labels of his bottles. He even wrote a book about the history of perfumes and had it printed on scented paper. An inquisitive traveller and natural innovator, he is said to have devised one of the first non-toxic mascaras (eye make-up remains a house speciality to this day).

Rimmel's two sons inherited the business after his death in 1887, and the brand continued to flourish under their leadership before entering a long period of mixed fortunes. After the Second World War, it was resurrected by advertising executive Robert Caplin and his sister Rose. They downplayed the brand's luxury heritage in a move that anticipated the 1960s democratization of fashion and beauty, launching the first self-selection counter dispenser. It was one of the moments in history when London quite legitimately considered itself the world capital of style: fashion designer Mary Quant popularized the era's emblematic garment, the mini-skirt, and went on to launch make-up in startling metallic hues.

Rimmel bounced between various owners in the 1970s and 1980s, before ending up in the grasp of Coty in 1996. Just as L'Oréal appropriated the persona of New York City as a brand identity for Maybelline, Coty associated Rimmel closely with the youth, energy and colour of London. 'With Rimmel, changing your look is as easy as hopping on the London Tube and switching from Soho to Camden, from Portobello to Notting Hill,' reads its website eagerly. In 2001, Rimmel signed up the ultimate British supermodel, Kate Moss, as its official face. It has since added other names to its roster, but it retains its 'streetwise' London-centric image and accessible pricing.

Another brand that might be described as a 'relative' of Max Factor is MAC, originally founded in Toronto in 1984 by Frank Toskan and its innovative marketing director, the late Frank Angelo, who died at the age of only 49 in 1997. Two years before the tragedy, they had sold 51 per cent of the business to Estée Lauder. William Lauder told them, 'The day I understand what you're doing, you're doing it wrong' ('Cosmetics company soars by making its own rules', *Toronto Star*, 5 October 1995).

The pair knew only that they wanted to do things differently to others. Their company was originally called Make-Up Art Cosmetics. Like Max Factor, they aimed for the professional market first.

Born in Trieste, Frank Toskan had arrived in Alberta with his parents at the age of eight, and then wound up in Toronto when they visited a cousin and decided to stay on. After school he started working as a photographer, making up his models too. As is often the case, dissatisfaction drove his desire to start a business. He disliked the narrow range of colours available to him – 'among other things, many of which didn't work on non-white skin' – and which he felt were being foisted on women by beauty companies that were obliged to push 'this season's colours'. He hated the glossy finish that reflected too much light in photographs.

He teamed up with Frank Angelo, an entrepreneur who was running a chain of beauty salons. They dreamed of a make-up brand for everyone: 'All ages, all races, all sexes.' Their plan was to begin selling 'to professional make-up artists and models, and then branch out from there'. Toskan recruited a second-year chemistry student who was dating his sister to help him cook up his product. 'I didn't have to ask anyone whether it was good enough. We were working in the business. We knew how it looked on the streets, we knew how it looked on a runway.'

Rod Ulmer, of a chain of department stores called Simpson's, was one of the first to spot the potential of the brand and give the Franks the space they needed to bond with their customers. 'I knew that this was a new generation of entrepreneur that reads the consumer a lot more accurately than the big corporations,' he told the *Toronto Star*, adding that MAC genuinely put service before profits. 'When you talk about servicing the customer without getting sales – that's radical.'

Ulmer had to reassure store managers who were sceptical about the look of MAC's sales staff. These were hardly pristine white-lab-coated 'beauty consultants': they dressed in black and often had pierced noses. Ulmer soon found that MAC was outselling established brands. It appealed to a young, hip audience by talking their language. For one thing, it refused to test its products on animals. It was an early proponent of recycling, offering customers a free lipstick if they brought in six empty tubes. Before long, supermodel Linda Evangelista and superstar Madonna were wearing MAC colours, without any endorsement deal or advertising campaign. The Franks did not do any advertising.

Except when they were helping others. Shortly after the brand was founded they launched the MAC AIDS Fund. Part of its income was derived from Christmas cards designed by children with AIDS. But the most significant initiative was the launch of the Viva Glam line of lipsticks and lip glosses, all the proceeds of which go to the fund. One of its early faces was the leggy black transvestite entertainer RuPaul, a choice that underlined MAC's all-embracing attitude to beauty. More recently, Lady Gaga took over. The buzz provided by her immense social media presence – more than 20 million Facebook fans and over 8 million Twitter followers – turbocharged the traditional print advertising to such an extent that Viva Glam raised US$34 million in 2010, equivalent to the total amount raised by the line in its first 10 years ('The Lady Gaga effect', *Fast Company*, 18 February 2011).

MAC took beauty out of sleek but staid salons and made it alternative and fun. Others in the industry began to notice the single-colour pots that allowed users to mix their own preparations, the camera-friendly formulas, the black packaging and the sales staff who looked as though they belonged in a funky downtown tattoo parlour. Estée Lauder was smart enough to snap it up first.

MAC's close relationship with make-up artists has fused it with the worlds of entertainment and fashion. The MAC Pro program is open to 'makeup artists, aestheticians, cosmetologists, hairstylists, fashion stylists, nail technicians, costume designers, models, on-air talent/performers, and photographers'. Members receive discounts, access to professional products and invitations to master classes and networking events. MAC also has a team of make-up artists who work backstage at runway shows and movie sets all over the world.

The result is that, when consumers buy MAC products, they feel empowered and creative. It's as though they are part of the fabulous world of professional make-up artists.

MAKING UP IS HARD TO DO

The lipstick was on the wall: after MAC a whole generation of make-up artists became entrepreneurs.

Take Bobbi Brown, who by the early 1990s had worked with photographers like Bruce Weber, Arthur Elgort and – in her breakthrough assignment – Patrick Demarchelier for an American *Vogue* cover featuring rising young model Naomi Campbell. Like Toskan and Angelo, Brown was dissatisfied with the products on the market, which delivered an overly artificial look. She wanted make-up that looked natural – almost as if the model wasn't wearing any make-up at all. 'Make-up was really extreme in the 80s – white skin and red lips and contouring. I loved more of the healthy, natural, simple skin,' she told *Inc* magazine ('How I did it', 1 November 2007.) 'I... hated most of the lipsticks on the market. I wanted it to be creamy and not dry, to stay on a long time, to not have any odour at all, and to be colours that look like lips.'

She shared this idea with a chemist, who helped her devise her first lipstick, Brown Lip Color, which was in fact a pinkish brown. Nine other brown shades followed. A chance meeting with a Bergdorf Goodman cosmetics buyer at a dinner party led to the line being sold at the store. It made its debut in 1991, and 100 lipsticks were sold within a day. The range expanded to brighter and bolder colours, as well as foundations, which were yellow-based instead of pink – an innovation. From her work Brown knew that most women – be they black, Asian or Caucasian – had yellow-toned skin. In 1995, Bobbi Brown Cosmetics was acquired by... Estée Lauder, which wanted a stable of hip beauty brands to counterbalance its establishment image. According to Brown, Leonard Lauder told her: 'We want you because you're beating us in all the stores... and you remind me of my mother when she started.'

Under Lauder, the brand ramped up its marketing. It shifted its New York headquarters to 'a cool downtown loft' and created advertising with more drama and movement than the conventional portraits. Brown said, 'Our advertising photographs were more editorial, like we were working for a magazine. A regular brand would never do an advertisement with smashed lipsticks. Now you see it all the time. We were one of the first brands to regularly use black models and show them as brides.' Like MAC, Bobbie Brown acknowledged the wide diversity of ethnicities in the United States. She showed young America a face it recognized.

Another make-up artist who launched his brand in the slipstream of the MAC revolution was François Nars, a Frenchman who'd grown up in the 1970s reading French *Vogue* and being inspired by the edgy fashion shoots of photographers like Guy Bourdin. He studied at the Carita make-up school in Paris and went on to work for the very fashion magazines he'd so admired, forming a glamorous trio with photographer Steven Meisel and hairstylist Oribe Canales.

Forced to combine different brands to achieve the dramatic looks he wanted, he created a range of nine lipsticks and launched them in 1994 through fashionable department store Barneys. The line quickly grew, jumping off shelves thanks in part to hip, minimalist black packaging designed by Fabien Baron. Nars shot the advertising himself, drawing on techniques he'd learned from Meisel and others. He chose unconventional models – like Alek Wek, a stunning Sudanese-born British girl with an oval face and shorn hair, or Karin Elson, a translucent redhead – and made them look ethereally beautiful: not so much natural as supernatural. Another crucial touch was the provocative nomenclature of the line: shades called Orgasm (a best-selling blush), Deep Throat, Striptease and Sex Machine.

It's a high-fashion, nightclub kind of brand, but apparently Nars remains in touch with reality. 'On the runway you sell a fantasy – it's very theatrical… But when I create the colours in my line, I think about the women who are actually using them,' he told the website Style.com ('Beautiful lives: François Nars').

Shiseido Cosmetics acquired the Nars line in 2000. To celebrate, Nars bought an island in French Polynesia, called Motu Tané. But he held on to creative control of his brand, opening its first stand-alone store in New York in February 2011. Characteristically, the space combines distressed black wood floors with a blazing splash of red lacquer. Summing up the brand, Barneys creative ambassador Simon Doonan described it as 'tough chic… memorable, anti-conformist'. He added, 'François offers women drama and definition with graphic brows, bold colours. He offers them a little idiosyncrasy, self-expression and individuality. Think Frida Kahlo, Ava Gardner or even Simone de Beauvoir!' ('François Nars: behind the makeup, a low-profile artist', *New York Times*, 9 February 2011).

Cosmetics have been linked with fashion for decades, but what make-up artist brands offer – apart from the stardust of their links with designers, photographers and models – is a promise of professionalism. If the products have been designed for the hectic, artistically demanding environment of the runway, there's no reason they shouldn't deliver in everyday life: creativity and efficiency in one slick package.

Never one to miss out on a good story, Chanel also sells the fantasy of the 'star' make-up artist. It spends a great deal of time promoting the global creative director of its make-up line, Peter Philips. The Belgian make-up artist graduated from the Antwerp Academy, which is historically linked with avant-garde Belgian designers like Martin Margiela and Ann Demeulemeester. He turned to make-up after a stint helping backstage at the Paris fashion shows. 'I saw the make-up teams and realised you could make a living out of doing that... I always did my friends' make-up in the 1980s; they'd ask, "Can you do my eyes?" and I was good at it. So when I realised that in fashion you could also do make-up, I was intrigued' ('Peter Philips: Chanel's golden boy', *Independent*, 17 August 2008).

After a successful career working for style magazines and fashion designers, he now collaborates with Chanel designer Karl Lagerfeld on the brand's runway shows and advertising. Philips says he once 'associated make-up with beauty parlours', which is exactly the point. Linking cosmetics to the work of make-up artists in a fashion show context ensures that they seem thrilling, dynamic. It justifies seasonal collections and constant renewal, as well as a harmonizing of hair, make-up and clothing that Max Factor would have recognized.

The glamour of the catwalk goes hand in hand with Chanel's pricing – a Rouge Allure lipstick costs US$32 from its online store – and opulent packaging. One veteran beauty journalist told me:

> If it's value for money you're after, you might as well use a lipstick from [French supermarket chain] Monoprix. When you buy Chanel, you're paying for the logo engraved into the tip of the lipstick, the gorgeous gold tube, and the mythology of the brand. Nobody can see any of that on your lips, but it makes you feel good to have the object in your handbag.

She adds that lipstick is a recession-proof treat – an affordable luxury, a way of boosting your confidence without breaking a 50.

Of course, MAC is not the only pure beauty brand to align with professional make-up artists. Estée Lauder signed up Tom Pecheux as its creative director in November 2009. Other names include Gucci Westman at Revlon and Aaron de Mey at Lancôme.

Besides lending credibility and cachet to brands and offering makeup-application tips, these artists often create internal training videos, talk to the press, make appearances and aid in product and packaging development. They generally make it their job to perpetuate the idea that any woman can be a paragon of pulchritude and happiness if she can find the right shade of foundation.

('It's your makeup artist's autograph that I want',
New York Times, 20 March 2008)

One of the most successful make-up artists in the world is Britain's Pat McGrath, who rose to fame working with fashion editor Edward Enninful at the influential style magazine *i-D* in the 1990s. She collaborated with John Galliano on some of his most outrageous catwalk shows and was chosen by Giorgio Armani to create his cosmetics range. McGrath is black, which is important, because she caught the cosmetics bug from her mother: 'She was always mixing up colours because there wasn't anything out there for black skin' ('The shape of things to come', *Time Style & Design*, Spring 2003).

McGrath is global creative director of Max Factor.

BEAUTY TIPS

✳ Max Factor brought skills gleaned in the dressing rooms of the Imperial Russian Grand Opera to the emerging world of Hollywood in the 1920s.

✳ In the early years he had the market practically to himself, and became the king of movie 'make-up' – a term he popularized.

✳ Cosmetics had become demonized, initially for their toxic qualities but later because of their associations with courtesans. Hollywood brought make-up back into the mainstream. It also exported Western canons of beauty worldwide.

✳ Max Factor pioneered celebrity advertising, using Hollywood stars to promote his products, but innovation in product and packaging design was the real key to his success.

✳ Max Factor's rival in Great Britain was Rimmel, which co-opted the streetwise image of London as its brand identity. The brand is closely identified with British supermodel Kate Moss.

✳ Max Factor is still known as 'the make-up of make-up artists'. Its global creative director Pat McGrath is one of the most famous make-up artists in the world.

✳ In the 1990s, make-up artists dissatisfied with the range of colour cosmetics on the market began launching their own brands: MAC, Bobbie Brown and François Nars are standout names.

✳ Many beauty brands now employ make-up artists as creative advisers and mouthpieces; they imply artistry and authenticity.

THE 5 PER CENT
SOLUTION

'People don't just buy smells; they buy stories.'

There is a legend about Marie Antoinette's attempt to evade the guillotine. In the first part of the story, the Queen leaves the Tuileries Palace under cover of darkness. She is dressed in the plain black clothes of a governess, her bodyguard at her heels. They get a little lost in the narrow streets around the palace, but finally rendezvous with the rest of the royal family – the King, the Dauphin, his sister, assorted servants – in the rue de l'Echelle. There, a small carriage whisks them to the outskirts of Paris, where they transfer to a larger, custom-built travelling coach – a *berline* – which rattles off into the night, bound for a Royalist stronghold on the north-eastern frontier.

If the plan works, they will have escaped the wrath of the Jacobin revolutionaries and what amounts to house arrest under the watch of Lafayette's national guard. If not, they will have only a few months to live.

In most versions of the tale, the royal family are spotted in the small town of Sainte-Menehould by an observant postmaster, who thinks he recognizes the King's profile from a banknote. He gallops on ahead to organize the arrest of the fleeing royals further down the road.

The escape bid ends at Varennes, where the suspect coach is halted by a mob of local citizens. When Marie Antoinette emerges, there can be no doubt as to her identity. Although anxiety has turned her hair white, radically altering her appearance, her perfume gives her away. Only a queen, it is argued, could afford such an exquisite fragrance.

Along with her family, Marie Antoinette is escorted back to Paris and the looming scaffold. The symbolism is perfect, and perfectly Parisian. The King is recognizable from his noble profile – but the Queen is betrayed by her scent.

OLFACTORY NOSTALGIA

In his fascinating (2006) book *The Secret of Scent*, the perfumer Luca Turin reveals that the traitorous fragrance was likely to have been supplied by the Paris perfume house Houbigant, founded in 1775 by Jean-François Houbigant of Grasse.

Houbigant's boutique at 19, rue du Faubourg Saint Honoré was called *A la Corbeille des Fleurs* (The Flower Basket). In the words of the sign outside, it sold 'gloves, Powders, Pomades and Perfumes; also the genuine vegetable Rouge which he has perfected to the highest degree'. Unlike Marie Antoinette, Houbigant survived the revolution – Napoleon is said to have carried a selection of the house's fragrances in his campaign chest as his army rampaged across Europe. Houbigant had been wise to locate his boutique on the most fashionable street in Paris, and he did not hesitate to profit from an early form of celebrity endorsement.

It is significant that Houbigant came from Grasse. With its benevolent climate and abundant supplies of jasmine – introduced to southern France by the Moors in the 16th century – this Provencal town surrounded by lush countryside became the capital of the French perfume industry. Originally the area had been famous for its tanneries, but a fashion for perfumed gloves, begun by Catherine de Medici and her sister Marie, prompted the leather merchants to begin cultivating aromatic plants. Today Grasse supplies more than two-thirds of France's fragrances and is home to many of its most prominent perfumers.

Of course, perfume is far older than the 18th century. To find its origins we must revisit the Egyptians, those beauty pioneers, whose religious rites were accompanied by wafts of scented smoke. (The word 'perfume' derives from the Latin *per fumum* – 'through smoke' – and for many of us, even today, the odour of incense is the smell of church.) Perfume was also applied to statues of the gods – and the dead were perfumed for their voyage through the afterlife. The Egyptians built veritable laboratories where they could extract essence of lotus, iris or lily by pressing the flowers or macerating them in hot oils.

However, Houbigant is an important name in the history of scent because the house created the first perfume containing a synthetic ingredient. Perfumer Paul Parquet composed the fragrance in 1882. It was called Fougère Royale, or 'Royal Fern'. As Luca Turin observes, this was a step towards the marketing-driven modern perfume business because 'ferns... have no smell, and there is nothing royal about them'.

The magic ingredient was a synthetic version of coumarin, which is generally described as smelling like freshly mown hay. In its natural form it is heavily present in tonka beans. So why recreate it chemically? Writes Turin: 'The main justification for using man-made material, then as now, is that you can get it cheaper than by extracting it from the real thing.' Today, he adds, synthetic ingredients are more popular with perfumers than natural materials, which are extracted from plants picked 'mostly in Russia and former Yugoslavia'. These get 'heaped on to trucks, carted to the nearest extraction plant and stirred with some hot solvent. The good stuff is extracted from the plant and later steam-distilled from the mixture.'

Turin argues that natural materials are 'fragile, variable and often... damaged'. They are also highly complex. While single chemicals are notes, natural materials are fully formed compositions, which makes the perfumer's task far more difficult when he or she sits down to write the symphony of a fragrance.

An Italian family acquired the rights to the Houbigant name in 2005 and began relaunching its most famous fragrances, including Fougère Royale and the 1912 Quelques Fleurs. It's doubtful that these scents bear more than a passing resemblance to the originals – but in a world full of designer fragrances, vintage is fashionable. Gian Luca Perris, Houbigant's executive vice-president, told *Forbes* magazine: 'After the recent crisis, there is a cry for authenticity, real quality, not just putting things together in a certain way, putting a nice label on it and selling it for a very expensive price' ('Names you need to know: Houbigant', 7 December 2010).

Should you buy into this idea, your search for a retro fragrance may lead you to Jovoy, a perfumery on the rue Danielle Casanova in Paris. There you may be lucky enough to meet the voluble, enthusiastic François Hénin, the proprietor of the business. Hénin got embroiled in the perfume industry by chance, as a trader of raw materials in Vietnam. He became intrigued by the quest for elusive odours and, with a cousin, resurrected Jovoy, a brand originally launched in 1923. Hénin speaks of its founder, Blanche Arvoy, with some affection.

'She was very ground-breaking, very ahead of her time,' he says. 'She was the first to use a vaporizer, for example. Her perfumes were firmly aimed at the sort of young women who could be seen strolling *les grands boulevards* on the arms of their rich "uncles". By today's standards, her fragrances were not subtle. They were opulent, aggressive. They were designed to turn heads.'

Hénin relaunched several of Jovoy's scents, including Oriental, Terra Incognita and the flirtatiously named Quand? (When?).

But the boutique is something different again. As Hénin made his way around the industry, attending trade shows and conferences, he bumped into others who were running vintage or niche perfume brands. The boutique brings his favourites together under one small but stylish roof. Alongside the fragrances of Jovoy you'll find scents from LT Piver (1774), Dorin (1780) and Rancé (1795). The latter, says Hénin, made Napoleon's favourite cologne: 'He used to drink it.'

An Italian barber, Gian Paolo Feminis, created the first *eau de Cologne* in the city of that name in 1709. It was a blend of grape spirits, neroli oil, bergamot, lavender and rosemary. It was sold not only to disguise body odour, but also to cure stomach aches, disinfect the gums and 'clean the blood'.

Hénin loves such details and admits that most people don't just buy smells; 'they buy stories'.

But at his boutique, customers do not sample the perfumes directly from their exquisite flacons. The fragrances are contained in rows of anonymous brown bottles. 'We encourage customers to try the fragrances, to immerse themselves in them, to locate the scent that suits their personality, before being seduced by the bottle and the packaging. In that respect, we're turning the modern perfume business on its head, putting the fragrance first and the image after. You'll find no images of famous actresses here. We're offering an antidote to the 'celebrity mania' that has infected the industry.'

There was a precise moment when the coquettish world of perfume that François Hénin loves began to cower before the rapacious marketing machine that the fragrance industry became. It was when Gabrielle 'Coco' Chanel pointed at a vial in a line-up of 10 sample fragrances and said: 'Number five.'

COCO AND 'LE MONSTRE'

By 1921, when No. 5 was launched, Coco Chanel was already a successful fashion designer who had parlayed her streamlined vision of women's clothing into riches and celebrity. The death in a car crash of her playboy lover Boy Capel had left her at first heartbroken, and then inhabited by a steely, bitter determination. (Rather like the Eiffel Tower, Chanel is best appreciated from a distance, snobbery and anti-Semitism being only two of her less lovable qualities.)

You will be aware by now that fashion designers do not create fragrances. That is the job of perfumers – sometimes referred to as 'noses'. These days, most of them work for giant companies like Firmenich, Givaudan, International Flavors and Fragrances (IFF) and Symrise. They create not only beautiful perfumes, but also the everyday aromas of bathroom products, detergent and snacks.

Chanel's 'nose' was Ernest Beaux, who had previously worked at the perfumer A Rallet & Company. One might assume that Beaux jumped at the chance when Chanel asked him to create her first fragrance, but according to Tilar J Mazzeo, author of *The Secret of Chanel No. 5* (2010), he had misgivings. 'Creating a scent for a couturière, after all, was still largely uncharted territory. That summer, Coco Chanel would be only the third designer in history to venture into the field.'

Eventually she persuaded him and, after listening to what would now be called a 'brief', he set to work designing her dream fragrance. One of its key ingredients was jasmine from Grasse – lots of it. 'She wanted the most extravagant perfume in the world,' writes Mazzeo.

Extravagant, yes – but also severe. Like many of the heroines of this tale, Gabrielle Chanel came from a lowly background. Her mother had died of tuberculosis when she was 12, forcing her father, 'an itinerant peddler', to abandon Gabrielle and her two sisters at a convent called Aubazine, in the Corrèze region of south central France. Something of the austerity of this place, with its whitewashed walls and scrubbed stone floors, lingered in Chanel's soul. Later, she scratched a dubious living as a singer in provincial cabarets: she earned her nickname with a saucy rendition of a song called *Qui qu'a vu Coco*.

So that was Chanel No. 5: the nun meets the showgirl.

The severity was provided by synthetic substances called aldehydes, which come in many forms but are often described as the smell of cold and cleanness. The fifth vial in the series that Beaux prepared for Chanel contained a surplus of these. It touched the designer's emotional core and became Chanel No. 5, an unapologetically synthetic fragrance for the machine age. The designer placed it in a stark Art Deco flacon. Square-shouldered, it was inspired by one of Boy Capel's whisky flasks.

A bottle of Chanel No. 5 is sold every 30 seconds. In a world where fragrances stay no longer on the market than they do on the skin, the 90-year-old brand is still packing a punch. No mere fragrance, it is a legend, a rite of passage, a monument. Chandler Burr, the perfume critic of the *New York Times*, refers to it as 'le monstre'.

Back in 1921, it did not explode on to the marketplace on the back of an aggressive advertising campaign. It was introduced stealthily.

Chanel launched Chanel No. 5 by wearing it to a dinner party in Cannes. As she had predicted, people asked her what it was. Next, she gave bottles to her favourite clients as Christmas gifts. They came to her boutique asking for more – and so did their friends.

Chanel No. 5 was well on its way to becoming the olfactory recognition code of the Parisian elite when the designer did an extraordinary thing: she sold the rights to the brand.

Today, the fashionable rich meet at gallery openings and charity dinners, at runway shows by star designers, at red carpet events in Cannes and Hollywood and behind the velvet ropes of exclusive clubs and restaurants. In 1923 they met at the racetrack in Deauville, which is where Chanel was introduced to Pierre and Paul Wertheimer, owners of the perfume company Bourjois.

The firm had its roots in the theatre, having been created in 1863 by an actor who invented easy-to-apply stage make-up that he began selling to the public. Alexandre-Napoléon Bourjois acquired the business four years later, finding himself with a hit on his hands in the form of 'Rice Powder from Java', which 'softened and whitened' the skin. His successor, Emile Orosdi, expanded the offering, adding nail varnish, lip colour and heady perfumes designed to be sprinkled on to handkerchiefs. Pierre and Paul's father, Ernest Wertheimer, a former tie salesman, bought half of the business in 1898. When his sons got involved, they took Bourjois to the United States and prosperity.

Coco Chanel handed them almost total control of her perfume business, settling for just 10 per cent of the profits. The move seems insane in retrospect – and Chanel was to bitterly regret her decision – but at the time it made perfect sense. Chanel was a fashion designer; she knew nothing of the perfume industry. Without the Wertheimers, Chanel No. 5 might have remained the signature scent of a tiny clique in Paris. With them, it conquered the world.

Tilar J Mazzeo is highly critical of the Wertheimers' initial marketing approach, especially their decision to 'bury' Chanel No. 5 amidst a range of similarly named products – Chanel No. 1, Chanel No. 2, Chanel No. 11, Chanel No. 14, Chanel No. 20, Chanel No. 21, Chanel No. 22 and Chanel No. 27, to be precise – but the catalogue they sent to US retailers showed a firm grasp of the flowery tautologies of luxury speak: 'The Chanel perfumes, created exclusively for connoisseurs, occupy a unique and unparalleled place in the history of perfume… Mademoiselle Chanel is proud to present simple bottles adorned only by their whiteness, precious teardrops of perfume of incomparable quality, unique in composition, revealing the artistic personality of their creator.'

And so on. In fact, the disproportional success of Chanel No. 5 *despite* their cock-eyed marketing strategy finally persuaded the Wertheimers to pile their advertising cash behind it in the 1930s.

The fragrance also managed to fend off competition from a rival with a suspiciously similar formula. L'Aimant (The Magnet) was put out by a company owned by an old acquaintance of Chanel's, François Coty. Corsican by birth, François Spoturno had adopted a tweaked version of his mother's maiden name, Coti, and trained as a perfumer in Grasse. In 1904 he'd launched a perfume based on concentrated flower oils, La Rose Jacqueminot, which proved wildly successful. Coty combined a love of scent with a talent for packaging: he worked with René Lalique to design sculptural Art Nouveau bottles that would have sold even without their contents. By the time Chanel created No. 5, Coty was running an empire. (His fragrance business funded a noxious political career: in 1922 he acquired the newspaper *Le Figaro* and turned it into a journal of the far right; later he funded Fascist organizations.)

In 1926 he acquired a company called Chiris, which itself owned A Rallet & Company, where Chanel's perfumer Ernest Beaux had learned his trade. With this purchase, Coty obtained the formula for Rallet No. 1, an earlier creation by Beaux. In fact, as Coty suspected, Beaux had based the formula for Chanel No. 5 quite closely on it. When Coty released L'Aimant, a slightly adapted version of Rallet No. 1, he was essentially launching Chanel No. 5 by any other name.

It was too late. Writes Mazzeo: 'Chanel No. 5 was the most famous fragrance in the world. It had soared during the economic bubble of the 1920s and, in an era dedicated to the pursuit of incomparable luxuries, it had become one of the most coveted.'

It was around this time that Coco realized her error and began considering ways of wresting back control of the brand – something she never managed. As she watched from the sidelines, Chanel No. 5 continued to sell throughout the economically turbulent 1930s. The Wertheimers had scaled back production of the other numbered fragrances and focused on their best-seller. As their advertising suggested, it was 'worn by more smart women than any other perfume'.

The fragrance secured its iconic status during the Second World War, when the Wertheimers took the risky decision to distribute it through retail stores on US military bases (the commissary post exchanges, or 'PXs'). Selling the brand tax-free in such an environment could have leached out its luxury status, but, as Mazzeo observes, 'no one expected to find opulent boutiques and glitzy showrooms in a war zone'.

Chanel No. 5 became the fragrance of freedom, 'part of a world before the war, a world of glamour and beauty that somehow had survived'. This allowed the brand to enter the 1950s under a halo of erotic nostalgia – every guy who'd been overseas had bought a bottle for that special person, or maybe for two or three of them.

True to form, Coco had spent the war shacked up in the Ritz with a Nazi officer. Even as the perfume she barely owned continued to fly off shelves, she was forced to hide out in Switzerland, her reputation in tatters. When she finally returned to Paris to resurrect her fashion line in 1954, she was obliged to turn to the Wertheimers for support. They responded by taking full control of the Chanel brand. They had long owned her perfume – now they owned her too. The resentment festered until the day she died, aged 87, on 10 January 1971.

In the 1960s the business was managed by Pierre's son, Jacques, but he appears to have been more interested in the Wertheimers' horse racing and breeding activities than in running a fashion house. Meanwhile, the ubiquity of Chanel No. 5 was in danger of rendering it passé. In the United States it was very much your mother's perfume – if not your grandmother's. When Jacques's 24-year-old son Alain took the reins in 1974, he swiftly set about remedying the situation, re-establishing the scent's elite positioning by taking it out of drugstores and slashing the number of retail outlets from 18,000 to 12,000.

The enduring popularity of Chanel No. 5 can be attributed to the advertising work of Jacques Helleu, the brand's artistic director, who joined the house in 1956 at the age of 18 and worked there until his death in 2007 at 69. His father, Jean, had held the post before him. With the exception of Chanel herself, nobody had a better understanding of the brand's DNA.

In 1968, Helleu recruited Catherine Deneuve as the face of Chanel No. 5. Coco Chanel might have approved: glacial yet sultry, the blonde actress captured the tension that lay at the heart of the fragrance. The previous year, in the film *Belle de Jour*, she had played a beautiful, bourgeois woman who staved off ennui by trying her hand at prostitution.

The Chanel campaign cemented Deneuve's international stardom and underlined the perfume's iconic status. The print ads are deceptively simple – there is Deneuve's flawless face, shot by Richard Avedon, next to the unmistakable flacon. Helleu recognized that the boldly minimalist bottle was nothing less than a glass logo. All his subsequent ads would feature it strongly. One of them simply showed the bottle, above the words 'Share the fantasy' (the 'bottle as logo' approach has also been used by vodka brand Absolut and, to an extent, by Coca-Cola).

TV executions shot for the US market made full use of Deneuve's French accent and faintly husky delivery. When she talked of placing a drop of Chanel No. 5 'in a special place – behind the knee', she made that hollow of skin sound like the ultimate erogenous zone. 'You don't have to ask for it,' she purred, as the bottle came into shot. 'He knows what you want.'

Helleu repeated this trick again and again, teaming the bottle with beautiful actresses under the lenses of famous photographers and directors. TV and cinema advertisements became increasingly extravagant, reaching their zenith with Nicole Kidman's 2004 romp through a blockbuster ad directed by Baz Luhrmann, who had shot the actress in the film *Moulin Rouge* three years earlier. (Kidman played the kind of showgirl-courtesan that Coco Chanel would have recognized.) The ad is either wincingly camp or unashamedly romantic, depending on your taste. Either way, Kidman was not complaining: she reportedly pocketed US$12 million for the three-minute commercial.

Advertising perfume is a notoriously tricky business. Obviously it's impossible to demonstrate the main product benefit, so you're left with vague notions of sex and romance, wrapped around imagery that expresses the atmosphere the scent is formulated to evoke. The results are often pretentious and entirely lacking in warmth or humour, not to mention any kind of narrative. Chanel's are better than most, but by no means better than award-winning ads for products in other categories.

When Helleu died, *Vogue* paid homage to him. '[He] was the driving force behind the house's iconic ad campaigns, which have… established Chanel as a key brand name in the modern consumer market' ('Jacques Helleu remembered', 1 October 2007). Chanel's global CEO, Maureen Chiquet, said in a statement: 'His larger-than-life personality, immense talents and unique vision have defined Chanel as the ultimate house of luxury, with an unparalleled global presence… He succeeded in bringing Chanel into the 21st century as a leader in the world of exclusivity.'

This might have somewhat wounded Karl Lagerfeld, designer of the brand's fashion collections. But as Coco discovered when she emerged from her Swiss redoubt, the fashion industry is fuelled by fragrances. It's no coincidence that, during the brand's fall/winter 2009 haute couture show, the models stalking the runway were overshadowed by towering replicas of the Chanel No. 5 bottle.

A FANTASY IN A BOTTLE

Yves Saint Laurent knew all about the importance of fragrances to the fashion industry. The designer's blockbuster 'oriental' scent Opium transformed the fortunes of his house; by its 30th anniversary in 1992 the company was earning more than 80 per cent of its income from fragrances and cosmetics. This is why, when giant luxury conglomerates like LVMH and PPR sign up young designer labels, almost the first thing they do is encourage the newcomer to launch a perfume.

In her (2002) biography of Saint Laurent, French journalist Laurence Benaïm describes the launch of Opium as 'a superb communications lesson'. Saint Laurent had already set the scene with his 'Chinese' collection: 36 pieces veined with gold and fringed with fur, a hallucinogenic blend of *Shanghai Express* and a Tintin adventure. 'Less than a year after the death of Mao, Saint Laurent celebrated the excesses of Imperial China,' writes Benaïm.

Opium was launched in Paris on 12 October 1977. 'Opium is the femme fatale, the pagodas, the lamps!' gushed Saint Laurent in the presentation brochure. His intention, he wrote, was to bottle 'the moment a man and a woman look at one another for the first time'. The red flacon was based on the samurai's *inro* (China and Japan apparently being somewhat confused in the designer's dreamscape), a lacquered carrying case for coins, seals, inks and medicine. Saint Laurent created the flacon with the designer Pierre Dinand, who was able to suggest the enigmatic gloss of lacquer in nylon. To this he added, threaded through the stopper, a fine black cord ending in a tassel, as well as a delicate golden chain around the bottle's neck.

The advertising image featured Jerry Hall shot by Helmut Newton. She reclined in an embroidered oriental blouse, lips parted, eyelids lowered, lost in languorous ecstasy. The picture was taken at Saint Laurent's own apartment; he styled the shot and dressed the model, right down to her rings. The slogan? 'Pour celles qui s'adonnent à Yves Saint Laurent' (For those who abandon themselves to Yves Saint Laurent).

European sales hit US$30 million in one year. When Opium was launched in the United States, on 25 September 1978, Saint Laurent took over a 1911 sailing ship called the *Peking*, moored at the South Street Seaport Museum in New York, garlanding it with flowers and lanterns, adorning it with pagodas and a giant Buddha. A glut of celebrities and 32 TV crews turned up for the launch party; fireworks spelled out YSL in the starlit Manhattan sky.

Inevitably Opium provoked a scandal – the Coalition against Drug Abuse wanted to know how YSL could name a fragrance after a drug that had killed millions? – whipping up a media typhoon and playing right into the hands of its creators. By the end of the year, Opium was the most notorious fragrance since Chanel No. 5. Women understood that the scent was an invitation to escape, a fantasy in a bottle.

The designer Thierry Mugler may have had Opium in mind when he used Jerry Hall as the face of his own fragrance, Angel, in 1992. But this new scent was very different. Tooth-achingly sweet, with notes of patchouli, praline, caramel and vanilla, it kicked off a trend for 'gourmand' perfumes. Mugler said it should make you 'almost feel like eating up the person you love'. To add to its weirdness, it was pale blue and came in a flacon shaped like a star.

Perfume critics did not like Angel, but its candyfloss odour appealed to women across many age and income groups. Plus, it was different. Thierry Mugler was a relatively small brand, so the company could afford to take a risk: there were not as many marketing dollars at stake as there were when Dior or Gucci launched a perfume. Mugler was having fun – and that playfulness was evident in the result. Finally, there was the time factor. Fragrances come and go with alarming speed, but Angel's sales built steadily over several years. Perfume has a viral quality – the 'What are you wearing?' effect – that does not take hold overnight. Thierry Mugler's star as a designer may have been falling, but the blue perfume in the star-shaped flacon became a best-seller.

The business of scent is not built on designer names alone. Many celebrities have lent their identities to fragrances. The phenomenon is often held to have started with Glow, by Jennifer Lopez, launched with Coty in 2002. It was a huge hit and prompted the singer and actress to launch a handful of spin-off scents. But it was by no means the first of its kind: Sophia Loren launched Sophia back in 1981; Cher's Uninhibited appeared in 1987; Elizabeth Taylor gave us White Diamonds in 1991.

Glow was merely 'the modern incarnation of the celebrity perfume', as Chandler Burr puts it in his (2007) book *The Perfect Scent*. By racking up millions of sales in a short space of time, it launched a trend that drew many other celebrities to the market. It's fair to say that Coty dominates the celebrity scent category, with potions from Sarah Jessica Parker, Gwen Stefani, Beyoncé Knowles, Celine Dion, David and Victoria Beckham, Faith Hill, Halle Berry, Kate Moss, Kylie Minogue and Lady Gaga, among others. This is escapism at its most basic: the comforting unreality of screen or glossy magazine distilled and bottled.

The company founded by the marketing-savvy Corsican – Gabrielle Chanel's best 'frenemy' François Coty – is now the world's largest fragrance concern, with annual sales of US$4 billion. Owned by Benckiser and firmly based in the United States, it has interests in cosmetics, toiletries and skincare, but 65 per cent of its income derives from fragrances.

THE COMPOSERS

As we've established, companies like Coty do not create perfumes. They are licensing, marketing and distribution operations. The perfumers are elsewhere, using their extraordinary olfactory skills to compose a scent from a client's brief.

Céline Ellena is a third-generation perfumer from Grasse. Her father, Jean-Claude Ellena, is the in-house 'nose' at Hermès. This is a very unusual position: alongside Hermès, only Chanel and Guerlain have exclusive perfumers (Jacques Polge and Thierry Wasser respectively). Céline is currently independent, but she has worked at Symrise and a Grasse-based company called Charabot.

Like many perfumers, Céline learned her trade at the Institut Supérieur International du Parfum de la Cosmétique et de l'Aromatique alimentaire (ISIPCA), the perfume school in Versailles. You'll need a chemistry degree and the backing of a perfume company before being considered for admission. After that, the school accepts just 15 students a year, based on a written test and a presentation to a professional jury. 'That's when you begin to realize', says Céline, 'that perfume is a tough business.'

Let's say you're lucky enough to be employed by one of the big perfume companies – what happens then? What is your day like?

Once upon a time, a perfumer sat before a rack of glass vials called an 'organ'. Each of the vials, of course, contained a smell, either synthetic or natural. By combining them in different quantities, the perfumer would arrive at a new fragrance.

Now the perfumer sits in an office before a computer. Having considered the smells that she might need to create the fragrance currently swirling around in her head, she turns to the database of raw materials on the computer. Each material has a price, so the perfumer can add and subtract elements to find out how much the formula she has in mind might cost. The smells are kept in labs staffed by technicians, who use high-precision scales to blend tiny drops of liquid according to her instructions. The resulting concentrate is added to alcohol to form a sample, which is taken to the perfumer's office.

There is pressure on the perfumer to keep the cost per kilo of a fragrance as low as possible. 'Ten years ago,' writes Luca Turin in *The Secret of Scent*, 'a fine fragrance used to cost $200–300 per kilo. These days $100 is considered expensive… The cheapness of the formula is the reason why most "fine" perfumes are total crap.'

There is also pressure on the perfumer to create a hit, which is why many fragrances are slightly adjusted versions of those that have gone before. Perfumers are constantly sniffing samples of recently launched fragrances to keep themselves up to date.

'To save time, perfumers have been known to mix the formulae of existing fragrances,' says Céline. 'So you might hear them say, "It's 80 per cent J'Adore and 20 per cent Nina by Nina Ricci." In the trade we call that a "twist".'

One of the great skills of a perfumer is the ability to reverse-engineer a fragrance by smell. Perfumers keep an enormous library of aromas in their heads – something that can seem akin to a superpower to those of us who are not in the business.

'Actually, building an olfactory memory is not the hardest part,' says Céline. 'You learn the smells by heart. The real skill lies in knowing what the different elements will give you when they're combined. Because in perfume, one plus one equals three. If I combine a synthetic called ionone, which smells a little like irises, with aldehyde C14, which resembles peach, I get apricot.'

Céline agrees that the generally low standard of perfumes is partly due to strict budgets, but she also blames tight deadlines. 'At a big perfume company you don't have time to think, to explore, to do your own research. You're often working on several different briefs at once. Add to that a lack of willingness among the clients to take risks, and you end up with a pretty bland selection on the shelves.'

There is an important cultural factor at play too. Since the 1970s, consumers in the developed world have been surrounded by an extremely common aroma found in detergent. To almost all of us, this smell equals 'clean'. When it is not present in a perfume – say, one that favours natural over synthetic aromas – we tend to find that fragrance a turn-off. Ergo, most perfumes smell largely of detergent. Our noses have been brainwashed.

The birth of a new perfume begins with a client – an LVMH, a L'Oréal or a Coty – deciding that it wants to launch a fragrance. It may need to replace a fading brand, or to follow a trend ('orientals' are in this season). The product manager contacts three or four of the big perfume companies, which dispatch their sales and marketing teams. Not their perfumers: that role is played by somebody called an 'evaluator', who combines perfumery and marketing skills. The evaluator and her colleagues pick up the brief, which is generally a written document: target demographic, olfactory family, which fragrance it should resemble (or not) and so on.

Céline says, 'On a good day, the team from the perfume company is alone in a meeting room with the client. Occasionally, the brief is presented to a handful of competing perfume companies at the same time. The commercial team are expected to take notes and bring them back.'

I wonder aloud how much input a fashion designer has into the creation of the fragrance that bears his or her name.

Céline says: 'If the designer's contract with the parent company means that they have effectively signed their name away, then they are barely consulted. They might be brought in at the end for a quick sniff, but otherwise their opinion is irrelevant. Perfume is not their métier. Needless to say, the *public* are told that the designer was heavily involved in the creation of the fragrance. But that is marketing.'

I later pose the same question to Judith Gross, global director, fragrance and natural ingredient marketing at International Flavors and Fragrances (IFF). 'It depends,' she says, citing Giorgio Armani as a particularly hands-on designer. 'Deep implication in the process from A to Z is quite rare.'

The same goes for celebrities, naturally. Gross acknowledges that the perceived presence of a designer or a celebrity during the creation of a perfume can be an important part of the marketing strategy. 'The perfumes that really work are those that tell a convincing story; they bring the consumer into their world.'

With approximately 400 perfume launches a year, you need a convincing story in order to stand out. Gross estimates that the 'juice' represents only 5 per cent of the price that the consumer pays for a bottle of perfume. The rest of your 70 dollars goes on packaging design, advertising – including the celebrity endorser's fee – and distribution.

The perfumers are not involved in any of this. They don't even see the flacon, which is the responsibility of specialist design agencies.

Once the commercial team returns from the client meeting, the brief is given to a group of perfumers, who compete internally to come up with the formula that the company will present to the client. This must be done within a time frame of 15 days to three weeks. The submissions deemed worthy by the evaluator and the sales team are then taken to the client. The result is that the client ends up with a choice of five or six fragrances from different perfume companies. Once the client decides on the fragrance it likes, the other companies are out of the picture – having earned not a single penny.

'After that, the real job begins, because the client always wants modifications,' says Céline. 'Too floral, not floral enough...'

The fragrance is tested on focus groups to determine how it might perform on the market, followed by more modifications. The entire process, from brief to launch, can take between one and two years.

It sounds like a disheartening business – until I ask Céline to describe what it's actually like to create a perfume.

'For me, it starts with an image,' she replies. 'It might be a shape. I might, for instance, want to create something that smells round. Or it could be the memory of a journey. Once, I wanted to create a perfume that felt like plunging your hands into a pile of feathers. Another time, I was thinking of Marlon Brando's T-shirt in *A Streetcar Named Desire*. After that, I write down the formula that might recreate the feeling I have in mind. It sounds strange, I know, but it's possible to create smells that have textures: rough, smooth, metallic. You lift the bottle to your nose, and suddenly you're experiencing a sensation.'

And that, despite the harsh realities of the perfume industry, is a kind of magic.

BEAUTY TIPS

* The 'juice' in a perfume bottle amounts to only 5 per cent of its price – the rest goes on packaging and marketing.

* Perfumers say strict budgets and tight deadlines mean that the standard of so-called 'fine fragrances' is generally low.

* Tired of conventional brands, some consumers are rediscovering perfumes first launched in the 18th century.

* Chanel No. 5 remains the world's most famous fragrance. Gabrielle Chanel initially promoted it via stealth marketing.

* It owes its success partly to sheer longevity, but also to advertising that exploits its heritage: actresses who evoke the spirit of Coco Chanel alongside the iconic bottle.

* The viral effect of perfumes means that they often require time to propagate among consumers.

* But beauty companies prefer to focus on advertising-driven novelty in the hope of creating an instant hit.

THE LURE
OF LUXURY

*'There are trends in beauty,
just as there are in fashion.'*

Sitting in the reception of Parfums Christian Dior in Paris feels like waiting to embark on a luxury vacation in outer space. I can imagine the same ambience of spotless calm, the same dove-grey furnishings, an identically immaculate reception desk garnished with a silvery logo. If the elegant woman who entered a moment ago had floated past me rather than clicking across the floor on spike heels, I would not have been surprised. I expect to hear the compressed sigh of an airlock as she vanishes into the heart of the building.

The fashion designer Christian Dior started his fragrance business in 1947, with the perfumer Serge Heftler-Louiche, at the very moment he launched his first collection. Their debut fragrance was Miss Dior, inspired, it's said, by the designer's sister Catherine. The following year, Parfums Christian

Dior had already opened offices in New York. Dior was well aware of the power of a fashion brand to attract consumers to ancillary products: in 1950 he licensed his name to a range of neckties and accessories in the United States. Dior Rouge lipstick appeared in 1955, although the skin cream Crème Abricot did not arrive until 1963, six years after his death. Ten years later, Parfums Christian Dior launched a range of skincare products under the name Hydra Dior.

It's skin that I'm here to discuss today. Edouard Mauvais-Jarvis is the brand's scientific director. As he welcomes me with a handshake, I note that he looks younger than the 41 my Google search indicated him to be, which makes him a convincing ambassador.

'The relationship between fashion designers, skincare products and consumers depends on legitimacy,' he explains, once we're installed in his modest office. 'By launching a perfume at the same time as his first collection, Christian Dior was particularly visionary. His name was associated with the world of beauty right from the start. Make-up followed fairly quickly – it is, after all, a fashion accessory.'

Skincare took off rather later, partly because the perfumes division was sold off and only reintegrated with the fashion company when it became part of LVMH (Moët Hennessy Louis Vuitton) in 1988. Parfums Christian Dior is still run as a separate business, meaning that it has little do with Christian Dior, the fashion brand. But the combination of its luxury positioning and the perceived legitimacy of Dior in the beauty sector keeps customers coming back for more.

Mauvais-Jarvis assures me that there is more to the products than sleek packaging, however: 'We play a leading role in skincare research. In fact, we share our research with the other brands within the LVMH group, such as Guerlain, Givenchy and Kenzo, thanks to our laboratories in Saint Jean de Braye. We have 260 researchers, which may seem quite a small number compared to the likes of L'Oréal, but we also work with exterior partners, such as Stanford's Institute for Stem Cell Biology and Regenerative Medicine.'

Stem cell research has proved fertile terrain for skincare marketers. As stem cells have the power to renew themselves, the theory is that epidermal stem cells should be protected – or even boosted – in order to ensure that they do their job of keeping our skin looking fresh and radiant with maximum efficiency. Such is the thinking behind Dior's best-selling Capture Totale anti-ageing line, long promoted with advertising images of an apparently ageless Sharon Stone. It defends stem cells with TP Vityl, a topical constituent derived from vitamin E. This is what skincare marketers mean when they talk about 'active ingredients' – elements that have a job to do, rather than simply being part of the delivery vector, such as a colouring agent or fragrance.

Beauty companies tend to promote active ingredients with language that reflects their brand DNA. For instance, La Prairie (owned, like Nivea, by Beiersdorf) makes much of its Swiss origins, equating the pure air and snows of its homeland with health and purity. Thus it assures us that its Cellular Power Infusion contains 'the stem cells of Swiss red grapes and extract of Swiss snow algae'. This somehow explains why it costs almost 500 dollars a pot. Anyway, let's return to Mauvais-Jarvis.

'I believe a smaller team with exterior partners is more flexible than an enormous research department that is practically a company within a company,' he says. 'In this business, you have to be reactive, because it's important to be first on to the market with a discovery.'

Such partnerships are good for academic institutions too; they suggest the scientists are grappling with real-world issues, and in any case there is a financial incentive. 'It's not a donation,' Mauvais-Jarvis stresses. 'Our researchers work together. It's a scientific approach – financed, admittedly – but there is a genuine exchange of opinion and expertise.'

Not that scientific discoveries immediately lead to the launch of new products. Indeed, a discovery can 'lie in a drawer', metaphorically speaking, until Dior works out how best to use it. 'We're constantly talking to consumers about their needs and desires, so we know when the time is right to launch a product. I compare it to the touch screen you have on your iPhone. The technology had existed for years, but Apple worked out the best way of incorporating it into a product.'

The fact is that most beauty companies have a marketing plan that stretches months or years into the future. They know exactly when they need to renew or replace existing product lines. Occasionally they may be forced to react quickly to a launch by a competitor. In both cases, they turn to the research department.

Mauvais-Jarvis denies that marketing drives research, but he agrees that they must be 'in accordance'. He adds: 'There is no point in launching a new product before the market is ready. We're in business, after all. There are trends in beauty, just as there are in fashion. There is even a seasonal aspect: we know we launch anti-ageing products at the beginning of the year, whitening creams in Asia in March, slimming and toning creams in the spring.'

He cites the launch of Dior's Capture Totale One Essential serum as the perfect example of research and marketing working in parallel. (A serum is richer and more intense than a cream.) The product derived from research Dior's scientists had been doing with the Pierre and Marie Curie Institute in Paris into the ageing of proteins. The key was the discovery of the proteasome, a protein found within cells that acts as a miniature 'recycling factory', ridding cells of toxins or converting them into healthy proteins. This natural process – and here's the kicker – slows with age, meaning that our skin cells accumulate more toxins as we grow older, resulting in lines, discoloration and a dull complexion. Dior's answer was a product containing its patented ingredient Perle de Longoza, extracted from the Longoza plant in Madagascar, which is capable of – you guessed it – enhancing proteasome activity.

'The idea of One Essential serum is that it gives your skin an overall boost and prepares it for other skincare products,' says Mauvais-Jarvis. 'It answered, to be honest with you, a trend in the market for universal serums, which other companies had launched but we did not yet have in our range. We had known about the effect of the proteasome for years, but had not found the right way of using it. Now, alongside the marketing team, we developed a concept that worked.'

The full force of Dior's promotional machine went into action. The bottle itself, designed by packaging company Rexam, was a work of art. It was a deep, lustrous red, with a pump dispenser hidden by a silver metallic cap, a style reprised by the product description and brand name. Sharon Stone was shot for the print and poster advertising campaign, and samples were sent to obliging beauty journalists and bloggers.

The 'skin boosting super serum' was 'an extraordinary success', says Mauvais-Jarvis. It earned a mention in LVMH's financial results for the first quarter of 2010, which described it as 'performing well'.

WHERE SCIENCE MEETS STATUS

The desire to blind consumers with science has led to the equivalent of an arms race in the industry, as each brand attempts to outdo the other with its latest find. They patent their findings and boast about these patents in their advertising claims: for example, Estée Lauder signals '20 patents worldwide' and '25 years of DNA research', emphasized by a golden double helix, for its Advanced Night Repair cream.

Since 1991, Chanel has run the Centre de recherches et d'investigations épidermiques et sensorielles (epidermal and sensory research and investigation centre) (CERIES), which grants a €40,000 annual award for ground-breaking research into skincare. One of Chanel's weapons in the skincare wars is Xavier Ormancey, the brand's director of active ingredient research. Ormancey traipses through remote regions of the earth in search of exotic plants that may help reduce the effects of ageing. It can often seem as though he does this purely for the entertainment of journalists.

'Ormancey, 42, scours the globe in search of undiscovered natural ingredients that just might constitute skincare's next big thing,' wrote a *Times* reporter in 2006. 'Of late, his favoured destination has been Madagascar... Here not only has he seen off crocodiles and the mosquito-borne, joint-freezing chikungunya virus, but also scorpions, snakes, spiders and leeches. It is a spirit of adventure that has earned him the moniker of "the beauty world's Indiana Jones".'

Thanks to Ormancey's work, we read, Chanel is poised to launch an anti-ageing cream eight years in the making:

> The cream, Sublimage, has its origins in the northern extremity of Madagascar from whence, almost a decade ago, Ormancey received a tip-off about a species of vanilla tree bearing an amazing, life-giving fruit, of which only 13 specimens remained. Field tests of the Vanilla planifolia pod revealed that it comprised over 60 per cent active ingredient, in this case fruit polyketones, unrivalled even by antioxidant super-sources such as grapeseed or green tea.
>
> ('Beauty in full bloom?', *Times*, 2 September 2006)

Like celebrity endorsers, Ormancey and his adventures bring a human dimension to those slippery tubes of cream.

After the London *Times*, it was the turn of its New York-based namesake to wax lyrical. 'Whether he's following Tibetan monks through the Himalayan foothills in search of a rose that blooms only under snow, macheteing his way through the Peruvian jungle for a vine that is eaten by condors to heal snakebites or procuring recipes for ancient Indonesian beauty elixirs, Ormancey is Chanel's secret ecowarrior' ('Ecochic', *T Style Magazine*, 27 August 2006).

With journalists writing this stuff, who needs advertising? More recently, for the launch of Chanel's Essential Revitalizing Concentrate (the name sounds familiar), we find Ormancey on the trail of 'the Golden Flower of the Himalayas: the Golden Champa'.

Wherever the plant was discovered, it lay at the intersection of three marketing imperatives: the desire for new active ingredients, the need for compelling stories, and the increasing demand among consumers for natural products. Dior has what it calls 'gardens' dotted around the world: protected areas from which it sources natural active ingredients. We've already mentioned Longoza seeds from Madagascar; to this you can add rare flowers from Uzbekistan and, closer to home, the vines of Yquem in the Bordeaux region of France. It is extraordinarily serendipitous that these vines have age-fighting properties, as Dior parent LVMH owns Château d'Yquem, producer of some of the world's most expensive wine. It's the luxury industry equivalent of a bonus prize.

Luxury skincare is outrageously expensive, but let's not forget Helena Rubinstein's theory that the fashionable do not want to buy anything affordable. They are even happier when it's practically unobtainable. Take this clipping from the *New York Times*:

> You need more than just dough – you need pull. Kanebo's Sensai Premier is $1,320, when you can get it; Barney's New York sold out in less than two weeks. A 21-day supply of La Mer the Essence is $2,100, available by invitation only... How to explain the breathtaking numbers? 'You can buy a new designer handbag for fall, but you only have one face,' says Jose Parron, the image director at Barney's New York.
>
> ('Luxe creams – tags to riches', 16 October 2005)

It's the familiar luxury marketing equation: you can't afford it; you're not worthy; availability is limited – therefore you want it very much indeed.

Switzerland's La Prairie understands this perfectly well.

The brand has its roots in the Clinique La Prairie – now a separate entity – founded by Dr Paul Niehans in Montreux in 1931. At this exclusive establishment, Niehans experimented with what he called 'cellular therapy', which involved injecting fresh cells from lamb foetuses into his patients (this is explained on the clinic's website at www.laprairie.ch). The idea sprang from an experiment involving a patient with damaged parathyroid glands (which control the amount of calcium in blood and bones). Niehans injected the patient with a solution containing parathyroid cells from a calf. When the patient recovered, Niehans continued experimenting with animal–human cellular transplants. He concluded that the process extended life and even fought cancer. (The American Cancer Society dismisses this claim, saying that the treatment has never been scientifically tested.)

Predictably, the Holy Grail of a longer lifespan proved irresistible, and Niehans treated thousands of wealthy and influential clients, from Gloria Swanson to Pope Pius XII. The link between La Prairie and the elite was established.

In 1976, five years after Niehans's death, Swiss banker Armin Mattli bought the clinic. He launched La Prairie Cosmetics, a range of skincare products whose marketing emphasized the clinic's reputation in the cellular therapy field. The line was sold off in 1982, when it passed first to the US Cyanamid Company and then to Sanofi. In 1987 it was acquired by Georgette Mosbacher, a businesswoman and 'vivacious socialite' who had been married to Fabergé chairman George Barrie and was now the wife of oil tycoon and Republican party fundraiser Robert A Mosbacher. As CEO of La Prairie, she proved a dynamic force, turning the ailing brand around with a camera-ready personality and a knack of motivating sales staff that recalled Estée Lauder. In 1991 she sold the brand to Beiersdorf for a reported US$45 million.

Today La Prairie plays on its salubrious Swiss heritage, its swish packaging and its 'patented Cellular Complex' – rarely seen without the word 'exclusive' attached – to lure a mature and well-off target market. Branded spas within luxury hotels help maintain its profile within this group. The key to Cellular Complex seems to be the inclusion of glycoproteins, which stimulate cell repair. But, as a source in the beauty trade observed, there is no reason why this should work when applied to the skin. 'You'd have to go much deeper to have any effect. Consumers are essentially paying for fragrance, texture – and status.'

In the summer of 2010, selected beauty journalists were invited by La Prairie to The Modern restaurant at New York's Museum of Modern Art, where the brand was launching a handful of new products. It typically does this between four and six months before launch, so the editors have plenty of time to discover the merchandise before closing their September and October issues – the thickest and most advertising-stuffed of the year.

The journalists were wooed with drinks and nibbles and handed branded La Prairie notebooks and pens. The products being launched included Cellular Radiance Emulsion SPF 30 (US$425), Anti-Ageing Neck Cream (US$200) and two holiday gift sets (US$950 each). A *New York Times* reporter described the brand as 'the Apple computer of the beauty world', adding, 'Its packaging is gorgeous: silver, white, clear and sleek. Its prices are high. And it emphasizes face-to-face customer service. Most of the selling is done at kiosks in department stores… where potential clients are dabbed and spritzed with products, and quizzed about their skin care needs' ('Mimosas and caviar for breakfast', 10 June 2010). At the event, Lynne Florio, president of La Prairie, said that the brand liked to 'speak to the press and to our customers as often and as intimately as possible'.

The profusion of glossy magazines and the regularity with which editors are hosed with free beauty product by PR people – as well as the advertising clout of the brands themselves – explain the absence of critical discourse within the sector. The journalist Janet Street-Porter once savaged beauty editors as 'traitors to their own sex' who 'churn out the column inches of drivel for these products, and act as propagandists for the cosmetics industry' ('Why beauty editors are the real villains', *Independent*, 22 October 2000).

Had Street-Porter been writing today, she might have widened her aim to include the majority of beauty bloggers.

So are consumers duped by luxury beauty companies and their glossy familiars? That is far from certain. It seems more likely that they want to believe. They enjoy the whole chain of experience: talking to the 'beauty consultant' in the store, taking the streamlined object home, opening it up, and applying a cream whose colour, texture and fragrance have been designed to deliver an optimally pleasing sensation as it glides coolly on to their skin. Throughout the process, they cling to an irrational yet thoroughly enjoyable optimism.

Another fabulously pricey brand is Sisley, the French beauty company created in 1976 by Count Hubert d'Ornano, whose father was one of the founders of Lancôme. D'Ornano and his wife Isabelle were keen art collectors, so they named their brand after the Impressionist painter Alfred Sisley. Their story – way ahead of its time – was natural plant extracts. Sisley calls its process 'phytocosmetology', which involves blending natural active ingredients in a way that heightens the effect of each individual component.

'Some people tell us they prefer to use one of our creams rather than go to a restaurant on a Saturday night,' Isabelle once said ('Sisley: the house of beauty', *Times*, 9 October 2008).

Her comment goes right to the heart of luxury beauty. For many purchasers of creams, efficacy is not even half the point. A cream is a source of comfort, a self-indulgent treat, a way of feeling better about the day to come. That's why beauty products continue to sell during a recession. Consumers are not addicted to the result, but to the feeling. Imagining the opulent spa or the brave eco-scientist hacking his way through a tropical rainforest is part of that experience.

Still, it's worth bearing in mind that the main ingredient of most skincare products – from the cheapest to the most expensive – is water.

BEAUTY TIPS

✳ Haute couture fashion brands were quick to move into perfume and make-up, establishing a legitimacy in the beauty sector.

✳ They followed up with creams as their consumers turned to combating wrinkles rather than simply hiding them.

✳ They invested in research departments in order to compete with the likes of P&G and L'Oréal.

✳ Research into 'active ingredients' drives the stories that are used to sell creams.

✳ Beauty brands compete to discover the latest active ingredient and bring it on to the market first.

✳ The cosy relationship between beauty brand PRs and beauty journalists smoothes the marketing process.

✳ Consumers buy not only efficacy, but also experience: the retail environment, the packaging, the fragrance, the texture.

✳ They also buy status: beauty is a high-margin business because many consumers are willing to pay for a luxury cream – or unwilling to pay for a cheap one.

HOW TO LAUNCH
A CREAM

'You have to dramatize science.'

I find myself wondering: 'How exactly does all this work? I understand why people buy skin creams, but what happens before they come on to the market? What's the process?'

So I find someone to ask: a friend of a friend, who works as a product manager at a major beauty company that has already been mentioned in these pages. She spoke on condition of anonymity, but let's call her Caroline.

As we've established, skincare trends come and go almost as fast as fashion fads. Plant extracts, antioxidants, peptides, stem cells, bio-electricity: all of them have had their time in the sun. Beauty companies watch one another like hawks to ensure that they don't miss out on a new active ingredient.

'You constantly monitor what your competitors are doing,' confirms Caroline. 'You want to be sure you're maintaining your fair share of the market, so you may find yourself launching a product to react to the competition or respond to a success story, but that's by no means the only impetus. When you have a successful range of products there's natural erosion. You can maintain interest by launching an extension to the range, or you may have to repackage and relaunch the entire line, changing the marketing message entirely.'

That's when you need to contact the laboratory and find out if there's a new active ingredient – a new story to tell. 'Everything starts with a concept. You actually sit down and write this – and a lot of what you write typically ends up in the advertising copy at the end of the process. You take that concept to the laboratory and discuss it with them. They can tell you whether their research supports your concept. You go back and forth for a while adjusting your concept until it agrees with the research, and finally you've got a coherent story to tell the consumer. A good example of this, in my view, is Vichy's LiftActiv Derm Source. Vichy is basically targeting the papillary dermis, the layer of skin below the surface – the epidermis – which it has renamed the 'derm source' in its marketing. This implies that it is the source of all your skin problems and that, by targeting it with a plant extract, they can improve the elasticity and radiance of your skin.'

A beauty brand may launch two or three products based on the same story, with others to follow if it proves successful. For an anti-ageing product this might be one serum, one cream and maybe a serum for the skin around the eyes. If the product is focused on hydration, the range might be larger because of the different skin types: dry, oily or combination. A range can gradually expand to embrace 10 or more products. 'Lately there's been a trend for launching the range with the serum,' says Caroline. 'Women are getting into the habit of applying a serum that prepares the skin for other beauty treatments.'

The laboratory then makes up samples, conducting tests to see how the active ingredients react with the commonplace elements that go into a cream – water, preservatives, colour, fragrance, slip agents and so on. The type of packaging is decided on very early too, partly because the chosen material may react negatively with the ingredients. ('I remember one cream that actually melted the plastic,' Caroline recalls.) The packaging is also a vital part of the storytelling process, so it's important to get it right. This involves various meetings between the marketing team, the design agency and the packaging producer, with numerous debates and adjustments. Moulds need to be prepared, slots booked at factories; glass containers require a particularly long lead time.

The product manager then receives several sample creams of different consistencies. 'Texture is very important – we have sensorial specialists who work exclusively on that,' says Caroline. 'But it's also quite subjective. I tend to always like the same type of cream. Usually a few of us test it to determine which is the most popular.'

If there is any doubt, the sensorial specialist is asked to make a decision about which texture delivers the most pleasing experience.

Once a sample has been validated, the cream is sent to a test centre to find out how it goes down with consumers. Volunteers take part in blind tests with competitive products. They're also asked to use the cream for between 15 days and a month, to see how it affects their skin (see 'Welcome to Cosmetic Valley', below). The sample groups are small – as few as 30 women. This enables the beauty companies to claim that '80 per cent of women tested noted an effect on their skin'. Positive test results give the product manager ammunition to convince the sales and marketing team – and ultimately the CEO of the company – that the cream merits the money and effort that will be put behind it.

While all this is going on, the product manager is working on the creative elements of the packaging and advertising. 'You're looking for the most attractive way of translating science into a scenario that sells the benefits of the product to the consumer.'

Another contact, this time at an advertising agency, tells me that there is not a great deal of difference between working on beauty brands and detergents. 'They both require the same skill,' he says. 'You have to dramatize science. With detergent, we're showing you how the enzyme or whatever it is eats up all the dirt on your clothes. With a skin cream, we're showing you how the active ingredient reacts with your cells. There's always a certain amount of scientific language and maybe one of those close-up illustrations you see in biology textbooks.'

The language of beauty marketing is a kind of surreal poetry. 'Natural', 'radiance', 'flawless', 'visibly reduces', 'enhances', 'renews', 'boosts', 'rejuvenates', 'revitalizes', 'replenishes', 'exclusive', 'patented', 'tested', 'proven', 'advanced': choose from a smattering of these, and add some science (extra points for the use of the words 'cells' or 'cellular') and preferably a few French words too. Many US beauty ads still prefer the word 'crème' instead of 'cream', because regulations once forbade the use of the word 'cream' unless it related to a dairy product.

Advertising restrictions concerning the beauty business are getting tougher. The United Kingdom's Advertising Standards Authority (ASA) regularly lashes out at claims it considers dubious, and as a result cosmetics companies regard the UK as one of the strictest regulatory environments in the world. 'If you get away with a claim in the UK, you can probably get away with it anywhere,' one beauty advertiser told me.

Digitally removed wrinkles and ingeniously manipulated statistics, alongside claims such as 'younger-looking skin' and 'reduces the look of fine lines', have provoked complaints from consumers, often upheld by the ASA, which has pressured the likes of P&G and Beiersdorf to withdraw certain ads. Ads for hair and eyelash products have come under fire, too, with L'Oréal and Rimmel, among others, facing criticism from the ASA for the use of hair extensions and false lashes. This is despite the fact that advertisers have begun peppering ads with small print that comes clean about the enhancements. Overseas brands are frequently obliged to adjust advertising copy for the UK market.

The beauty industry is becoming increasingly worried about this development. At the inCosmetics trade show in Munich in May 2009, cosmetics consultant Chris Gummer urged the industry to 'get tough with regulators'. 'They are being over-diligent about our claims and not really understanding the consumer,' he said. He suggested regulators be invited to cosmetics companies and shown consumer research. 'This is an area of perception, of beauty and emotion, and they need to know how consumers really respond to these products.'

He was convinced that consumers knew how to interpret claims and were not being misled. On the other hand, he agreed that cosmetics companies needed to be more diligent about the data they were providing. Particularly, he pushed for more in vivo tests (on live subjects) rather than in vitro (purely lab-based). 'In vitro only says something possibly will work or might work. It gives you a guide to take the next big expensive step to the in vivo trial' (www.cosmeticsdesign.com).

Caroline believes most consumers are willing victims. 'They're never 100 per cent convinced it will work. They're perfectly aware that there's an element of fantasy.'

Very often, that fantasy is symbolized by a celebrity. Some lines have an established star endorser, such as Sharon Stone for Dior's Capture Totale, in which case you just need to shoot her for the latest product. But if you're launching a new line – or relaunching an old one – you need a fresh face.

Caroline says: 'Between you and me, I think consumers are getting a little tired of the celebrity game. They are well aware that she's had little or no involvement with the conception of the product. But it's considered important internally. If you launch without a star, the industry thinks you have no confidence in your product. After all, if you're willing to sign up a celebrity for 8 or 10 million dollars, that sends out a message. I also think it's important for corporate morale. You tell yourself that all the stress and crap you put up with is worth it because you work in a glamorous industry.'

The combination of a big star and an intriguing science story will also attract the attention of the press. Caroline acknowledges the importance of beauty journalists – and, more particularly, of the awards handed out by glossy magazines. In France, the *Marie Claire Prix d'Excellence de la Beauté* is considered particularly prestigious. I was told major brand owners put pressure on magazines if their products are overlooked by such prizes. The conglomerates that now own the bulk of the world's luxury beauty brands wield tremendous advertising clout.

With positive press coverage in hand and a dazzling VIP figurehead beaming down on a whey-faced populace from posters, the product is ready to fly from shelves. According to Caroline, the journey from concept to launch takes 18 months.

During that time, it's likely that the product will have passed through France's beauty heartland. They call it Cosmetic Valley.

WELCOME TO COSMETIC VALLEY

Cosmetic Valley is more of a concept than a location – although it is a geographical area, spreading outward from the Ile de France like a blotch of spilled scent on a handkerchief to Tours in the heart of the country and Normandy in the north. Embracing over 200 laboratories, six universities and more than 7,700 researchers, as well as businesses concerned with every aspect of the beauty industry, it is the perfume and cosmetic sector's equivalent of Silicon Valley. Many French brands have research and packaging operations there; almost all of them have depended on it at one time or another. Jean-Luc Ansel, director-general of the association, says, 'Eighty per cent of beauty products on sale in duty-free shops come from this cluster.'

The development of Cosmetic Valley began in the 1970s, when beauty companies began quitting Paris and its suburbs for cheaper and more spacious accommodation in neighbouring regions. By the 1990s a busy hive of enterprises had grown up, but they barely communicated with one another. Cosmetic Valley was created to develop joint training and employment initiatives, organize conferences and trade fairs and promote the region as a single entity abroad. Growth accelerated in 2005 when it was named one of the French government's 'competitive poles', offering tax breaks to companies that relocated there. 'Cosmetic Valley plays an important role in maintaining the prestige of "Made in France" in the luxury and beauty fields,' says Ansel. 'It is a wellspring of innovation.'

While plenty of straightforward bottling and packaging goes on in the region, scientists there are also studying everything from the effects of biodegradable plastics on active ingredients to the use of ultrasound to measure the depth of wrinkles.

It is through Cosmetic Valley that I meet Patrick Beau, founder of a clinical trials centre called Spincontrol. One chilly October morning I pay him a visit in Tours, a staid but by no means unpleasant town whose handsome white houses are crowned with bruise-coloured slate.

Rather than the maze of glass-fronted laboratories I'm expecting, Spincontrol turns out to be an unassuming enterprise based in a small Art Deco building. Inside, it is clean but functional – more provincial clinic than luxury spa. It seems to have little to do with the glamorous actresses and gold-tinted posters advertising skincare products in Paris.

Beau himself is relaxed and friendly, with the bright blue eyes and faintly ruddy complexion of somebody who prefers fresh air to a laboratory. Escorting me through the corridors, he unlocks a door to a large storeroom. The shelves are stacked with white plastic tubs of cream in various sizes, all marked with a code number. 'The volunteers never know the brand name of the cream they're being asked to test,' he tells me. He picks up a tub and peers at its anonymous white contents. 'Even I'd be hard pressed to tell you what that is.'

All test subjects are volunteers recruited via word of mouth – Spincontrol has a pool of around 15,000 of them. A study can take anything from two months to a year, depending on the product and the demands of the client. 'First we need to know who their target market is and what they expect of the product. Then we'll propose different techniques in order to arrive at a tailor-made study that follows international regulations.'

Beau opens more doors, revealing various incomprehensible devices: steel frames equipped with chinstraps, spotlights and cameras. The company uses advanced photography techniques and software to analyse dark spots on the skin or circles under the eyes, and 'fringe projection' – projecting light on to the skin to obtain a microscopically detailed 3D image – to judge the efficacy of slimming creams and anti-wrinkle treatments. 'We were the first to bring fringe projection to France, a decade ago,' Beau tells me.

He founded Spincontrol in 1991, and it now has 42 employees in France, as well as outposts in Thailand and Montreal. He's also thinking of opening branches in India and Brazil. 'There is a growing demand for rigorous testing because the cosmetics companies are making increasingly ambitious claims for their products, while at the same time consumer groups are calling for more transparency. Obviously, the results would be questionable if the brands conducted tests themselves.'

Spincontrol has obtained ISO certification as well as official approval from AFSSAPS – the French health products safety agency – as an independent 'place of biomedical research'. Beau stresses, 'We are impartial. We don't advise the brands on what they can or can't say. We just give them the facts. What they do with the data is up to them.'

I ask him about the small sample sizes. 'A typical study involves 30 people,' he confirms. 'But that's all you need, especially if you are considering a very specific target market. If you think about it, the smaller the number of people tested, the more the product is proved effective if there is a measurable change.'

He admits that the way the data are used might leave brands open to criticism. 'They are more likely to say "reduced wrinkles in 95 per cent of women tested" than "reduces wrinkles by 5 per cent", for example. They tell the story to their advantage.'

I'm surprised to hear that there is any real change at all, but Beau assures me that some creams can have an impact, if not a dramatic one. 'In any case, I don't think you can reduce creams to their efficacy. They're also designed to provide pleasure: the packaging, the fragrance, the texture. We've conducted well-being tests proving that the use of cosmetics reduces stress.'

He does believe, however, that anti-ageing creams have begun to supplant conventional make-up. 'Once upon a time, if people had wrinkles and blemishes, they hid them. But now they hope that, even without cosmetic surgery, they can get rid of them.'

BEAUTY TIPS

* Beauty brands constantly monitor their competitors and often launch creams to catch up with the latest trend in active ingredients.

* The launch of a new cream begins with a concept – literally, a story – built around the latest research.

* The skill of beauty marketers is to 'dramatize science' in a way that convinces consumers the cream will improve their looks.

* But consumer groups are cracking down on exaggerated claims by beauty brands, led by the Advertising Standards Authority in the United Kingdom – considered the toughest regulatory market.

* Products are tested by independent clinical trial laboratories – but the results are often manipulated in advertising copy.

* Celebrity endorsers embody the fantasy element of beauty branding – although they are also considered important for a brand's prestige within the industry.

THE QUEST FOR
ETERNAL YOUTH

'You would be better off spending the money on a good bottle of pinot noir.'

When Catherine de Medici came to Paris, she brought with her Italian cuisine, Renaissance beauty treatments and rumours of daggers and poison. Yet while the people called her Madame Snake, throughout her long marriage to Henry II of France she stoically resisted skewering his mistress, Diane de Poitiers, upon whom he publicly showered his affections. Indeed, he was wearing Diane's colours when a splintered lance pierced his brain during a jousting tournament.

Following the king's death, Diane was banished from court. But Catherine did not need to poison her. The king's former favourite managed that on her own.

Diane's mistake was to have a doctor who was also an apothecary. These early druggists experimented with all sorts of dubious treatments, including the use of mercury and gold as elixirs of youth. The pseudo-science of alchemy – which, of course, involved transforming baser substances into gold – gave rise to many superstitions about the metal, including a link with immortality. Gold was immutable, went the thinking, so those who consumed gold were guaranteed eternal youth. For Diane, this seemed to work. Although she was 20 years older than the king, she is said to have looked the same age. In later years, a courtier noted that she remained as 'fresh and lovable' as she had been at 30, and that her skin was 'of great whiteness'.

In 2008, a French toxicologist named Joël Poupon analysed a lock of Diane's hair, which was preserved at her former home, the Château d'Anet in Eure-et-Loir. Poupon is somewhat addicted to solving ancient medical mysteries. Until 2005, nobody knew what had caused the illness and death at 28 of Agnès Sorel (1421–50), mistress of King Charles VII of France, to whom she bore three children. Working with a colleague – Philippe Charlier, a forensic archaeologist – Poupon established that she had been a victim of mercury poisoning. While this may have been a beauty treatment, murder could not be ruled out. In 2008, the same team established that the purported 'holy remains' of Joan of Arc – bones discovered in a labelled jar in the attic of a Paris pharmacy in 1867 – were in fact those of an Egyptian mummy and a cat.

Now Poupon and Charlier turned their attention to the enigma of Diane's ageless beauty. The strands of hair, contained in a locket, showed a high concentration of gold. Poupon deduced that she had been a regular drinker of a liquid gold potion – gold chloride and diethyl ether – probably added as drops to a glass of wine.

'Gold is not enormously toxic,' Poupon told me, when I visited him one afternoon at the Lariboisière hospital, a gracious 19th-century Parisian building whose vaulted walkways surround a therapeutic garden. 'Nor is an overdose necessarily fatal. But over time it made her weak. Her hair was extremely fine, her bones brittle. Anaemia explains her ethereal pallor.'

Poupon and Charlier were also able to study Diane's bones, which were being returned to their original resting place at Anet from the mass grave in which they had been dumped during the Revolution. Tissue residues contained doses of gold and mercury.

'My guess is that, like many women of her time, Diane was intrigued by alchemy,' said Poupon. 'The word has a ring of mystery about it today, but in fact it was the forerunner of chemistry. The term derives from the Arabic *al-kimia*.'

This itself is derived from the Persian *kimia* or 'elixir'. The search for the key to youth proved to be the undoing of Diane de Poitiers. She died at the age of 66, but not of natural causes.

THE EMPEROR'S NEW SKIN

Gold is still used as a beauty treatment. A number of creams claim to contain it, notably La Prairie's Cellular Radiance Concentrate Pure Gold, 'newly developed peptides join Pure Gold, suspended in a colloidal gel', and its Cellular Treatment Gold Illusion Line Filler, a 'glamorous, gold-infused potion'. Products from other brands have featured diamond and gold powder and 'black pearl extract'. They are not dangerous – except to your bank balance.

Despite its effects on her health, Diane de Poitiers may have been right to ingest gold rather than rubbing it on. No anti-wrinkle cream can turn back time. Some have a temporary effect on signs of ageing, usually by puffing out the skin to hide fine lines: this can be done using any common moisturizer. Other active ingredients play a variety of roles. Peptides are said to stimulate the healing process and promote the production of collagen or elastin; alpha-hydroxy acids (AHAs) remove dead skin cells and promote a smoother appearance – but at high doses can effectively strip the skin; antioxidants can counteract sun damage; coenzyme Q10 is held to have antioxidant properties; Retin-A is used to treat acne, but may also have a drying effect... I could go on.

In 2007, the US consumer watchdog Consumer Reports tested 10 of the best-selling anti-wrinkle creams on a group of women, aged 30 to 70, over 12 weeks – far longer than the creams suggested it would take for positive effects to become visible. The tests used technology very similar to that described in the previous chapter. They revealed that the products did smooth out some fine lines and wrinkles – among some testers – but that 'even the best performers reduced the average depth of wrinkles by less than 10 percent, a magnitude of change that was, alas, barely visible to the naked eye. Moreover, the luxury-priced skin-care offerings didn't work any better than the drugstore brands.'

Interestingly, when the women were asked their opinion about the effectiveness of the creams tested, they found it difficult to judge, '*and their opinions bore no relation to how well the products performed based on objective measures*' (my italics). As ever, then, beauty is in the eye of the beholder. Consumer Reports has since conducted similar tests on anti-wrinkle serums ('improvements were minor') and eye creams ('none came close to eliminating wrinkles').

One of the most startling denouncements of the skincare sector came in 2000, from Body Shop founder Anita Roddick (see Chapter 18, 'Ethical, organic and sustainable'). Addressing the Cheltenham Literature Festival during a tour to promote her book *Business as Unusual*, she said, 'Moisturisers do work, but the rest is complete pap. There is nothing on God's planet, not one thing, that will take away 30 years of arguing with your husband and 40 years of environmental abuse. Anything which says it can magically take away your wrinkles is a scandalous lie.' With a wry smile, she added, 'You would be better off spending the money on a good bottle of pinot noir' ('Wrinkle cream is pap', says Roddick, *Telegraph*, 19 October 2000).

The condition of your skin is the result of a complex blend of factors including genetics, diet and exposure to the sun. None of the skincare marketers I spoke to convinced me that their products worked, but they were more persuasive when they suggested creams could defend the skin against future damage. Dior's Edouard Mauvais-Jarvis pointed out: 'If you looked at a 40-year-old woman in the 1970s and compared her skin to that of a 40-year-old woman today, you'd see a dramatic difference. We've made enormous progress – and the only thing stopping us from making even more progress is regulation.'

In other words, if cosmetic creams were any more effective, they would become pharmaceutical products and subject to far more lengthy and stringent testing.

Similarly, Spincontrol's Patrick Beau described a photograph he'd seen of Brazilian twin sisters. One had spent her life working in the open air on the family farm, while the other had left home for a more sophisticated existence in the city. In the picture, they no longer looked like twins. 'The one who'd spent her life toiling under the sun could have been the mother of the one who'd led a pampered urban life. Environment is everything. The sun is very hard on the skin.'

In a 1989 forum, the Japanese brand Shiseido (see Chapter 12, 'Beauty goes global') proposed the term 'successful ageing', instead of 'anti-ageing', suggesting that it believes in prevention rather than cure.

Are consumers duped by the claims made by the marketers of anti-ageing creams? Not necessarily: research by Mintel in 2011 found that 69 per cent of consumers in the United States – where the anti-ageing skincare market is worth US$832 billion – believed that 'how you age is mostly genetic, and external products are more hope than help'. Eight in 10 consumers said diet and exercise were the most important factors associated with ageing skin; 78 per cent said using sunscreen was the real key to preventing visible signs of ageing. While many consumers felt ageing was governed by diet, exercise and genetics, 69 per cent said the earlier you start using age prevention remedies, the better.

Beauty analyst Kat Fay said: 'There's a sizeable gap between opinion and practice. While there are no guarantees when it comes to anti-ageing skincare purchases, many women buy the products anyway with the hope of achieving visible results. They adopt the "It's better to try something than do nothing" approach.'

Just 24 per cent of US consumers reported using anti-ageing skincare products. 'Respondents aged 25–54 report the most likelihood to use facial skincare products with anti-ageing, wrinkle-reducing, and skin rejuvenating properties,' added Fay. 'This makes sense, as at age 25 many people are likely beginning to see the first signs of ageing and want to prevent further signs. Through middle age they are trying to reverse the signs; and after age 55 they are likely more resigned to ageing and less inclined to spend.'

Once you have them, wrinkles can only be eradicated temporarily with injections (of dermal fillers like collagen or muscle relaxant like Botox) or permanently by surgery.

But maybe there's another way of tackling the ageing problem. How about immortality, for example?

A TICKET TO FOREVER

There are few more pleasant towns than Arles in the south of France. Strolling in the extraordinary crystalline light along the ramparts beside the green expanse of the Rhône, or drinking a glass of rosé wine on a terrace in the Place du Forum while the lowering sun tints the ancient stones cinnamon, you feel as though life here would always be warmer, slower, easier – simply better.

And you may be right, because Arles was home to the world's oldest human being. Jeanne-Louise Calment died here in 1997 at the age of 122 years and 164 days. She met van Gogh when she was 13 years old. At the outbreak of the First World War she was already 39. She smoked two cigarettes a day from her early 20s until 120, when her doctor advised her to give up. She liked chocolate and the occasional glass of port. She had married well, and never had to work. When she was 92 a lawyer bought her apartment, on the agreement that he would move in after she died. She outlived him.

Calment attributed her long life to olive oil – which she put on food and rubbed into her skin – and an uncomplicated philosophy. 'I took pleasure when I could. I acted clearly and morally and without regret. I'm very lucky.' She also had an uncommon wit, even later in life. 'I've only ever had one wrinkle,' she said, 'and I'm sitting on it.' When, in her very old age, somebody bade her farewell by saying, 'Until next year, perhaps,' she replied, 'I don't see why not – you look pretty good to me!' ('Jeanne Calment, world's elder, dies at 122', *New York Times*, 5 August 1997).

Perhaps having a sense of humour is the key to longevity.

Others are not content to simply knock off early from work, rent a romantic comedy and break out the port and the olive oil. The quest for immortality is a serious business. A number of doctors, scientists and futurists have published books on the subject, popping up regularly on the conference circuit to share their theories.

Leading the charge is Aubrey de Grey, who at least has the right name for the job. Identifiable by a beard that would make Methuselah bristle with envy, de Grey is a maverick Cambridge-educated researcher who insists that ageing is not inevitable. He is convinced that it is possible to identify the components that cause human tissue to age – and fix them. Drawing on his training as a computer scientist, he describes it as 'an engineering problem'. He believes the first human who will live to 1,000 may be walking among us right now.

I can hear you scoffing from here, so let me assure you that de Grey is no lone eccentric. In 2009, with a team of supporters, he set up the SENS Foundation (www.sens.org). This is a registered charity that 'works to develop, promote and ensure widespread access to rejuvenation biotechnologies which comprehensively address the disabilities and diseases of aging' – in other words, regenerative medicine that repairs the wear and tear that causes us to grow old. The Foundation backs a network of students and researchers.

SENS is an acronym for Strategies for Engineered Negligible Senescence. It proposes directly targeting the causes of ageing – de Grey has identified seven of them, including cell loss, cell atrophy and mutations of the nuclear DNA that lead to cancer – in the hope of systematically wiping them out.

De Grey's ideas are inevitably controversial, but the scientists who criticize him can't make him go away. In 2005, MIT's *Technology Review* offered a prize of US$20,000 (half of which was put up by de Grey himself) for any molecular scientist who could prove that SENS was 'so wrong that it was unworthy of learned debate'. The purpose of the challenge was to 'determine whether de Grey's proposals were science or fantasy'. Nobody won, and at the time of writing the money is still on the table. The best that de Grey's critics could come up with was that his ideas were 'somewhat fanciful'.

Writing on behalf of the judges, Nathan Myhrvold, the co-founder and chief executive of Intellectual Ventures and the former chief technology officer of Microsoft, noted: '[E]very now and then, radical ideas turn out to be true. Indeed, these exceptions are often the most momentous discoveries in science' ('Is defeating aging only a dream?', *Technology Review*, 11 July 2006).

For his part, de Grey denies that he is an 'immortality merchant'. He just doesn't want people to get sick. He told the *Guardian* newspaper:

I don't work on longevity, I work on keeping people healthy. The only difference between my work and the work of the whole medical profession is that I think we're in striking distance of keeping people so healthy that at 90 they'll carry on waking up in the same physical state as they were at the age of 30, and their probability of not waking up one morning will be no higher than it was at the age of 30.

('Aubrey de Grey: We don't have to get sick as we get older', 1 August 2010)

Also noteworthy is the amount of publicity that de Grey's 'non-scientific' research has generated. As he puts it, 'Most scientists will get serious media exposure about twice in their entire career. And they'll get that because they've actually done an experiment that was interesting. Well, I don't even do experiments, right?... And I'm in the media all the bloody time.'

It almost seems as though – exactly as with anti-wrinkle creams – we want to believe.

A different and somehow spookier take on immortality is offered by Ray Kurzweil, a brilliant inventor – when he was 13, he turned telephone parts into a machine that could calculate square roots; later he taught computers to recognize and read text aloud – who essentially believes that technology will enable us to live forever. The downside is that we will all be computers.

Kurzweil's theory is based on a notion called 'the singularity'. The phrase was originally used to describe places beyond which the accepted rules of nature ceased to apply – such as the event horizon of a black hole. Later it became associated with the mind-bogglingly rapid advance of technology. Anybody who has seen the *Terminator* movies will be familiar with the theory: at some point, computers will become so smart that they will create more, even smarter computers, at which point they will take control of the planet and shuffle humanity to the sidelines. The moment when the machines achieve ascendancy is 'the singularity'.

Kurzweil has a less dystopian vision of the future. He is certain that, by 2029, we will have succeeded in reverse-engineering the human brain. This will enable us to create the software we need to build a computer that thinks like a human being, right down to experiencing emotions. As computing power is growing exponentially (it doubles every year), this new generation of supercomputers will inevitably be far more intelligent than ourselves.

Sounds like bad news, right? Not necessarily. Kurzweil points out that, while human intelligence will have been overtaken, human consciousness will continue to exist. Rather than a master–slave relationship, Kurzweil envisages the singularity as a partnership. Humans will integrate computers into their own bodies, forming hybrid beings that will naturally live longer than their purely biological forebears. Artificial intelligence will extend the abilities of our brains. Nanocomputers will work away inside us busily repairing what Aubrey de Grey describes as the 'damage' of ageing.

> Kurzweil predicts that by the early 2030s, most of our fallible internal organs will have been replaced by tiny robots. We'll have 'eliminated the heart, lungs, red and white blood cells, platelets, pancreas, thyroid and all the hormone-producing organs, kidneys, bladder, liver, lower esophagus, stomach, small intestines, large intestines, and bowel. What we have left at this point is the skeleton, skin, sex organs, sensory organs, mouth and upper esophagus, and brain.'
>
> ('Futurist Ray Kurzweil pulls out all the stops – and pills – to live to witness the singularity',
> *Wired*, 24 March 2008)

Immortality, then, is to be found in the overlap of the theories proposed by de Grey and Kurzweil. Regenerative medicine will allow each and every one of us to reach the ripe old age of Jeanne Calment, by which time we'll be able to radically improve our bodies using technology. Or at least some of us will. The theory also raises the spectre of a wealthy elite of supercharged immortals lording it over a bunch of obsolescent serfs. Already, the singularity has spawned a niche branch of medicine, with wellness counsellors advising clients on how to live long enough to make it over the 'first bridge' into extreme old age – by which time technology may have solved the problem of mortality.

Fortunately, there is a good chance that the singularity is science fiction. Previous seekers after immortality have proved consistently unsuccessful, as their gravestones attest.

And is the prospect of living forever really so appealing? Shortly before Jeanne Calment's death, she was asked if she wished she could hold out until the end of the century.

'No,' she replied. 'I've had enough.'

BEAUTY TIPS

✳   Much of beauty marketing is based on the quest for eternal youth – an age-old yearning.

✳   Renaissance beauties like Diane de Poitiers believed that drinking gold potions granted them a more youthful appearance. Gold is still used in some beauty products today.

✳   While moisturizer improves the appearance of the skin, there is scant evidence that anti-wrinkle creams have any significant impact, although they do have a placebo effect.

✳   Consumers are wary of the claims made by the marketers of anti-ageing creams, but feel that taking action is better than doing nothing: 'more hope than help'.

✳   They agree that creams can defend against future damage to the skin, particularly from overexposure to the sun.

✳   Fear of ageing has spawned an 'immortality business', with doctors, scientists and thinkers considering ways in which we might live forever.

✳   Approximately 100 billion people have lived on this planet to date. To our knowledge, the very oldest has lived to only 122.

BEAUTY

GOES GLOBAL

'Inequality is written on the body.'

'If we want to be a global brand, we have no choice but to adapt our products to different cultures and skin types,' says Dr Olivier Courtin-Clarins, one of the two brothers who run the French cosmetics brand Clarins. 'Do you know what the percentage of white people on earth is?' I venture a guess: 25 per cent? He shakes his head, smiles, and raises three fingers. 'Three per cent. We're not going to get very far if we market our products exclusively to white women.'

Clarins cites the Institut National d'Etudes Démographiques in France as the source of this figure. But what does the provocative term 'white people' mean? Of European ancestry? Or merely people with a light skin pigmentation? Courtin-Clarins mentions the word 'Caucasian', but even that is hard to define. The numbers I found on the internet, from sources far too unreliable to cite here, were closer to my estimate: about 20 per cent and falling. One suggested that the percentage of 'white people' in the world would have dropped to a single figure by 2040.

That the beauty industry will be forced to adapt to this new reality is ironic, given that it was responsible for establishing a cliché of beauty – tall, thin, fair-skinned – whose after-image is still visible today. In the late 19th and early 20th centuries, Western soap and cosmetics companies took with them to Asia and Africa colonial attitudes that associated fair skin with civilization and cleanliness. Later, the beauty industry and Hollywood joined forces to disseminate the ideal of the blonde bombshell. It was many years before beauty marketing broadened its messages to include a wider range of skin types and ethnicities; by then the damage had been done.

One thing is certain: beauty companies today are immeasurably more flexible than they were 40 years ago. Within the United States alone, the situation has changed utterly. The first significant step towards recognizing black women as a distinct and valuable target group for beauty products came in 1973 with the launch of Fashion Fair Cosmetics by the late John H Johnson, founder of *Ebony* magazine. From its first counter in Chicago at Marshall Field's (now Macy's), the company expanded to the UK and then to France, opening a counter at the Paris department store Printemps in 1984. Following in its footsteps, Maybelline, Max Factor, Revlon and L'Oréal were all marketing products to the African American market by the 1980s.

Still, it's worth noting that make-up artists launched their own lines in the 1990s partly because the range of colour cosmetics on the market did not seem to reflect the wide variety of American – and indeed international – skin tones they came across in their work. Bobbie Brown made her mark with an American *Vogue* cover featuring British black model Naomi Campbell; François Nars used British black model Alek Wek for his first advertising campaign. Neither model was recruited with the express intention of targeting a black audience.

Attitudes to race and beauty had changed, but the traditional beauty companies were slow to catch on. Their narrow perception of beauty in their domestic markets was mirrored abroad. This enabled local brands to assimilate their ideas and adapt them more effectively to local tastes.

JAPAN: THE WAKING GIANT

They called them the *kurofune*, the Black Ships. They were the American gunboats the *Mississippi*, the *Plymouth*, the *Saratoga* and the *Susquehanna*, and they sailed into Yokohama bay on 14 July 1853 under the command of Commodore Matthew Perry. His mission was to press Japan to open up to foreign trade and end a policy of isolation that had lasted more than 200 years. To underline his point, Perry staged a burial at sea, which required the firing of the ships' cannon in salute. A year later, the Japanese signed a treaty with the United States. Westernization had begun at gunpoint.

Starting in 1868, the Japanese government embarked on political, economic and cultural reforms aimed at allowing it to 'catch up' with the West. This had an impact on beauty: women slowly began to abandon the ancient practices of blackening their teeth and eradicating their eyebrows, although they continued to whiten their faces. They coaxed their looks towards an ideal of otherworldly attractiveness that was mirrored years later in the wide eyes of Manga characters.

Procter & Gamble inevitably arrived on the scene bearing its message of hygiene as a mark of Western civilization, ensuring a following among wealthy Japanese consumers. (P&G would one day acquire a major asset in Japan in the form of SK-II, launched in 1980 by Max Factor and based on an active ingredient discovered during the production of sake.)

But a visionary local entrepreneur emerged to satisfy the demand for 'Western' good looks. His name was Arinobu Fukuhara, and in 1872 he opened the Shiseido Pharmacy in the Ginza district of Tokyo. Attracting a well-off clientele, Fukuhara used the pharmacy as a base for launching a series of ground-breaking products: Japan's first toothpaste (as opposed to tooth powder) in 1888, Eudermine skin lotion in 1897 (this is still sold today, complete with the trademark red ribbon around the neck of the bottle) and in 1906 the first 'natural' skin-toned face powder, as opposed to the white product favoured by women at the time.

In the meantime, Fukuhara's son Shizo – a photographer – travelled to Europe and the United States, immersing himself in these foreign cultures. When he returned, he worked with his father to incorporate what he'd learned into the business. This led in 1916 to the establishment of a separate cosmetics division, complete with a stand-alone boutique not far from the original pharmacy. Another important step was the creation of an in-house design department, staffed by ambitious young artists who based their graceful style on the illustrations they'd seen in Paris fashion magazines. This resulted in a new Art Deco logo in the shape of a camellia, and a range of fragrances in packaging with distinctive arabesque graphics. The company established a reputation for supporting budding artists: in 1919 it opened a gallery at its headquarters; this still exists, having hosted more than 3,000 exhibitions and displayed the works of over 5,000 artists.

Shiseido was incorporated as a joint stock company in 1927, with Shizo as its first president. Over the coming years, it followed five management principles. They were: 1) quality above all – absolute excellence is pursued in everything created; 2) coexistence and co-prosperity – everyone associated with Shiseido must benefit in a consequent way; 3) respect for consumers; 4) corporate stability – respect for the company's past achievements and choice of intelligent goals for the future; and 5) sincerity – loyalty and honesty are the fundamental principles of business.

These principles drove many of Shiseido's innovations, notably a foresighted approach to customer loyalty, with the creation of the Camellia Club and a monthly consumer magazine. When pharmacies engaged in a price-slashing war to lure customers, Shiseido launched its chain store system, which obliged retailers to sell its products at fixed prices. Not only did this protect the upmarket image of the brand, but it also guaranteed margins for supplier and retailer and ultimately levelled the playing field for its customers.

The globalization of the beauty industry in the first half of the 20th century was slowed by economic turmoil and conflict. Shiseido moved into the US market in 1935 in a deal with the New York luxury goods store Mark Cross, but was forced to suspend sales with the outbreak of the Second World War. International expansion would not begin again until the 1960s, when Shiseido returned to the United States and entered Europe for the first time, through Italy.

Having sold a Western ideal of beauty to Japanese consumers, Shiseido cunningly reversed the idea with the launch in 1964 of a fragrance called Zen aimed at US and European customers. There was a growing interest in 'oriental' health practices such as acupuncture and yoga, as well as Japanese decor. The bottle featuring wild flowers and grasses on a jet black background was designed to cater to an American vision of Japanese art.

But attitudes to Japanese beauty were changing at home too. In the 1970s the 'Western' look was still fashionable, and Shiseido used many half-Japanese women in its advertising. But in 1973 it chose Sayoko Yamaguchi, a classical Japanese beauty with almond-shaped eyes and raven hair, as the face of its Paris collection. She remained an exclusive Shiseido model until 1988, helping the brand reinforce the idea that Japanese beauty was as desirable as its Western counterpart.

Unlike incomers who were keen to conquer what had now become the world's second largest beauty market, Japanese brands excelled at blending local and Western concepts to arrive at something quite unique. We've already met beauty pioneer Shu Uemera, who had worked as a make-up artist in Hollywood. He became the Japanese Max Factor, opening in 1965 a make-up studio that taught US beauty techniques to Japanese customers hooked on Hollywood movies. Yet his philosophy of simplicity and pureness had a distinctly Japanese feel. Uemera had suffered from tuberculosis as a youth, and beauty was associated in his mind with health and well-being.

Shiseido expresses the same belief: its Life Quality Beauty Centre provides advice on make-up techniques to individuals with skin concerns such as birthmarks or scarring. It also counsels doctors and social workers on how quality of life can be improved through cosmetics and skincare. In short, it extols the message that beauty products deliver both physical and emotional benefits.

Another entrant to the Japanese market was Kanebo, a textile company that introduced skincare products and cosmetics into its stores in the 1960s and had grabbed a fifth of the market a decade later.

With their rigid Hollywood ideals of beauty, Western firms initially struggled to compete with the more nuanced approach of local brands. But the incomers quickly stepped into one of the most important sectors in the Asian beauty market: that of skin lightening creams.

VANITY FAIR

As discussed in Chapter 1, the perceived attractiveness of lighter skin dates back thousands of years and at its most simplistic level is linked to the image of the pampered noble languishing in a shaded palace while peasants toil in the fields. This prejudice was no doubt reinforced by the white rulers of the colonial era. In India, the situation is made even more complex by the strict social stratification of the caste system, which clearly puts those with a darker skin at the bottom. One of the many disturbing repercussions of this is the notion that women with fairer skin are more desirable in both romantic and career contexts.

No surprise, then, that India is home to the world's most famous skin lightening cream, Fair & Lovely, launched by Hindustan Lever (now Hindustan Unilever Ltd) in 1978. Although the company is partly Indian owned, a 52.1 per cent stake is held by the Anglo-Dutch Unilever, creator of the Dove Real Beauty campaign. Fair & Lovely's marketing strategy in India has not changed since its launch: a promise of fairer skin within weeks of application – the website currently claims 'unmatched radiant fairness in just four weeks' – and advertising featuring Bollywood stars. The brand was rolled out internationally in the 1980s and is now sold across Asia, the Middle East and Africa.

Hindustan Unilever is at pains to stress that Fair & Lovely is not dangerous and is free of harmful or banned ingredients such as hydroquinone, steroids or mercury. Its patented formula is based on a skin lightening active called niacinamide (vitamin B3, also used to treat acne) blended with UVA and UVB sunscreens. That's right: Fair & Lovely works in part by ensuring its wearers don't get a tan.

Distasteful though its implications might be, Fair & Lovely was a huge success, spawning many imitators. Almost every major brand now has a skin lightening product: L'Oréal White Perfect Fairness Control ('NEW with melanin-vanish'), Yves Saint Laurent White Mode Repair Whitening Night Cream, Diorsnow Sublissime Whitening Moisture Cream, Shiseido White Lucent, Clarins White Plus HP... and so on. Chanel launched a product called Blanc Pureté in 2001, followed by the White Essential range in 2008. Its latest offering is simply called Le Blanc: 'beauty based on light, where radiance is revived from within'. The controversial nature of these products is apparent from the fact that advertising for them is practically invisible in Western markets.

The question now is whether the advertisers of such creams are blocking the emergence of a broader vision of beauty by continuing to insist that lighter skin is preferable. In a pugnacious article for the left-wing US political newsletter *Counterpunch*, Amina Mire described the trade in skin whitening creams as 'commodity racism'. She was particularly shocked by an advertisement for Vichy's Bi-White cream, which featured 'what appears to be an Asian woman peeling off her black facial skin with a zipper. As her black skin is removed a new "smooth", "whitened" skin with no blemishes takes its place. The implications of this image are blunt and chilling. Blackness is false, dirty and ugly. Whiteness is true, healthy, clean and beautiful' ('Pigmentation and empire', 28 July 2005).

In 2008, Brinda Karat, a politician and member of the All-India Democratic Women's Association, spoke out against the products, saying, 'It's downright racist to denigrate dark skin.' Temperatures were running high over an advertising mini-series created for the alarmingly named White Beauty, another Hindustan Unilever product. 'The popular mini series whitening cream advert portrays heart-throb... Saif Ali Khan preferring fair skinned starlet Nehan Dhupia over former love Priyanka Chopra, celebrated in Bollywood circles for her "dusky, wheatish complexion". But a lovelorn and shunned Chopra turns desperately to White Beauty cream, hoping its application would make her fairer and more appealing to 41-year-old Khan' ('Criticism in India over skin-whitening trend', 10 July 2008).

Aside from the occasional outburst in the press, there is little sign that attitudes are changing, either in India or in other markets where whitening products are popular. The notion that fair skin is desirable seems as ingrained in those societies as the idea in the West that a suntan implies a life of leisure and good health, despite overwhelming evidence that a bronzed skin is a damaged one.

THE NATURE OF BRAZIL

Talking of sun tans, Brazil must be the country most closely associated in the minds of Western consumers with beach life, not to mention body culture. European and US skincare marketers told me that it is also one of the most challenging countries for their brands because of the wide range of skin types there. This has led to the evolution of a large domestic beauty industry that is beginning to have an impact abroad.

As the trend forecasting company WGSN pointed out in 2008, 'Brazilian brands are poised to take advantage of the growing global trend for "natural" and "ethical" products' ('Brazilian beauty targets the world', 4 January 2008). Leading the charge is Natura, founded in 1969 out of a single store in Sao Paulo by the 27-year-old Luiz da Cunha Seabra. He had trained as an economist and was working at the Brazil outpost of Remington Electric Shavers when he decided to go into the skincare business. Even in those days, he emphasized the products' natural ingredients – company lore has it that he occasionally promoted the brand by giving a flower and his card to passers-by.

He was skilled at customer relations, taking time to explain his beauty formulations to those who visited the store. This led to the company's most important step, which was to abandon traditional retail and introduce door-to-door, or 'direct', selling along the lines of Avon (which remains its biggest rival). The move transformed the business. By the mid-1980s it was managing a network of 16,000 independent sales representatives – it calls them 'consultants' – and growth of 40 per cent a year. By recruiting motivated staff who could explain its products to customers on a one-to-one basis, in the comfort of their own homes, it had created a human connection between the brand and its target that few of its rivals could match.

Seabra brought in Guilherme Peirao Leal, a distributor, and Pedro Luiz Passos, an engineer who took charge of production, as partners. In 1986, they launched an anti-age product called Chronos – the first in the market to promote cell renewal – which sold 90,000 units in less than two months. The line expanded to embrace a wide range of skincare solutions. Meanwhile, Natura moved into Portugal, Argentina and Chile. At the same time, it was forced to compete with the incursion of the multinationals into its home market: cosmetic sales in Brazil grew from US$2.6 billion to US$5.7 billion between 1992 and 1996. Natura fought back by launching more than a hundred new products (Hoover's Company Profiles: Natura Cosméticos SA).

Along with its innovative direct selling approach, the company has been aided by the wide-ranging interests of its founder, which include Buddhism, Taoism, the writings of Carl Gustav Jung and the management theories of Peter Drucker. Seabra was an early adopter of 'sustainable' practices, taking care to ensure that none of the company's suppliers used child labour and investing a percentage of profits in social projects. Refillable packaging was launched as early as 1983. Sales staff are paid an average of 16 times higher than minimum wage, are given shares in the company and receive regular training in the latest skincare advances. Natura remains responsive to consumers, with a call centre to deal with enquiries from consultants and customers.

Seabra has not been afraid to rely on his instincts: he launched a line of products for infants (Mamãe e Bebê, or Mother and Baby) against the advice of his researchers. Like Shiseido, he believes cosmetics are vital for boosting well-being and self-esteem. Natura refers to this as *bem estar bem* (well being well). It also steers clear of exaggerated claims, saying that it aims to prevent signs of ageing rather than promising rejuvenation. Even before Dove, the company ran advertising featuring ordinary women instead of models.

By 2000 Natura had a portfolio of more than 300 products covering fragrances, skincare, colour cosmetics, toiletries, products for children and babies and nutritional supplements. Innovations were driven by one of the country's largest research facilities. In 1999 the company bought Flora Medicinal J Monteiro da Silva, whose model was based on the curative powers of Brazilian plants. This led in 2000 to the Ekos line of body care products, using natural ingredients sourced from Brazilian rainforests on a fair trade basis. The company believes this is a way of slowing deforestation.

Natura floated on the Sao Paulo stock exchange in May 2004. It expanded into Europe the following year with the opening of a boutique on the Left Bank of Paris – one of the first to blend a natural and sustainable offering with the trappings of a luxury brand, anticipating a trend that would take a firm hold of the beauty market by the end of the decade (see Chapter 18, 'Ethical, organic and sustainable'). The company now has a network of 800,000 direct selling 'consultants' in Brazil, Argentina, Chile, Peru, Colombia and France – not bad considering it started with only 70. Amusingly for those who buy into the 'sun, sea and sex' image of Brazil, one of its most popular products is a home bikini-line waxing product.

Taking their cue from Natura, a handful of Brazilian brands have begun marketing products to overseas markets by emphasizing both their naturalness and their origins. (This has been actively encouraged by a local trade body, the ABIHPEC, the Brazilian Association of the Cosmetic,

Toiletry and Fragrance Industry.) For example, WGSN identified Brazilian Fruit, a range of bath and body care products 'based on high concentrations of Amazonian butters and natural oils'. When it launched on the French and UK markets in September 2007, managing director Veronika Rezzani said: 'Our objective is to introduce to the world products that bring out the "Brazilian-ness", with aromas, flavours and the enormous variety of natural assets from our country.' The brand's flagship line is called Caipirinha, after the ultimate Brazilian cocktail.

Brazil generally has a positive image abroad – it's difficult to imagine a stroppy London taxi driver confessing an instinctive dislike of Brazilians, in the way that he might voice a prejudice against the Germans or the French – but the country's preoccupation with beauty has a negative side. In social, romantic and career terms, a perfect body is almost as desirable in Brazil as a fair complexion is in India.

In 2007 an anthropologist named Mirian Goldenberg, a professor at the Federal University of Rio de Janeiro, launched a book called *O Corpo Como Capital* (The Body as a Capital Asset) exploring the country's cult of physical perfection. In an interview with the news agency Inter Press Service, she said women from all classes felt compelled to 'invest heavily in their bodies', with obvious advantages for the wealthy. She pointed out that the country's market for gyms, cosmetics and plastic surgery vied with that of the United States, where incomes were 14 times higher. In Brazil, 'inequality is written upon the body... The market and society demands it... for instance, no woman can appear with grey hair.' Once again, in a country where skin tones run the gamut from pale to black, the emphasis is on slender and blonde. ('The body beautiful – women's ladder to success', 17 April 2008).

One of the world's most successful models is the sculptural blonde Brazilian Gisele Bündchen.

EASTERN APPROACHES

Beauty companies are keeping a close eye on upheaval in the Middle East, which has for some time been a promising market for premium brands:

one only has to stalk the luxury malls of Dubai to see why. In November 2010, *Global Cosmetic Industry* magazine published a report on the region by Euromonitor International. It commented: 'Beauty in the Middle East, particularly in the Persian Gulf, is a massive market for international brand owners – with the United Arab Emirates (UAE), Saudi Arabia and Iran being the biggest in terms of overall and per capita sales, along with Israel' ('Premium positioning, innovative retail hallmarks of Middle East beauty market', 5 November 2010).

As in other regions, economic recession failed to make much of a dent, as beauty products are perceived as 'an affordable luxury and a harmless indulgence'. The report noted that the average woman in the UAE spent an average of $73 on colour cosmetics in 2009, compared with $69 in the UK and $53 in France. It also signalled innovations such as Beiersdorf's Nivea Haus spa in Dubai, which 'uses only Nivea products for various pampering and healing treatments and also allows clients to purchase their Nivea products on-site'. Western department stores like Harvey Nichols and Debenhams are also present. Advertising restrictions are far less draconian in the UAE than they are in Saudi Arabia, allowing the Western brands to traffic their concept of beauty.

But while it is intrigued by the Persian Gulf and deeply attracted to Brazil – the latter is, after all, one of the favoured BRIC economies, along with Russia, India and China – the beauty industry is still preoccupied by Asia. According to figures from Euromonitor International, the region dominates the global skincare market, accounting for 40 per cent of total sales at the time of writing. This is not surprising given that – as one cosmetics marketer from Lancôme told me – many Asian consumers use as many as six different skincare products during each session before their bathroom mirrors, both morning and night. 'A cleanser, followed by a serum, followed by a hydrating cream, followed by something for the eye area, followed by a whitener, followed by a sunscreen. At night, replace the sunscreen with a night cream. In Europe, many women use just one or two products. America is in between.'

One of the most established markets in the region is South Korea, where women take an immense pride in their looks. There is a big demand for whitening creams; the nip and tuck business is also booming. In 2005, the BBC reported: 'Women of marriageable age are under intense pressure to look their best at all times… a women's magazine recently advised its readers to spend 30 per cent of their incomes on looking good… The buzz word these days is *ul-jjang*, literally "best face"' ('The price of beauty in South Korea', 2 February 2005).

South Korea too has an impressive home-grown market. This is dominated by AmorePacific, founded by Suh Sung-hwan in 1945, with Melody Cream as its first product. The company gained quick inroads by paying close attention to design: although its cream was produced in Seoul, the labels were printed in Japan. In the 1950s it benefited from an alliance with Coty of France to produce Coty Face Powder. It also published Korea's first beauty magazine, *Hwajanggye*. Its development from the 1960s onwards is somewhat analogous to that of Brazil's Natura. In 1963, it began sending its own beauty consultants to boutiques where its products were sold, in order to coach employees about its brand values and the needs of its consumers. This led to a move into door-to-door sales for the launch of the Amore brand of cosmetics in 1964.

Today, AmorePacific has standout brands at every level of the market. Its high-end line Sulwhasoo has international ambitions, with a flagship store in Hong Kong. The name comes from Sulwha, or 'snow flower', and 'soo', meaning excellence. Its natural ingredients are based on Korean herbal medicine. The short range includes a serum, cleansers, hair care and an eye cream. It does little advertising, preferring to communicate with women face to face in a department store environment, or via its website and bi-monthly magazine. It also has spas in South Korea and Hong Kong. Every year it launches a collectable limited edition compact demonstrating traditional Korean craftsmanship.

In an interview with WGSN, vice-president and brand manager Eric Hwang said the brand's sales in South Korea were between 11 and 12 per cent, similar to that of SK-II, Estée Lauder and Lancôme combined. He added that the brand had been built on samples and word of mouth.

> Since the brand's philosophy was established, there have been about a million samples released. Because we believe in the quality of the products, we want people to have a first hand experience. The evaluation is up to the users – we're here to provide opportunities. This is where we invest, and not in TV ads. The rule applies not only in Korea, but it has proven successful in Hong Kong as well. Through sampling and word of mouth, our sales grew as high as 50 percent in Hong Kong.
>
> ('Sulwhasoo: executive interview', 29 December 2010)

International visitors – particularly from Japan and China – have been flocking to Seoul to buy not only luxury products like Sulwhasoo, but good value mid-market products like Laneige and Mamonde, as well as the ubiquitous BB or 'beauty balm' creams that play the role of invisible foundation. Local make-up artists are now launching their own brands. Korean cosmetics have become outrageously trendy in China, driven by the 'Korean wave' of music and movies that has captured the imagination of the market. After Hong Kong, Sulwhasoo opened its first counter at Beijing's Parkson department store in April 2011.

But it will have to compete in China with the Western brands, which are unlikely to repeat the error they made when entering Japan, having learned how to act globally while adapting to local tastes. L'Oréal's Lindsay Owen-Jones was the acknowledged master of this approach. Here's Geoffrey Jones (no relation) again:

> The determination to stay relevant was evident in the evolving identity of L'Oréal Paris as it was taken around the world. The brand remained true to its position as representative of 'chic beauty', but the view that such chicness was no longer primarily French became widespread. The majority of the global spokesmodels of the brand ceased to be primarily French... the more global the brand became, the more local its models had to be.

While consumers liked the idea of Paris, it was just that – an idea, a collection of brand attributes, not a grey-stoned city with all the problems of any large capital. The trick was working out what the myth of 'Paris' meant to each group of consumers and tailoring the brand to them. As we've established, L'Oréal solved this problem with a team of international brand managers who could monitor each mega-brand in its respective market, tweaking global advertising approaches with the use of local celebrities and cultural references.

The practice is still not universal: the first hurdle is the cost of producing many advertising images featuring different models with various skin types. Then there is the hard fact of consumer demand. 'Even in Asia,' one source told me, 'customers respond to an international star like Julia Roberts. It's when we use a model who's big in Europe but not very well known over there that the local marketing people insist on replacing her with a local celebrity.'

The cosmetics marketers I spoke to were inevitably enthusiastic about China's economic boom. The country had a flourishing cosmetics market in the early 20th century – fuelled by Western brands and exposure to Hollywood movies – but the Sino-Japanese war signalled the end of this first phase, with a full ban imposed in 1966 at the beginning of the Cultural Revolution. Only when the country opened up again in 1978 did advertisements for beauty products begin to reappear. Procter & Gamble entered the market with Olay in 1988. Others followed, bringing their impressive advertising clout with them. Smelling cash, Western media brands jetted in too. A Chinese edition of *Vogue* launched in 2005. In 2010 researcher Kline & Company said sales of toiletries and cosmetics in the market would top US$17 billion.

Premium European and US brands are prized, although cultural differences are putting a slight break on development: a traditional preference for natural beauty means that many consumers are still wary of fragrances and make-up, but sales of skincare – including whiteners – are rocketing, especially among the urban young. The appeal of 'Western' looks has also provoked a rise in cosmetic surgery as wealthy young women sign up to have their eyes 'widened' via eyelid reshaping. Again, this may lead to a social stratification based on looks, with the rich sporting pale Westernized faces and the less wealthy remaining more authentically Chinese.

One area where Western brands have failed to make much of an impact in Asia – at least compared to the West – is that of anti-ageing products, perhaps because age is considered a sign of wisdom. But as Mintel reports, Western brands have tackled this by blending anti-ageing claims with whitening solutions. 'In India, Fair & Lovely, for instance, offers Forever Glow Anti-Ageing Fairness Cream with a vita-AHA complex, said to work in just four weeks.'

Elsewhere, BB creams have been adopted as a way of encouraging Asian consumers to buy into anti-ageing. 'Chinese company Dr Ci:Labo's BB Perfect Cream Enrich-Lift contains firming and lifting actives as well as helping to hide spots and blemishes. The product promises true multi-functionality as the company says it can be used as a toner, moisturising milk, sunscreen, make-up base, concealer and foundation.' It's the Swiss Army knife of beauty solutions.

Dr Olivier Courtin-Clarins told me that the company now tests on different skin types and formulates products for a wide range of cultural habits. 'I'm a scientist,' he told me, 'and I know that, if our company wants to be everywhere, I have to provide products for everyone. I can't change the nature of your skin, and I don't wish to change your culture.'

For the beauty giants, globalization is about far more than adopting local accents for advertising: actives and delivery systems discovered and developed in the West must be reconfigured to suit local preferences.

BEAUTY TIPS

❋ When Western cosmetics manufacturers began to expand globally in the late 19th and early 20th centuries, they exported a vision of beauty driven at first by colonial ideals and later by Hollywood.

❋ This reinforced an ancient preference for paler skin – which had connotations of nobility – and expanded the market for whitening products, which Western brands did not hesitate to exploit.

❋ A lingering preference for the Hollywood cliché of beauty – pale skin, blonde hair, slim physique, wide eyes – has driven a flourishing cosmetic surgery business in markets ranging from Brazil to South Korea.

❋ In Japan, companies like Shiseido and Shu Uemera stole a march on foreign incomers by adopting a more nuanced approach to beauty, which combined Western with local cultural references.

❋ Brands from Japan and Brazil have successfully repackaged elements of their local cultures for Western consumers: 'art, design and health practices' from Japan; 'natural beauty' from Brazil.

❋ Western companies slowly mastered a 'think global, act local' approach for their mega-brands, spearheaded by L'Oréal with its Maybelline and L'Oréal Paris brands.

❋ Far more brands now use local celebrities in advertising – but international stars have by no means disappeared.

❋ Door-to-door or 'direct' selling has proved hugely successful for brands in Brazil and South Korea.

❋ Spa culture also helped to spread the message about both local and global brands.

❋ China is the boom market for brands from Europe and the United States as well as from Japan and South Korea.

❋ Actives first introduced into Western products are being repurposed for local formulas, especially whitening creams.

A FACE IN THE CROWD
Finding a niche

'Our ambition is to be the
Apple of the beauty industry.'

As Anita Roddick seemed to suggest in Chapter 11, red wine is good for you. It is the central pillar of the French Paradox – the familiar belief that, although the French wolf down artery-clogging foods like cheese, steak-frites and patisseries with abandon, they enjoy relatively low levels of coronary heart disease. This led to speculation that drinking red wine reduced the risk of heart attacks. While the data behind the French Paradox turn out to be shaky, research has shown that red grapes contain antioxidant polyphenols, such as resveratrol, which may well have health benefits.

Most of us merely use this as an excuse for accepting a second glass of red wine with dinner. A French beauty brand named Caudalie encourages us to go several steps further, by rubbing wine-related products into our skins. What sounds like an odd notion is a palpable success, as a visit to Caudalie's offices in an elegant champagne-coloured building not far from boulevard Haussmann confirms.

There, marketing director Pauline Celier-Bony gives me chapter and verse on the Caudalie saga. More than anything, it's a valuable lesson in creating an independent brand with an identity strong enough to stand out in the crowded skincare sector. It attracts consumers by expertly playing on two notions: the French Paradox and the French art of living.

The story began at the Château Smith Haut Lafitte in 1993, when Mathilde Thomas and her now husband Bertrand took a group of students led by a professor of pharmacology from Bordeaux University on a tour of the vineyards, owned by Mathilde's parents. The professor, Joseph Vercauteren, remarked that the grape seeds discarded during the winemaking process contained potentially valuable antioxidants. Pursuing the conversation, Mathilde discovered that the by-products of winemaking were known for combating free radicals, one of the main causes of skin ageing.

Realizing that they had stumbled upon a business idea – and a way of further monetizing the vineyard – Mathilde and Bertrand partnered with Vercauteren to isolate the molecules that would turn those by-products into the active ingredients of a line of beauty products. In 1994 they launched Caudalie (the word is a unit of measurement referring to the duration of a wine's flavour on the palate) and patented the idea of 'vinothérapie'. They began with two creams and a nutritional supplement.

In a stroke of genius, they decided to distribute their product not through conventional beauty retailers like Sephora, but through pharmacies. Pauline explains:

> Caudalie's key market is successful women aged between 35 and 49. The conventional strategy of a beauty company is to sell a dream world, but we felt that selling through pharmacies better reflected the authenticity of our products. Although it's a glamorous brand, its products are reasonably priced and contain natural ingredients. We consider pharmacies our partners. Our sales people educate pharmacy staff about what our products can do and they pass this information on to our customers.

Caudalie also provides point-of-sale posters – which it considers more effective than press advertising – and keeps the brand front of mind with regular promotions, also carefully communicated to pharmacies by its sales staff. Pharmacies with a high footfall of the brand's target customers are selected for consumer events, during which the brand's beauty therapists are on hand to provide tips and an opportunity to test products. Pharmacies often sell out of their stock during one of these gatherings. By 2009, Caudalie was the leading anti-ageing brand across a network of 10,000 pharmacies.

The brand has proved skilled at building a database of consumers. Products come with an invitation to join 'Le Club' and benefit from special privileges. The invitation includes a customer code that can be tapped into a registration form on the brand's website. Customers must name the product they purchased, which provides a clearer idea of their preferences. Members of Le Club receive a newsletter and regular free samples. The brand now has a database of over 200,000 clients.

The website is available in 11 different versions, including Japanese, Chinese and Russian. From customer relationship management to the e-boutique, it has proved vitally important to the growth of Caudalie. Its address is clearly visible on packaging and advertising. One of the brand's most interesting innovations was the 'click to call' service. When visitors to the 'gift ideas' section of the site land on a product, underneath they see the words, 'Personalized consultation? We will call you within half an hour,' followed by a button marked 'Call me'. A click and a phone number later, they're talking to a Caudalie representative.

In 1999, Mathilde and Bertrand opened Les Sources de Caudalie, a five-star hotel and spa amidst the vines of Château Smith Haut Lafitte. This introduced clients to such delights as 'barrel baths' in red wine or grape marc, massages with grapeseed oil, grape blossom wraps and crushed Cabernet scrubs. There are also wine-tasting and cooking classes and a gastronomic restaurant. Even if you're sceptical about the treatments, the place is idyllic, from the perfectly judged rustic-luxe architecture to the wandering peacocks. The establishment proved so popular that Caudalie has opened a number of other spas: just outside Paris, in Brazil, in Turkey, within the Plaza hotel in New York (note the 'French Paradox Lounge') and in the Rioja region of Spain.

Spas play the same role – on a more impressive scale – as branded beauty salons within department stores. Beyond their basic utility as generators of cash, they encapsulate and concretize the brand's values. They also provide memorable experiences that inspire brand loyalty. Imagine if every time you use a tube of Caudalie cream you remember a pampered vacation in the gently sun-warmed Bordeaux countryside, when you felt more relaxed and contented, possibly, than you had in years. The building in Rioja, designed by Frank Gehry, is essentially a giant logo, with its purple-tinted metallic curls reflecting the towering peaks in the distance.

Not that Caudalie disparages more conventional marketing methods. Initially, its advertising was minimalistic and star free, focusing on grape and vine imagery. But in 2010 it recruited the Hungarian model Reka Ebergenyi as its 'face'. 'Beautiful, natural, feminine,' says Pauline. She confirms that the recruitment of the model underlined Caudalie's status as a successful brand.

Caudalie now has a whole panoply of skincare products, including an obligatory 'fix everything' cream, which it naturally calls Premier Cru ('your skin is regenerated and redensified, wrinkles are smoothed, the look of your skin is renewed and your complexion is even-toned. Smoother, firmer and more luminous, your skin looks visibly younger'). It has mastered every aspect of beauty branding, including the vocabulary, while delivering the extra tannic twist that enables it to compete with the luxury titans.

But what can you do if you don't have a vineyard and a scientist close to hand?

THE ABSOLUTION SOLUTION

When two marketing experts launch a beauty brand – watch out. For a start, they have a tendency to take a close look at what the rest of the market is doing with the sole aim of disrupting it, which was more or less the approach of Isabelle Carron and Arnaud Pigounides, founders of the emerging brand Absolution.

The pair were already entrepreneurs, having created a small but cool communications agency called Jak. (It stands for 'Just a kiss'. Arnaud explains, 'When you meet someone you like, if your strategy is good enough, the validation comes with a kiss. After that, anything can happen.') This attracted an impressive list of clients, ranging from Louis Vuitton and Vogue to L'Oréal and Christian Dior Cosmetics.

They both know branding backwards. Isabelle worked for a string of well-known agencies. Arnaud ran a call centre before running off to New York to play electronic music and set up an agency called Reflex. Then he came back to Paris to work for another agency, before meeting Isabelle at a dinner. They call Jak 'a strategy, design, creation and curiosity agency'. The seed of Absolution lies in the word 'creation'. Isabelle believes that an agency should create not just advertising, but products too. (This is by no means unheard of: the cult jeans brand Acne was launched by a communications agency.)

'I'd worked on beauty brands, but that's a world away from launching your own,' says Isabelle. 'However, I'd done some benchmarking and I got the impression that there were a lot of "me too" products in the industry. There was also an element of personal frustration because I'd never found a product that suited my skin.'

Wondering about this, Isabelle began to explore the mysteries of the skin by talking to scientists. 'What I discovered was that the skin is an ecosystem. It's an external organ, so it's always reacting to outside influences. I think of it as a communications interface. It's not in a fixed state; it's always adapting, reconfiguring. So if your skin is different every day, why would you always use the same cream?'

At the same time, she knew that customization was a growing trend in the luxury sector. The challenge, then, was to create a flexible, bespoke beauty system.

Arnaud says, 'Once the problem was clear, we realized we had to solve it. Creating our own brand would be a demonstration of everything the agency could do.'

The solution was intriguingly simple: a range of four soothing base creams that could be used on their own, but to which users could add an active-rich serum depending on their needs. There's a serum for dry skin, one for outbreaks, another targeting wrinkles and – finally – one to promote 'radiance'. The bottle's pump action delivers a bead of cream to the small concave dispenser at its top. Users add a pump of serum and then mix with a fingertip before applying to their skin.

'We didn't want to keep adding to the range,' says Isabelle. 'The idea was to launch a complete range of solutions at once. They're not segmented by age or even by sex, although there is a cream tailored toward men.' In addition, the brand is certified organic. 'More than 99 per cent of ingredients are of natural origin, far higher than is required for certification. Most products calling themselves "organic" only contain between 10 and 16 per cent. Not only that, but at least 60 per cent of our ingredients are produced by organic farming.'

Although Absolution mentions the 'organic' aspect of the brand in its marketing, this is not presented as a raison d'être. 'Today it should be a given,' Isabelle states. Her stringent demands, along with the unusual mix-and-match system, were 'a challenge for the laboratory', she admits. Despite this recourse to professional help, there is something handcrafted about the brand. When the pair launched it at the Beyond Beauty salon in Paris in 2009, they handed out brochures printed on thick recyclable paper and roughly stitched together on a sewing machine. They won the salon's Beauty Challenger award. Since then, the brand has landed a design award from *Wallpaper* magazine.

Arnaud is behind the brand's aesthetics, which are markedly different to those of its rivals, with dramatic black-and-white packaging that recalls both contemporary art and post-punk album covers. The website (www. absolution-cosmetics.com) continues the theme, with its handwritten text and drawings. The e-shop looks more like an underground fanzine. In fact, there's a touch of rock and roll about Absolution that makes the global luxury brands look distinctly conservative. Even the 'mixing' aspect brings to mind a raucous night at a club. Absolution is skincare for hipsters.

The distribution strategy reflects this positioning. Rather than being stocked by global chains, Absolution is sold through niche boutiques in bohemian parts of town – its first two outlets in New York were in Brooklyn – or distributors that share its cultish air, like London's Space NK 'apothecary'. In Paris, the brand has its own 'gallery', where you'll find bookshelves, an elderly piano and assorted creative types.

At that time of writing, Absolution was closing in on its first million and considering opening a spa.

'Our ambition', says Arnaud, with a wry smile, 'is to be the Apple of the beauty industry.'

He's half-joking. But it's the other half you should keep an eye on.

THE TALE OF AESOP

The first thing that happens when I walk into a branch of Aesop, the Australian beauty brand, is that an attractive young woman offers to rub cream into my hand. I accept, obviously, and find myself receiving a full-blown hand massage. It is sensual and rather shockingly intimate. I notice afterward that my skin feels smooth and smells great – in a herby, refreshingly masculine way – which it continues to do for the rest of the day. It's rule number one, straight off the book: if you want to sell a cream, get it on to your customer.

Despite its name, that's about the only thing Aesop does by the book. It was created by former hairdresser Dennis Paphitis who, as you may have deduced, likes stories. The product packaging is sprinkled with quotations, and when you land on the brand's website the first thing you see is a line from Carl Jung: 'As far as we can discern, the sole purpose of human existence is to kindle a light in the darkness of mere being.'

Straight away, you know you're not dealing with a conventional celebrity-driven beauty brand. The site also includes a newsletter offering bite-size reviews of books, art exhibitions, films, designer objects, gourmet restaurants and other cultural and lifestyle matters. The brand positions itself as part of the global creative community. All this might be rather wearing – not to say pretentious – were it not done with a light touch that nods to the irrepressible Australian sense of humour.

Paphitis originally ran a hair salon in Melbourne, where in the late 1980s he began experimenting with hair care products containing essential oils. Although these had been credited with mysterious life-changing qualities and had a whiff of the hippie about them, Paphitis was interested in their antibacterial and astringent qualities. When his potions proved popular, he moved on to a hand cream for the salon's in-house manicurist. Eventually he began working with a chemist. Now the brand has its own laboratory in Melbourne.

Suzanne Santos, who has worked with Paphitis almost since the beginning and is his 'product advocate' (a role somewhere between ambassador and chief marketing officer), says Aesop has always been inspired by 'science and the elegance of science'. The products contain mostly natural ingredients (like Caudalie, it is convinced by the antioxidant effect of grapeseed extract), but it doesn't boast about that, because it uses artificial ones too. Suzanne says, 'You'll never hear us saying we're "natural" and "organic". Brands that make that claim usually aren't being honest. We use man-made ingredients when they're essential for creating the best-quality product.'

Nor does the brand boast about its packaging, which is nonetheless one of the loveliest things about it: brutally simple striped black and cream labels on brown tinted bottles that recall beer bottles. 'Where possible, we avoid plastic packaging because it can disperse into the product,' Suzanne explains. 'We could have used green glass, but it turned out that brown was easier to find – maybe because of beer bottles.'

Paphitis himself has said that he wanted a 'consistent, monochromatic and understated approach to packaging' so people didn't feel 'violated' when they entered their bathrooms in the morning. Additionally, in its stores, Aesop shuns exterior packaging, such as cardboard boxes shrunk-wrapped in cellophane, which it considers a waste. The bottles are ready to be transferred from the stores directly to your bathroom shelf.

At the time I catch up with it, Aesop has 36 stores around the world and 300 employees. ('It's still a small company. Small enough that we know who's who,' notes Suzanne.) Each store is unique, designed to complement its environment and say something about the history of the neighbourhood. A store in the Aoyama district of Tokyo recycled materials from a demolished home nearby. Another in London's Mayfair has a Georgian air, with antique green walls, globe lights and giant white porcelain basins. And a store in Paris is entirely decorated with wooden slats inspired by the parquet floors found in the city's apartments.

Since the brand eschews advertising, the stores and their quirky interiors are marketing tools, often featured by design and architecture magazines and blogs. Suzanne confirms that Aesop also supplies products to selected restaurants and hotels. 'They usually come to us,' she says. 'It's a great way of communicating, but we have to be careful about it. We always go along to make sure that it's a suitable environment. If it's a restaurant, for example, we want the food to be excellent, no matter how stylish the decor might be. Dennis enjoys great cooking, and he certainly wouldn't want his products on display in a place with awful food. Uniqueness is important, too. A hotel doesn't have to be big – it could be five rooms on an island somewhere. It's about attitude.'

People have been known to leave their hotel and go straight to a department store to ask for Aesop products.

Word of mouth, as ever, remains the most prized marketing tool. Aesop is what is occasionally described as a 'dog whistle brand' – compelling to those on the right wavelength. 'Our customers tend to be urban, worldly, well travelled, curious and quite demanding,' says Suzanne. 'They have every right to be, because they're putting our product on their skin. We're highly aware of that responsibility.'

She accepts that Aesop is not for everyone. Because it uses largely natural ingredients, and dispenses with synthetic colours and fragrances, its products tend not to look or smell alike. 'Mainstream beauty products have an inoffensive odour and a deathly white colour. Ours can look and smell quite unusual in comparison.'

Paphitis himself is dismissive of the major cosmetics brands, which he describes as 'passionless products constructed by marketing departments and focus groups, and designed to exploit the vulnerabilities of people to appeal to those who would like to be lighter, slimmer, thinner, whatever'. He does not pay attention to them, but rather tunes them out as mindless clutter, like reality TV ('Skincare with soul', *Star*, Malaysia, 27 January 2008).

One thing you won't hear in Aesop's discourse is 'anti-ageing'. Says Suzanne: 'It is simply not in our philosophy. And that, I think, is quite radical.'

BEAUTY TIPS

✳ New entrants to the beauty market need unique ingredients, compelling stories and disruptive strategies to stand out.

✳ France's Caudalie combines the culture of winemaking and 'the French Paradox' with references to the French 'art of living'.

✳ Instead of selling through department stores, it formed close partnerships with pharmacies. Luxury spas also helped build notoriety.

✳ Caudalie considers customer relationship management vitally important, urging customers to get in touch via coupons within products and a club that can be joined via the internet. Its award-winning 'click to call' service offers personal consultations at the click of a mouse.

✳ Another French brand, Absolution, innovated via customization and eye-catching design.

✳ With the hip, rebellious look of an independent music label, it offers a distinct alternative to the mega-brands.

✳ It has carefully selected multi-brand retailers with fashionable, early-adopter customers in Paris, New York and London.

✳ Australia's Aesop has taken an intellectual approach – something notably lacking in the beauty industry.

✳ Rather than insulting the intelligence of customers, it suggests that they are part of a global creative community.

✳ The product packaging features literary quotations; the website includes a cultural newsletter.

✳ It never advertises, but attracts media coverage in design and style magazines with its idiosyncratic stores and unusual philosophy.

✳ It favours natural ingredients, and the expression 'anti-ageing' is banned from its vocabulary.

BEAUTY FROM
SHELF TO STREET

'The service that the customer receives in-store is a massive part of the value proposition for our brands.'

It's the height of the summer tourist season in Paris, and the giant Champs-Elysées branch of Sephora is packed. Shoppers swarm around the shelves, where hundreds of beauty and skincare brands are ranged in efficient A-to-Z order. Dozens of fragrances meet and mingle in the artificially cooled air, their top notes competing with the piped pop music. Attractive black-clad sales assistants are on hand to aid the indecisive, offering words of advice on scents and skin sensibility.

An acquaintance once suggested to me that Sephora was a cosmetics cathedral, with the giant S emblazoned at the back of the vast space playing the role of a crucifix. 'It's a place where people go to pray at the altar of youth,' he added. Today, there are plenty of worshippers.

Owned by French luxury conglomerate LVMH, Sephora can seem hard to avoid: every upscale district in Paris now appears to have its own branch. The chain's aggressive marketing – including a glossy cinema advertising campaign – heightens the impression of omnipresence. According to the brand's website, it has 265 stores across France and more than 250 in the United States, as well as a presence in 13 other countries, including China. The brand is named after the wife of Moses (the site does not mention that there's also a sinister ship called the *Sephora* in the Joseph Conrad short story *The Secret Sharer*).

Although it competes in France with Marionnaud and Nocibé, which are similar operations, it broke new ground by pioneering the concept of 'limited assistance self-service' in the fragrance retail sector. In other words, it dispensed with counters to give shoppers a wide choice in an environment that looked more like a record store – or an outrageously hip bookshop – than a perfumer. Suddenly, the barrier between customer and product had vanished. More recently, Sephora has launched a successful range of own-branded products, notably its Stri-Vectin SD anti-age cream in 2004, as well as diverting retail experiences like hair styling counters and nail bars. The result can cause something resembling culture shock among British consumers used to the staid interior design of Boots the Chemist, which resembles a cross between a laboratory and a supermarket.

In keeping with its black and white decor, Sephora has a chequered history. In fact, it was once owned by Boots.

The British chain came to France in 1970, opening its first store on rue de Passy. In 1976 it launched the Sephora brand as a joint venture with the department store group Nouvelles Galeries, which it later acquired. However, the Sephora of that period was more like the traditional Boots, with a mid-market positioning and without any of the retail innovations mentioned above.

Meanwhile, an altogether more visionary retailer named Dominique Mandonnaud had founded a chain called Shop 8, starting in 1969 with a modest space in Limoges. Mandonnaud brought the self-service concept that had revolutionized grocery retail – in the form of supermarkets – to the perfume sector, which was still dominated by the kind of genteel boutiques that greeted customers with a bell tinkling over the door, or mask-faced vendors selling a single brand from behind a counter in a department store.

In 1988, Mandonnaud acquired eight perfume stores in Paris and converted them to his ground-breaking format.

The next chapter came in 1993, when Boots sold its 38 Sephora stores to Shop 8's holding company, Altamir ('Boots on march into Europe,' *Independent*, 19 November 1995). Innovating once again, Mandonnaud opened his Champs-Elysées flagship, which at 1,300 square metres launched the cosmetics cathedral concept and provided a template for future stores. More than a shop, it was a destination: tourists popped in to witness the exotic sight of luxury cosmetics being sold in a discotheque, only to walk out laden with potions and fragrances, their purses lighter than air and a bemused look of pleasure on their faces, as if they'd been freebasing Aldous Huxley's soma.

In 1997, LVMH acquired Sephora, moving the retailer into its third phase of development. The company opened its first store in New York in 1998; after that it expanded in Europe and entered Japan. The next target was Eastern Europe, but Sephora's energy began to dwindle in 2001, accompanied by a downturn in sales. In 2003, incoming CEO Jacques Levy and European managing director Natalie Bader-Michel began to rehabilitate the chain, bringing in a selection of new brands from the United States, launching Sephora-branded products and encouraging more interaction with customers, including beauty makeovers by consultants. By now Sephora had shrugged off its image as a fragrance retailer and emerged as a luxury perfume and cosmetics superstore.

'Sephora is beginning to reap the fruits of its facelift,' read a headline in the French business magazine *Les Echos* on 25 January 2006. Nothing better illustrated the chain's new strategy than its own Stri-Vectin SD anti-wrinkle cream 'made by a laboratory in Salt Lake City, sold exclusively at Sephora and selling like hot cakes despite its high price of 125 euros'. In the same article, Bader-Michel admitted that the Sephora-branded products, sold at a 'strong margin', had played a decisive role in the chain's return to profitability.

Visiting Sephora is an entertaining experience, but it can also be an irritating one. The advice that sales staff hand out is not always objective. When a particular skincare brand has done a promotional deal with the store, chances are that's the brand they're going to recommend. Sales are tracked in real time so staff can ensure that they're reaching their targets.

This can annoy beauty companies too. The chairman of one independent skincare company told me, 'We need to be in Sephora, but with certain reservations. I get the impression we're third in line behind Sephora's own products and brands owned by LVMH.'

For that reason, his preferred environment is the department store, where he can manage his own branded universe and train sales staff to interact with customers.

Along with beauty salons and their larger, more opulent cousins, spas, department stores have played a vital role in the history of the beauty industry. Many of the pioneers we met in the early chapters of this book wore out a great deal of shoe leather trying to convince salons and department stores to stock their products. They went to extraordinary lengths to attract the attention of buyers: early in his career, François Coty famously shattered a bottle of his Rose Jacqueminot fragrance on a countertop at the Grands Magasins du Louvre; the appreciation of customers who crowded around to ask about the delicious scent led to it being taken on by the store. Beauty entrepreneurs from Estée Lauder to Bobbie Brown owed their success to department stores.

Sephora is part of the 'selective distribution' market favoured by luxury beauty brands. What that means is an exclusive environment, usually with at least one beauty adviser or make-up artist on hand to 'educate' customers and nudge them towards buying. Upmarket surroundings – flattering lighting, numerous mirrors and lacquered surfaces – are part of the brand story: confirmation that beauty companies are selling not products, but lifestyles.

William Lauder said as much at the Global Department Store Summit in New York in 2010:

> The service that the customer receives in-store from the consultant is still a massive part of the value proposition for our brands. Crème de la Mer is at the top of our brands pyramid, selling for US$190 in Saks, so of course it is important to match brands like that to the right environment... The level of service the customer receives reinforces for her why she chooses to shop in this environment, why she chooses the brand and why she is prepared to pay a premium (WGSN.com, 15 July 2007).

THE LEGACY OF MR BOOT

Historically, Boots the Chemist lies at the other end of the spectrum: a highly democratic destination selling a host of health, beauty and pharmaceutical products in a self-service environment. The business was started in 1849 by John Boot, a former agricultural worker who began selling herbal remedies from a small store in Nottingham, in part to help employees of the area's new textile factories, many of whom could not afford a doctor. John died in 1860, but his widow Mary continued running the shop along with his son Jesse.

It was Jesse who transformed the business from a single store into a flourishing chain. First he began to buy stock in bulk, which enabled him to keep prices down: his advertising promised 'Health for a shilling'. Additional branches were opened across Britain. By the outbreak of the First World War, Jesse owned 550 stores. Retiring just shy of his 70th birthday, in 1920 he sold the business to the United Drug Company of America. Under US ownership the chain expanded to 1,000 stores. In an elliptical twist to the tale, a group of investors led by Jesse's son – John Boot – bought the business in 1933. John launched the Boots No. 7 skincare line in 1935, packaging it in eye-catching blue and yellow and advertising it as 'the Modern Way to Loveliness'. Today Boots claims No. 7 is 'the UK's leading cosmetics and skincare brand'. It has a charismatic creative director in Lisa Eldridge, a make-up artist who has worked with a glittering array of photographers, designers and celebrities, as well as hosting a popular blog (www.lisaeldridge.com).

On 5 July 1948, health secretary Aneurin 'Nye' Bevan launched the National Health Service, providing free government-funded healthcare for all, with the words, 'We now have the moral leadership of the world.' Boots – which had long been a dispensing chemist – was now more than ever a vital community hub, continuing the tradition established by its founder during the industrial revolution. But it also evolved as a health and beauty retailer, introducing supermarket-style self-service in the 1950s. It merged with Alliance Unichem in 2006 to form Alliance Boots, which was acquired the following year by Alliance's former executive deputy chairman Stefano Pessina and a private equity firm.

Boots has stores around the world – in Norway, Russia, Thailand and the Netherlands – but it is an inescapable element of the British high street.

Its customer loyalty card, the Boots Advantage Card, launched in 1993, has 16.7 million 'active' members in the UK (it defines active as members who have used their card at least once in the past 12 months), enabling the chain to gather vast amounts of data about its customers' shopping habits. In their (2001) book *Romancing the Customer*, Paul Temporal and Martin Trott describe it as 'the largest smart card retail loyalty scheme in the world', suggesting that 40 per cent of transactions in the store are linked to the card.

Boots has made the card almost impossible to turn down. Customers collect four points for every £1 spent in store or online, one of the most generous schemes in the country (one point is more typical). Card holders can then spend points on a wide range of items in the store. Boots has also installed Advantage Points Extra Offers kiosks in selected stores: by inserting their cards into an ATM-style terminal, customers can check their points balance, receive money-off coupons and learn about promotions exclusive to card holders. This has the added advantage of driving traffic to stores.

The clinical, no-nonsense interior of Boots stores can recall airport duty-free shops, but neither their customers nor the brands they stock are the same. Since their establishment in 1946 – when the first one opened at Shannon Airport in Ireland – duty-free spaces have become a vital retail channel for upmarket beauty brands. They particularly appeal to frequent-flying male consumers, who tend to shun traditional beauty emporia but feel at home in the bland surroundings of the duty-free shop, where they can kill time between flights.

A key player in the sector is a company that started life in 1960 as Duty Free Shoppers, now known as DFS Galleria. It was launched in Hong Kong by entrepreneurs Charles Feeney and Robert Miller, who spotted an opportunity to target 'the emerging Japanese traveller' when they secured the exclusive concession for duty-free sales in Hawaii. Their operation evolved into what their website describes as 'the world's largest travel retailer' (www.dfsgalleria.com). Since 1996 the company has been partly owned by LVMH.

There is another, entirely different distribution channel, which for me has a ring of nostalgia about it.

AVON CALLING

'Ding dong, Avon calling!' My mother would chime the advertising slogan when she brought our breakfast to the table, making us laugh. The ultimate door-to-door beauty sales company, Avon was already a legend when it launched the campaign in 1958. Such was the ubiquity and staying power of the phrase that my mother was still singing it decades later. In the 1970s the company changed the name of *Outlook*, its magazine for sales representatives, to *Avon Calling*.

Avon's reps buy its products at a discount – between 20 and 25 per cent – and then sell them at full price, pocketing the difference. Overseeing them are 'sales leaders' who manage teams of representatives and earn commission from their sales. Sales reps tour their territory leaving brochures with potential clients, returning to pick up orders later. The job is not for everyone: reps are required to trudge the streets, and the most successful have a knack for sales. You don't have to look far online to find disgruntled ex-Avon ladies whose earnings did not live up to their aspirations. But with more than 6 million reps worldwide and US$10 billion in annual revenue, somebody at Avon is making money.

Suitably enough for an industry that knows how to tell a good story, Avon was started by a bookseller. His name was David H McConnell, and in the late 1800s he was hawking books from door to door in New York, providing samples of the fragrances he concocted at home as sweeteners. When McConnell noticed that women were far more interested in his scents than in books, he decided to focus on perfume.

But he needed help – and on his bookselling rounds he had come across many impoverished women with time on their hands. What if he could help them and their families while also growing his business? His plan was to take women on as independent contractors, leaving them free to manage their time and their territory.

Mrs PFE Albee of New Hampshire, a 50-year-old wife and mother of two, became the first representative of what was then the California Perfume Company in 1886. Just over a decade later, the company had 5,000 representatives. As the company's website says, 'at that time it was practically unheard of for a woman to run her own business. Only about 5 million women in the United States were working outside the home, let alone climbing the ranks of any corporate ladder. That number accounted for just 20% of all women.' They were domestics or factory workers, and their wages were a fraction of men's (www.avoncompany.com).

With its door-to-door model – more formally known as 'direct selling' – the company literally advertised itself, although it did place a print ad in *Good Housekeeping* magazine in 1906. It also began expanding internationally, with representatives ringing doorbells in Montreal, Canada from 1916. The brand name did not emerge until 1928: McConnell had visited Shakespeare's birthplace, Stratford-upon-Avon, and was so enchanted with the town that he named a range of products after it. The California Perfume Company would be renamed Avon Products in 1939.

Over the years, Avon has aligned itself with the cause of empowering women – and in 1986, when the hundredth anniversary of the Statue of Liberty coincided with its own centennial, the company sponsored a project to restore the iconic 'Lady Liberty'. It has run the Avon Foundation for Women since 1955, the Avon Breast Cancer Crusade since 1992 and Speak Out against Domestic Violence since 2004. The company donates hundreds of millions of dollars a year to causes related to or supported by women. (It's interesting to note, however, that Avon did not get its first female CEO until 1999: the remarkable Andrea Jung has stayed in the top slot for more than a decade.)

Avon has innovated on the product front too: in 1986 it launched Bioadvance, one of the first skincare products to use stabilized retinol. In 1992 it launched Anew, another skincare cream, this time pioneering the use of alpha-hydroxy acid (AHA).

As its worldwide expansion continued, the company moved into China in 1990, but was forced to switch to a traditional retail model eight years later when the government banned direct selling. It shifted back to its original strategy when the ban was lifted in 2006. Today, Avon is the world's biggest direct seller, selling fragrances and cosmetics door to door in 120 countries. As we've seen, it inspired beauty innovators like Natura in Brazil and Amore in South Korea.

The development of Avon can be compared to the market research techniques pioneered by Procter & Gamble in the 1950s: like Doc Smelser's door-to-door interviewers in their hats and gloves, Avon's women sales representatives – self-employed, motivated – created a complicity with their customers that made traditional advertising almost an afterthought. Not only that, but they were self-recruiting.

In an interview with the *Financial Times*, CEO Andrea Jung said: 'The macroeconomic global dip created a dynamic that forced us to double down on our founding principles… We saw a big uptick in the numbers of direct salesmen.'

During the recession, Avon focused sales on 'value' products and turned its attention to recruitment. In 2009 it ran a commercial during the Super Bowl broadcast in the United States – this was later extended globally. 'We featured Avon representatives who had lost their jobs [elsewhere] and talked about how they were now running their own business, how they could never be fired. By half-time our phones were jammed. We took the campaign global and gained both market share and number of sellers wherever we ran it. It's the most cost-effective campaign we've done and it was at the heart of the financial crisis.'

Jung is overseeing Avon's expansion into emerging markets – she sees the Middle East, India and Africa as the most promising, with Turkey and South Africa showing the fastest growth – but she adds, 'For me, the biggest emerging market isn't a country, it's women. We have 600 million people living on a dollar a day, and two-thirds of those beneath the poverty line are women. When a woman takes on an earning role, family health and education improve. The societal impact is huge' ('Woman at the top: Andrea Jung', *Financial Times*, 16 November 2010).

With markets still to conquer and representatives to recruit, Avon isn't about to stop calling.

BEAUTY TIPS

❋   Upmarket beauty brands set great store by department stores, where their counters and beauty consultants add to the impression of status created by other elements of the marketing strategy.

❋   Sephora revolutionized the 'selected distribution' channel by pioneering the concept of 'limited assistance self-service'.

❋   It provides an upscale environment where shoppers have access to a wide range of fragrances and skincare products on a self-service basis, but can ask assistants for advice.

❋   In-store beauticians and nail bars add to the dynamic atmosphere.

❋   Assistants are often pre-programmed to recommend the brands that have done promotional deals with Sephora.

❋   The UK's Boots the Chemist sells mass-market health and beauty products in a self-service environment.

❋   Its loyalty card is one of the most generous in the sector and has been widely adopted. It enables the company to tailor its offering to the shopping habits of customers.

❋   Avon cut out intermediaries by pioneering door-to-door sales of fragrances and cosmetics. It's now the world's biggest direct seller, with more than 6 million reps.

❋   The Avon lady creates a complicity with her customers, earning their trust and becoming a recognizable figure in her community.

❋   Avon benefits from economic downturns because it can recruit more sales representatives among women (and occasionally men) who have lost their jobs elsewhere.

DIGITAL

BEAUTY

'Today's big thing is tomorrow's cautionary tale.'

The digital world evolves so rapidly that I had two meetings with the man who agreed to be my informant about what beauty brands were doing online. There were perhaps eight months between our first rendezvous and our second – during that period, he told me, a great deal had changed.

He asked me not to use his name or that of the company he works for. It's an upmarket French cosmetics brand – one of the biggest in the world. Xavier, as we'll call him, heads the digital department there. When we first met, he had complained that many beauty company executives, particularly at the luxury end of the market, were uncertain about the possibilities of digital, which they regarded as a bolt-on resource rather than a central pillar of their marketing strategies. He added that digital agencies were not used to the extreme sense of detail that luxury brands required when communicating with their audience: historically the web had not been an aesthetic environment.

'What's happened since then is the gradual merger of specialist web agencies with traditional advertising agencies,' he says. 'As a result, the agencies have been pushing their digital expertise among their clients. The result is that we're now open to doing something a little more sophisticated than just putting a video – a glorified TV ad – online.'

He mentions the social networks, which have exploded since our last meeting. Like most brands, Xavier's has a fan page on Facebook. Unlike many of its competitors, however, it has a coherent strategy: announcements on Facebook are planned months in advance to reflect the entirety of the brand's communications: product launches, advertising, competitions and so on. Comments posted by consumers are monitored, and responses are carefully thought through rather than being dashed off. 'The trick with Facebook is controlling the conversation rather than letting consumers run away with it.'

Facebook has evolved into a valuable customer relations marketing tool. 'Visitors to the fan page are interested just as much in what other customers are saying as in what we're saying. I've seen research suggesting consumers have only about 20 per cent confidence in a product that's been advertised; but they have 80 per cent confidence in one that's been recommended by another consumer online.'

Social networks resolved a problem facing many beauty companies: a lack of direct contact with the customer. Their brands are often sold through retailers rather than from an owned environment, so it's difficult for them to develop relationships with those who buy their products, or to build customer databases. Thanks to loyalty cards, the distributors have a great deal of data, but they keep it to themselves because they see the brands' e-commerce sites as competitive with their own online operations. Social media short-circuit the distributors and put brands face to face with customers again.

Another advantage of a Facebook fan page is that it's entirely transparent: consumers know that it is being run by the brand. 'There was always something manipulative about brands commenting on forums or blogs about beauty issues. There was a temptation to arrive in disguise, to chat with customers without saying you were a brand. On the occasions consumers found out they considered it extremely intrusive.'

One notorious example of this was the French blog *Journal de ma peau* (Diary of my skin), which appeared in April 2005. The blogger was identified only as 'Claire', a woman of a certain age. But the blogosphere was not fooled: both on the blog and within the community, bloggers commented that Claire's posts read rather too much like advertising copy, which was exactly what they turned out to be.

'Diary of my skin' was a fake blog launched by L'Oréal-owned French skincare brand Vichy and the advertising agency Euro RSCG to promote a product called Peel Microabrasion. When Vichy confessed, it faced a storm of criticism from bloggers and something very close to ridicule by the marketing press. In retrospect the case was a landmark in other ways: it taught L'Oréal and its rivals a great deal about interacting with consumers online. The aftermath of the disaster was that Vichy changed its tack and developed a branded blog that allowed consumers to ask for advice about their skincare problems.

'Consumers like to engage with brands,' says Xavier. 'We're not necessarily seeking advice that will enable us to develop or change products. We're a luxury brand, so we're supposed to be one step ahead of consumers in terms of innovation. But we're inviting them to join the family, so to speak.'

Xavier's comments are echoed in reports from across the beauty sector. In early 2010, *Advertising Age* reported that Procter & Gamble had overcome 'serious reservations' about the use of Facebook as a marketing tool. 'Now, the world's biggest marketer wants all of its brands to get a presence on Facebook… and has recently opened a research-and-development office in Palo Alto, California, not far from Facebook's headquarters, in an effort to co-develop capabilities in digital and social media.' The article added that P&G rival Unilever had turned to Facebook to promote its men's personal care brand Axe. 'The page has become a place to host viral videos the brand launches, and Axe recently added a human face aimed at appealing to its male clientele – Jennie from Axe, actually part of the brand's team at PR shop Edelman' ('Once skeptics, brands drink the Facebook Kool-Aid', 22 February 2010).

Use of Facebook will evolve – or maybe it won't. 'One of the problems of this job is that the ground is always shifting beneath your feet,' says Xavier. 'Who a couple of years ago could have predicted the almost complete desertion of Myspace? Today's big thing is tomorrow's cautionary tale.'

This raises the subject of Twitter, for which Xavier finds little use 'beyond straightforward PR purposes'. He adds, 'People use it as a news resource, not for conversations. Something like 80 per cent of Twitter accounts are inactive.'

I wonder aloud where all this leaves blogs. Years after the Vichy fiasco, the web is still crammed with people blogging with varying degrees of professionalism about cosmetics. One standout name is Michelle Phan, who set aside a straightforward blog to become a 'vlogger' on YouTube, uploading video make-up tutorials that eventually reaped millions of views. She was so successful that Lancôme signed her up in 2010 to make videos showcasing its products. Retailers such as Boots and Sephora use blogs to add 'branded content' to their online shopping sites. And make-up tutorials are a by-now-familiar aspect of the brands' own websites.

The relationship between brands and bloggers is almost as vexing as the one between brands and journalists. Traditional beauty journalists are in thrall to their advertisers and deluged with free cosmetics. Any hope that bloggers might represent an independent voice beyond the controlling arm of the brands' PR departments has long gone – they too receive free products and invitations to chic launch parties, making them as straitjacketed as their print cousins when it comes to offering an objective viewpoint.

'The problem with recruiting bloggers for PR purposes is that there are just too many of them,' says Xavier. 'Even the best ones don't rise to the surface in Google searches, so you have to stumble across them or hear about them from someone else. Strategically, that doesn't make much sense for the brands. There's also the fact that, as soon as they're regarded as being too closely tied to one particular brand, readers begin to feel that they're too commercial and move on.'

Still, he acknowledges that brands should work with bloggers. 'The question for me is: are they part of social media, or are they press? Most brands treat them like journalists but, since brands have recruited social media specialists, responsibility for building relationships with bloggers could move out of the PR department.'

At the time I first met Xavier, he was grappling with the implications of the iPhone and the iPad. Beauty brands swarmed into this new media space with applications. Nail products brand OPI, for example, launched a free virtual nail bar allowing users to access the whole range of more than 200 colours and match them with their skin tone. The result could be saved and the phone could then locate the nearest OPI retailer. L'Oréal also plunged in with a free app allowing users to browse make-up looks, watch tutorial videos and receive personalized product recommendations after providing details about their skin and hair.

'We were all pretty excited about apps – at first,' says Xavier, 'but once everyone had launched one the space became less interesting. People tend to download an app, play with it a few times, then let it lie dormant. I must have downloaded about 50 apps on my phone – I regularly use about five of them.'

He believes a mobile site that can be accessed via myriad devices is far more interesting. Mobile communications, in general, interests beauty brands a great deal. For example, the L'Oréal app included a barcode scanner allowing users to access product-related tips and advice in-store. Once again, this kind of application allows brands to bypass the retailer. As we've established, vendors at retailers tend to recommend whatever product they've been told to push that week. Barcode scanning devices that link consumers directly to brands' websites could be the answer. 'I can talk directly to my customer while she's still at the point of sale,' explains Xavier.

The one thing we haven't discussed among all this digital strategizing is the humble website.

'It's the hub: the departure point for all the content the brand creates. It should also provide unique content: science videos, launch videos, tutorials and so on.' And e-tail, presumably? 'Yes, but for me the main vocation of a website is one of image building. E-tail is important, but an online shop usually achieves the equivalent in sales of a single flagship store, so it's never going to replace your other points of sale. That's why you have to be careful to provide other content. A purely commercial site would have a negative impact on your image.'

The internet has also allowed beauty companies to address the sensitive problem of ethnicity: it is easier to depict different skin types online than in a costly traditional advertising campaign.

Websites have been used as a way of prompting potential customers to ask for samples – you may remember the Caudalie case from Chapter 13 – but Xavier says postage costs and logistics make this a daunting exercise for all but the biggest brands. An alternative has emerged in the United States in the form of a beauty club called Birchbox (www.birchbox.com). Membership costs US$10 a month. For that, members receive every month an elegant brown box containing four or five product samples: not sachets of foil, but the kind of mini bottles and tubs that end up travelling to exotic climes in your toiletry bag. If they like a product, customers can buy the full-sized version from the brand's site via a link on the Birchbox website. Each box is based on a theme – for example, organic products – and customers can also ask for boxes tailored to their needs.

Co-founders Hayley Barna and Katia Beauchamp, who met at Harvard Business School, say they created Birchbox 'to help women cut through the clutter of the beauty world to find products that really work for them'. They've signed deals with a wide range of 'brand partners', including Kiehl's, Korres, Marc Jacobs, Serge Lutens, NARS and Stila, to name a few. Barna and Beauchamp pay nothing for the samples. But the advantage for the brands, obviously, is that they are exposed to a self-selecting audience of discerning potential customers.

'We realized that, when people walk into Sephora, you opt out of making a choice to learn more because there is so much to choose from,' Beauchamp told the *New York Times*. 'With four or five samples a month, you can really sink your teeth into a new product and decide if you want to buy the product in a full size' ('Birchbox aims to simplify the business of beauty', 20 April 2011).

The service was officially launched in September 2010 – by April the following year more than 22,000 people had signed up. Beauchamp said she got the idea for Birchbox during a stint at Estée Lauder, when she saw how much money beauty companies spent sending out samples or including them with larger purchases. 'Including a gift with a purchase to an existing customer makes it very difficult to track that investment... Birchbox is a way to track that return and give them data about purchasing behaviour.'

She added that early research suggested around 20 per cent of its subscribers went on to purchase full-sized products after testing a sample. The site also incorporates a blog about beauty trends.

Advances in technology are constantly making the online experience richer for consumers. 'It's great that they can upload photographs of themselves and then experiment with make-up, for example,' Xavier says. 'Augmented reality will transform the shopping experience, too, with virtual mirrors that allow you to test looks without the need to apply actual product. The borders between screen and reality are coming down.'

The size and mutability of the digital world make it a daunting environment for any company. In 2010 Unilever was one of a number of organizations that sent executives on a digital safari to Silicon Valley to explore the opportunities available to them. 'The marketers visit Google, Facebook, Apple, Twitter, Microsoft, Amazon and Yahoo in search of digital solutions to marketing problems – a clear acknowledgement that today's digitally savvy consumers are forcing the hands of brands that continue to spend the bulk of their marketing dollars on traditional advertising' ('Clients go direct to tech', *Adweek*, 13 February 2011).

Unilever's chief marketing and communications officer Keith Weed told a conference: 'The most challenging thing I see right now is the amount of choices out there... You physically cannot get through the day without being bombarded with all of these messages, and the way you get through the day is by engaging with the brands you want.'

In other words, brands must fully harness the communications power promised by digital media. Right now, they're painfully aware that social media like Facebook – and the consumers themselves – are writing the script. Beauty brands, those great storytellers, must find more compelling ways of doing what they do best.

BEAUTY TIPS

✳ Social media are the new playing field, but brands worry that consumers 'control the conversation'.

✳ Brands have recruited social media specialists to ensure posts are in line with overall marketing strategy and to monitor comments.

✳ Social networks are seen as valuable customer relationship management tools that enable brands to bypass retailers and talk directly to customers.

✳ Beauty bloggers are useful for PR, but are seen as difficult to manage. Most of them are not well referenced by Google, meaning that they do not appear high up in search results.

✳ Readers are turning off beauty blogs as bloggers form closer relationships with brands, limiting their objectivity.

✳ Online 'sample clubs' may provide an alternative way for brands to reach potential customers.

✳ Mobile devices and tablet media have potential, but a 'me too' effect has led to clutter. It's difficult to design a compelling app.

✳ Mobile may be another way of bypassing the retailer by allowing users to consult directly with brands while browsing in-store.

✳ Websites are becoming portals giving customers access to a wide range of digital content created by brands.

✳ Even the biggest beauty companies worry that the digital world is too vast and unpredictable to master.

✳ They need to approach digital as a 'tool kit', selecting the elements that enable them to build their story without feeling obliged to leap into every new digital space.

UNDER
THE KNIFE

'Quackery was outlawed in medicine over a century ago, but it is in danger of returning in the cosmetic surgery industry.'

Of all the global beauty industry trends, the rise and acceptance of aesthetic surgery treatments – as well as interventions like Botox and dermal fillers – is the most remarkable. In 2007, the American Society for Aesthetic Plastic Surgery (ASAPS) said it had noted a 437 per cent increase in the number of procedures over the previous decade, with annual spend reaching US$13.2 billion.

A couple of years later, the same organization reported that a tough economic climate had hardly affected the trend at all. Its survey showed that 51 per cent of all Americans, regardless of income, approved of cosmetic surgery. Gender-wise, 53 per cent of women and 49 per cent of men said they would consider a procedure; 67 per cent of Americans said they would not be embarrassed if their friends learned they'd been under the knife. Alarmingly, the youngest age group, 18- to 24-year-olds, were the most likely to consider aesthetic surgery for themselves, now or in the future.

In Europe the situation is similar, with the British Association of Aesthetic Plastic Surgeons noting annual increases of more than 5 per cent, to around 40,000 procedures a year. In France, a magazine called *Perfect Beauty*, devoted to cosmetic surgery and other medical makeover options, hit newsstands at the beginning of 2011. It is distributed through kiosks, cosmetic surgery clinics, beauty salons and luxury hotels, as well as the Eurostar and Thalys high-speed train services. Along with surgery, it covers anti-ageing products, dieting, skincare, fitness and spas. 'Today, cosmetic surgery is no longer taboo or just the domain of celebrities,' commented editor Brigitte Dubus.

In Italy, the venerable cosmetics brand Santa Maria Novella (or to give it its full name, Officina Profumo – Farmaceutica di Santa Maria Novella, founded in Florence in 1612) sells a Plastic Surgery Support skincare line. For example, the Face Recovery Kit contains 'products to reduce the initial consequences and discomforts following cosmetic procedures like face lift and eyelid surgery'. It includes Face Calming Water to reduce puffiness, as well as Papaya Gel, owing to its 'excellent antioxidant properties', and an aloe cream that 'acts on skin texture leaving it softer and smoother'. The kit also includes 'balsa cream which helps improve scar appearance and quality'. It's a brilliant marketing idea that says a lot about the brand's target demographic, as well as its struggle to conquer the US market.

In other parts of the world, as we've seen in Chapter 12, aesthetic surgery is flourishing as young women struggle to conform to globalized 'norms' of beauty. The internet and the falling cost of international travel have also led to 'cosmetic surgery tourism', says the ASAPS. 'Popular destinations include Argentina, Brazil, Costa Rica, Dominican Republic, Malaysia, Mexico, Philippines, Poland, South Africa, and Thailand. These destinations offer everything from "safari and surgery" to "tropical, scenic tour" vacation packages.'

Wendy Lewis, the author in 2007 of a book called *Plastic Makes Perfect*, has pointed to a shrinking tolerance for imperfections as 'advancements in cosmetic treatments offer promises of beautification and age reversal'

('Aesthetic surgery update', WGSN.com, 3 December 2008). Once again, her words raise the spectre of a two-tier society based on those who elect – or can afford – to pay for a procedure or not.

With aesthetic surgery becoming more mainstream, I wanted to find out how well the industry was regulated. How could customers be certain that a cosmetic surgeon was a respected professional and not a charlatan with a scalpel? I put the question to Nigel Mercer, president of the British Association of Aesthetic Plastic Surgeons (BAAPS).

'On an international level the industry is largely self-regulating, with associations like our own setting standards,' he replies. 'We're currently pressing for common European standards. Of course standards are not laws, and the legal situation varies broadly. France has strict laws; Belgium has no laws at all. In the UK we police our membership: we monitor what they're doing, how they're doing it and complication rates.'

Mercer admits that many aesthetic surgeons operate outside the regulatory framework. Others agree. An article in the *British Medical Journal* explains bluntly: 'Any General Medical Council registered doctor can practise as a "cosmetic surgeon" in the United Kingdom' ('The hard sell in cosmetic advertising', 16 March 2010).

Mercer says, 'A combination of media coverage driving increased customer demand on the one hand and greed on the other has created a potentially disastrous situation.'

He advises those considering a procedure to liaise first with their doctor, who should be able to refer them to a named surgeon. (Occasionally general practitioners refuse to recommend cosmetic surgery, forcing the patient to short-circuit the process and go directly to a clinic. Mercer warns that, if patients go to a clinic, no matter how good, they will be operated on by the doctor who has the first slot available, not the best one for their problem.) Never rely on reports in the media or, especially, advertisements. In fact, the BAAPS has called for an outright ban on advertising – a situation that already exists in France.

A casual scan of the inside back packages of the British editions of *Elle* and *Vogue* reveals a rash of ads for breast reduction and enhancement, 'fat removal' and 'body contouring', somewhat lowering the tone but perfectly in context with publications that weave a fantasy of glamour and physical perfection.

Advertising by cosmetic surgeons in the UK is regulated by codes of practice established by bodies such the General Medical Council and the Advertising Standards Authority – the advertising industry's own self-regulatory organization. As the *British Medical Journal* puts it: 'UK and European law, professional rules, and government monitors… which oversee the advertising of prescription drugs, make few specific references to cosmetic surgery… Because cosmetic surgery clinics are not aimed at treating disease, their advertising is exempt, and regulation falls almost entirely with the advertising industry itself.'

Mercer says: 'The GMC states that doctors cannot 'advertise' and that any entry, on a website or telephone directory, for example, must be factual only. The ASA states that any advert must be 'legal, decent, honest and socially responsible'. But even in markets like France, where advertising is banned, online advertising is extremely hard to regulate. And online is where most advertising is done these days.'

Regulation of Botox injections and similar treatments is also lax in Europe. As you may know, Botox derives from botulinum toxin, one of the most powerful neurotoxins on the planet, which paralyses muscle nerve endings. In the 1970s scientists discovered that botulinum toxin type A could be used in small doses to treat crossed eyes and muscle spasms. Its smoothing effect on wrinkles was first documented in 1989. In 2002 the FDA announced regulatory approval of botulinum toxin type A – marketed under the name Botox Cosmetic – to treat frown lines. Widespread publicity about the use of the treatment by celebrities – with pictures of the smooth-browed stars accompanied by hypocritically disapproving headlines – attracted the attention of the public. In 2009 there were 5 million procedures in the United States alone.

In the UK, high street chemist Boots began offering Botox injections for £200 as early as 2002. It has since stepped back from this and other beauty treatments to return to its roots as a retailer. But the press coverage that accompanied the move reinforced the idea that Botox was almost as problem-free as an anti-ageing cream. In fact, the Botox Cosmetic website clearly states that it 'may cause serious side effects that can be life threatening'. These include 'problems swallowing, speaking, or breathing, due to weakening of associated muscles' and a 'spread of toxin effects' resulting in 'loss of strength and all-over muscle weakness, double vision, blurred vision and drooping eyelids, hoarseness or change or loss of voice (dysphonia), trouble saying words clearly (dysarthria), loss of bladder control, trouble breathing, trouble swallowing' (www.botoxcosmetic.com).

Frankly, it sounds as though ingesting gold might be safer.

Tales of botched interventions involving the injection of fillers surface regularly. Nigel Mercer has written scathingly about regulation in the medical journal *Clinical Risk* (2009):

> In the USA, there are only a handful of fillers with FDA approval… whereas in the UK there are over 100 on the market. Why the difference? In the USA, the products undergo testing as a 'drug', but in the UK they are tested as a 'device' and so only have to pass 'CE' mark [it stands for *Conformité Européenne* or European Conformity] requirements, which relate to standards of production, not of efficacy. Drug testing is lengthy and expensive but CE marking is not.

Mercer calls on the European Community to adopt FDA-like testing. He adds: 'Permanent and semi-permanent fillers all come with a greater incidence of complications, which may not be correctable… Quackery was outlawed in medicine over a century ago, but it is in danger of returning in the cosmetic surgery industry.'

There is little doubt that the fashion press is largely behind the normalization of aesthetic surgery. Opening a copy of a magazine recently, I happened on an article about 'an anti-aging oracle' who had started out as a cardiologist before she was encouraged by a friend to give cosmetic dermatology 'a go'. She added that she 'just taught myself, really'. The whole thing looked to me like a huge flashing warning light, but the doctor's customers clearly have confidence in her, so much so that she now has a second house in the country and an impressive wardrobe of designer clothing.

Nigel Mercer confirms that aesthetic surgery has become more acceptable. 'People are more open in talking about it, particularly in the affluent section of society.' As for the types of procedures that are being undertaken, they have evolved very little over the past few years: nasal surgery, breast reduction, liposuction and tummy tucks are all high on the list. An increased use of Caesarean sections has led to a demand from women who wish to correct scarring.

'Facelifts are in decline,' Mercer adds. 'Botox has almost replaced brow lifting.' He's also noticed a slight increase in male patients, who opt for eye pouch removal, liposuction and the removal of pectoral fat. When I ask him about procedures worldwide, he answers, 'It's a globalized market. There's pretty much an international standard of beauty.'

What's the Holy Grail of cosmetic surgery? I imagine that it's gaining height, but apparently this is quite easily achievable – if painful and expensive. The treatment is growing in popularity in China, where the tall are seen as socially advantaged. Orthopaedic surgeons saw through the tibia and the fibula below the knee, without touching the bone marrow. Heavy metal braces are screwed into the patient's legs. Every day for four months, these are expanded to slowly stretch the leg. The bones regenerate to fill the gap. The tendons and arteries magically stretch too. Four months of this torture gets you two to three inches.

'Actually, it's fine lines around the mouth.' says Mercer. *What?* 'The Holy Grail of aesthetic surgery is improving the lines around the mouth,' he repeats. 'It's because they're so tiny. Lasers and chemical peel don't work very well. That's something I'd like to see improved upon.'

The phenomenon is quite common among smokers – another good reason to give up, because, even if you survive your habit, cosmetic surgery may not be able to fix your looks.

BEAUTY TIPS

* Aesthetic surgery has become acceptable, with a rise in the number of treatments of over 400 per cent in a decade in the United States.

* Only approved by the FDA in 2002, Botox was used by 5 million people in a single year in the United States just seven years later.

* A globalized standard of beauty has led to a flourishing cosmetic surgery market in Asia and Latin America.

* Italian skincare brand Santa Maria Novella sells a Plastic Surgery Support line.

* Reports in the press – particularly in fashion magazines – are largely responsible for the normalization of cosmetic surgery.

* A new genre of consumer magazine informing readers about aesthetic surgery has sprung up.

* Regulation around the world is weak: in the UK, anybody who has qualified as a doctor can open a cosmetic surgery clinic.

* Advertising is also under-regulated: even in markets where it is banned, such as France, clinics advertise online.

THE NEW
MALE ORDER

'We have lived through the era of emancipation
for women; now we're witnessing the
emancipation of men.'

If you'd lived in 19th-century Paris – and you'd been a gentleman of a certain substance – how much time would you have spent in the bathroom?

The question is raised and partially answered by a visit to the magnificent Hôtel Jacquemart-André, a manor house that was once home to banker and art collector Edouard André and his wife Nélie Jacquemart. The 1875 building offers a fascinating glimpse into the lives of a fashionable couple from that era. It is preserved intact, as if they have just stepped out for a moment. You can stroll through the vast ballroom, pause for reflection in the cosy drawing room or poke your nose into the library.

The most interesting room is inevitably the bedroom. Or perhaps I should say 'the bedrooms', as Madame and Monsieur had separate boudoirs. Edouard's is the one we're after. Note the pale pink upholstery – a bold choice that nonetheless works when combined with the chocolate and gold tones of the rug, the ivory walls and the dove grey doors. It's the equivalent of wearing a pink shirt with a sombre tie.

Off to the right is a vast dressing room. Lined up before the mirror – which takes up almost an entire wall – are crystal decanters of cologne, essential oils, soaps and other unguents. The sparkling containers alone would put a modern metrosexual to shame. And yet our man was a Protestant financier who had been awarded the *Légion d'honneur*. Edouard André had powerful people to impress, and he needed to look immaculately turned out.

There has been much talk recently about the growth of the men's grooming industry. In fact, there is nothing new about this habit. It's only for the past 50 years or so that men have been encouraged to equate masculinity with a lack of vanity. If you were able to pay a visit to the Roman Empire, for example, you'd hear yelps emanating from the bathhouse as hair is ripped from men's ears, nostrils and backs. Less painfully, Roman men were shaved daily by barbers who plied their trade in the street. From the dawn of time until the mid-20th century, gentlemen plucked, barbered and perfumed themselves with unselfconscious abandon.

So what happened? Two world wars can't have helped: fighting men got used to plain old soap and a slash around the chops with a razor, if they were lucky. There was no time for dandiness when you were busy trying not to get killed. My own grandfather's sparse morning routine seemed to confirm this theory. He'd apply shaving soap with a brush, shave himself briskly with a so-called 'safety razor' – it took lethal screw-in blades – rinse off the residue with hot water and then slap his cheeks with an aftershave appropriately named Brut. And that was that. This approach got passed down to the next generation.

Always a pioneer, Estée Lauder noticed that things were changing back in the 1970s. As the liberating dress codes of the 1960s hippie movement filtered into the mainstream – looser clothing, brighter colours, longer hair – men were becoming flashier, more flamboyant, dressing with a touch of the peacock about them. She embarked on two experiments that were to influence the male grooming sector for decades to come. The first was

Aramis, which she had launched in 1964 as an aftershave and cologne. Now she began to expand the range, until by 1978 it constituted more than 40 products. It was also selling 'an estimated US$40 million annually; this compared to US$175 million for the Estée Lauder division and US$80 million for Clinique', according to Lee Israel. However, the line was dominated by the fragrance and cologne, the success of which Estée attributed to 'strong masculine appeal, good packaging, good and long-lasting fragrance, status pricing, and clever distribution'.

The December 1977 edition of a trade magazine called *Soap/Cosmetics/Chemical Specialties*, also cited by Israel, provided further analysis of the explosion of the male fragrance market:

> More disposable income in the hands of black and Hispanic people who have never been influenced by the Anglo-Saxon taboos about the use of male fragrances; more money in the hands of teenagers who found fragrance an expression of rebellion against their no-smell, conformist heritage; more disposable money for non-essentials in dual-income households... advertising and promotion associating fragrance with sports, good grooming and national celebrity, especially designer names.

The formula for selling cosmetic products to men has hardly changed since. Along with sport, men appreciate the language of technology and science: they approve of functional products, which made Clinique ideal for them. Clinique Skin Supplies for Men made its debut in 1976 with smart gunmetal packaging and the familiar three-step process, augmented with a masculine twist: 'Clean, exfoliate, moisturise. Gets your skin in its best shape for your best shave.' Promoted as a three-minute regime, it has now considerably broadened into a range of 29 different products, including hydrators, face washes, blemish solutions and bronzing creams.

In 1987, Estée Lauder introduced Aramis Lab Series for Men, 'high-performance, technologically advanced skin care, hair and shaving essentials' developed by 'the elite team of doctors, scientists and skin care specialists of the Lab Series Research Centre'. The range is now simply called Lab Series, having disassociated itself from Aramis. The tech-speak of its marketing language remains intact.

Lauder undoubtedly blazed a trail, but the evolution of the male grooming sector began to accelerate in the early 1990s. Companies like Unilever and Procter & Gamble were aware that half the population was still not spending enough on beauty products. There was money to be made, but how to get men to spend?

The metrosexual offered them a way forward.

Journalist Mark Simpson coined the term in an article for the *Independent* ('Here come the mirror men', 15 November 1994). The piece was inspired by an exhibition called 'It's a Man's World', an exhibition of male-oriented brands organized by *GQ*. Simpson seized on this as evidence of a new breed of male. 'Traditionally heterosexual men were the world's worst consumers,' he wrote. 'All they bought was beer, fags and the occasional Durex, the Wife or Mum bought everything else. In a consumerist world, heterosexual men had no future. So they were replaced by the metrosexual.'

The metrosexual crossed the Atlantic when the term was picked up by Marian Salzman, then chief strategy officer at the advertising agency Euro RSCG Worldwide, who produced an influential report on metrosexuality and marketing to men. Key to the metro's appeal was that he embraced the consumption habits that had previously been the preserve of gay men – or of women. The report rocketed across the media. 'Metrosexual' became shorthand for a new, marketing-friendly male that advertising agencies were determined to conjure into existence. Soccer star David Beckham became the poster boy for metrosexuality: a married sporting hero who was perfectly at ease with his off-pitch role as a fashion icon. A further step was the US TV series *Queer Eye for the Straight Guy*, in which straight men gratefully accepted grooming and lifestyle tips from a troupe of gay advisers. Suddenly, the metrosexual entered popular culture.

Although evidence of the metrosexual's existence was limited – a survey by a US ad agency in 2006 determined that only a fifth of the population fitted the description – the message that it was OK to moisturize filtered through. The word 'metrosexual' was abandoned as ordinary men slowly integrated his habits. It was as if they realized that they could enjoy masculinity and good looks too – a power drill and a grooming regime. In 2009 the researcher Kantar Worldpanel estimated that, in the UK alone, spending on men's skincare products had risen by £22 million in one year, bringing the total up to £592 million.

Its research found that the impetus for purchasing men's grooming products usually comes from their female partners – either because women are fed up with men furtively borrowing their moisturizer, or simply because they want their man to look and smell better. It's no coincidence that an award-winning 2009 ad for Old Spice body wash in the United States began with the words 'Hello ladies'. The preposterously handsome hero, Isaiah Mustafa, then explained to his female viewers how 'your man' may not look as good as him, but could at least smell like him – all this while wrapped in a towel and transitioning in one take from a bathroom to the deck of a yacht and, finally, to horseback.

The ad was so pitch-perfectly ironic – advertising a product aimed at men by satirizing ads for products aimed at men – that it appealed to everyone. The advertising agency, Wieden & Kennedy, went one step further by creating online videos featuring Mustafa – still clad in his micro-towel – responding to consumers' comments about the ad on Twitter, Facebook and YouTube. This in turn generated more comments and questions: the agency replied with even more video responses from Mustafa. As Teressa Iezzi explains in her (2010) book *The Idea Writers*: 'The results were staggering – on their first day, the responses got nearly 6 million views on YouTube and by day three had surpassed 20 million views. One week after launch, the videos had been viewed 40 million times, making Old Spice the most viewed branded YouTube channel ever.' In the month after the 'responses' went live, Old Spice sales were up 107 per cent. Humour, self-deprecation and interaction – and never forgetting that women are an audience for men's products – are a winning mixture in the male grooming market.

That's not the end of the story, however. Marketing men's products to women assumes the presence of a female partner. But men are staying single for longer – and divorcing sooner. For long periods of their lives, they are forced to shop on their own. Genevieve Flaven of the trend consultancy S-Vision told me: 'Men are changing because the context in which they live their lives is changing. They are evolving because of the evolution of women. This is a huge chance for men to change the identity and roles that have been imposed on them for centuries. They will retain their masculinity, but it will be a new kind of masculinity. We have lived through the era of emancipation for women; now we're witnessing the emancipation of men.'

Unilever touched on men's exploration of their own identity when it launched Dove Men+Care range at the end of 2009. This was aimed at men over the age of 35. Unilever hoped to repeat the success of its Axe brand (known as Lynx in the UK), originally launched in 1983 as a deodorant body spray but later extended to shower gels, skincare and hair care. It had appealed to much younger men by straightforwardly yet humorously suggesting that smelling great was the best way to get a girl.

Dove Men+Care was a somewhat riskier proposition because the brand was already identified with women, via both its advertising and the associations of purity and gentleness conjured up by the word itself. The centrepiece of the launch was an advertising spot called 'Manthem', which celebrated – in a light-hearted fashion – the various aspects of manhood. To the galloping tune of the *William Tell* overture, a song detailed all the challenges that guys face on the road to maturity. Play sport, meet a girl, go to college, play the fool, grow up, get married, have a family, work till you're 60 and plan for retirement. And these are just a few of the things on the list. Why d'you have to do all of them? 'Because you're a man!' The message was clear: men were proud of and at ease with their role. In an interview with the website eMarketer, Kathy O'Brien, vice-president and general manager of Unilever Skin in the United States, put it cleverly: 'For Dove Men+Care, it's about celebrating the unsung moments where men are most comfortable with themselves, including literally being comfortable in their own skin' ('Unilever's Dove dives into male grooming', 6 April 2010).

Going into more detail about the range, O'Brien said, 'While men's overall interest in personal care is not as strong as women, men are becoming more sophisticated in grooming desires, but still want a simple routine. We also know that 51 percent of men are already using women's skin care products and many men trust and use Dove.'

The campaign made its debut during the Super Bowl, one of the world's most watched live sporting events and a showcase for advertising creativity. As O'Brien pointed out, this enabled the ad to reach not just men, but families: 'a captive audience of over 100 million consumers effectively reaching both men and women'. She added that the brand intended to have 'a significant presence in platforms where we can engage and interact with our target male consumers and the women in their lives who are, many times, the primary shopper in the household'.

The ad generated comments from men on Twitter, feeding the social media element of the campaign.

O'Brien stated that 'the real growth opportunity in men's care is outside of shaving'. But marketing to men means focusing on their centres of interest, and in the bathroom their centre of interest is often their razor blade, which is why men's skincare lines tend to start with a core shaving product and then swirl outwards in a constellation of post-shave healers, moisturizers and anti-wrinkle potions. The P&G-owned Gillette dominates the shaving business, with a 70 per cent slice of the market. It also has a vast range of skincare products for 'before, during and after the shave', from balms and lotions to face washes and scrubs. And of course it's skilled at using the language and imagery of sport, having signed faces ranging from David Beckham to Roger Federer and Thierry Henry over the past decade.

Gillette's strongest competitor in the mass-market male grooming sector is Nivea for Men, launched in 1986, whose widening range of products can be seen on supermarket shelves. They express the fresh, healthy, no-nonsense sprit extolled by the core brand. French giant L'Oréal is also convinced by the potential of the male sector. It markets a range of skincare products under the L'Oréal Paris Men Expert label. At the upper end of the market, Jean Paul Gaultier, Dior, Clarins and Lancôme all have lines for men. Lancôme launched its range in January 2007, with rugged British actor Clive Owen as its face. It was the first time a male Hollywood star had become the face of a skincare range.

The depiction of male role models in advertising has created problems of its own. Men are increasingly being confronted with the inadequacy of their own bodies – something only women had to put up with until the 1990s. The turning point is generally cited as 1992, when Calvin Klein launched a poster campaign featuring the rapper 'Marky' Mark Wahlberg clad only in briefs, his muscled body taunting the flabby executives who strolled past the giant billboard in Times Square. The casual clothing brand Abercrombie & Fitch deploys similar imagery. The 'perfect' male body is now gym-honed yet sexually ambivalent, as it is entirely free of body hair. Sales of depilatory products for men are up, and body hair removal is a feature of a new generation of male-oriented spas. Having successfully traumatized women all over the world, the beauty industry now seems determined to standardize male attractiveness too.

A quirky French brand called Nickel, launched by Philippe Dumont in 1996, has become an expert at speaking men's language. An admirer from a rival brand told me: 'Men aren't really interested in hearing about the universe of a brand or being told the story of a product. They just want to know what it does. Nickel realized that straight away. Its flagship product is called Morning After Rescue Gel. It ditched the whole language of claims that had been adopted for women's skincare in favour of a chatty, amusing style, as if you're talking to your best pal in a bar. Even the packaging looks indestructible.'

Similarly, Nickel opened a series of men-only spas, starting in Paris, before taking the concept to New York and London. 'That's the other thing about men,' my informant continued. 'For both shopping and treatments, they want their own space. They don't like the beauty sections of department stores. They don't like Sephora. They want to walk into a distinctly male environment. Duty-free shops are just about anonymous enough for them, but department stores should reconfigure their offering to make sure all men's products – clothing, accessories and skincare – are in a separate area, preferably on a separate floor.'

The beauty companies have managed to globalize the male grooming trend too: demand for 'post-shave' and anti-age products has risen in Asia and Latin America. Euromonitor International reports that between 2004 and 2009 the annual male grooming market in Latin America (Mexico and Central and South America) grew from US$2.44 billion to US$4.87 billion, or 99.6 per cent.

However, after a period of explosive growth in the global men's grooming market, there are signs that the demand is beginning to slow. British high street chemist Boots pulled out early, abandoning in 2001 plans to open a chain of stores specifically for men after testing the concept with pilot operations in Bristol and Edinburgh. Sephora has visibly reduced its selection of skincare products for men. The sector stumbled during the recession, as its value was undermined by special offers and promotions.

Christian Courtin-Clarins, the chairman of Clarins, told me: 'The trend really began with sunscreens; even if they weren't convinced by other products, men got into the habit of protecting themselves in the sun. This convinced the beauty companies that there was a wider market for men's skincare. It did well among early adopters: people who worked in sport and entertainment, and of course gay men who already purchased cosmetics but were attracted by packaging and formulations that better suited their needs. After that, slightly later adopters came along. The market expanded rapidly starting in 2000. And then it stopped. Now we get the impression we've reached a sort of ceiling. The market will continue to grow, but far more slowly than it has over the past decade.'

Courtin-Clarins is convinced, however, that men 'remain peacocks at heart'. Men still want to be seductive charmers, he says, 'even though we'd only admit it to ourselves.'

Perhaps Axe had it right all along. Throughout time, men have been persuaded to preen themselves by the common urge to attract a sexual partner. Returning to the home of Edouard André and Nélie Jacquemart, you'll recall that they had separate bedrooms, which was common at the time. This may explain Edouard's interest in maintaining his looks. When you're obliged to seduce your own wife every evening, you certainly don't want to let yourself go.

BEAUTY TIPS

∗ Estée Lauder was one of the first to note and react to men's 'secret peacock' side in the 1970s.

∗ She developed a language that contained references to sport and science, but without resorting to jargon.

∗ In the 1990s the 'metrosexual' was enthusiastically adopted by marketers, even though he proved elusive in reality. Sports stars and actors helped to grow the market, however.

∗ Men like straightforward information about products. Tell them what it does – no preposterous claims, no frills.

∗ Humour doesn't hurt: it helps men feel less awkward.

∗ The shaving ritual is the ultimate 'man moment' of the day and a good place to get them started on a skincare regime.

∗ Women are a legitimate target for products aimed at men – but there are more single men around these days.

∗ Men use the internet as a discreet shopping channel and are open to advice about products.

∗ On the street they prefer a separate retail experience, tailored to their needs and interests.

∗ The rapid growth of the men's skincare sector has eased, but an ageing demographic and a mainstream adoption of products offer plenty of room for optimism.

ETHICAL, ORGANIC
AND SUSTAINABLE

'From an idealistic fringe notion
into a mainstream concern.'

I first came across the Body Shop as a child, walking in the streets of Bath, appropriately enough, with my parents. I was attracted by the name of the store: I imagined it selling spare arms and legs. When we went inside, I was disappointed to find that the shelves were stacked not with spare limbs in cellophane, but strange pastel-coloured potions in clear plastic bottles. It smelled funny, too.

There's a lot that smells funny about the Body Shop, as it turns out. But the controversy comes later. The company started with a brilliant concept and a woman who seems to have been as inspiring as she was exasperating: the late Dame Anita Roddick. Her life was a mesh of contradictions – an anti-capitalist who made a fortune, a marketing genius who hated branding, an outspoken critic of the cosmetics industry who sold her business to

L'Oréal – but she changed the beauty landscape. The combination of natural ingredients, eco-consciousness and human rights activism that charged her brand's image was a new and potent mix. It seduced a generation infused with the values of the late 1960s.

Roddick herself grew up in Littlehampton, Sussex, not far from the seaside town of Brighton, where in 1976 she would open her first store. Her childhood was as bohemian as her soul: Anita Lucia Perilli was raised as the daughter of Gilda and Donny Perilli, Italian immigrants who ran a café. Later, Gilda divorced Donny and married Henry, her lover and Anita's natural father. Anita would often speak affectionately of Gilda, a force of nature who tooled around town in a Jaguar and went ballooning when she was 80.

After school, Anita failed to get into the Central School of Speech and Drama in London. She could have become an actress; instead, she turned her business into a stage, never failing to put herself in the spotlight whether it was to sell an ideal or a shampoo. For the moment, though, she wandered: Paris, Geneva (where she worked at the women's rights department of the International Labour Organization), Asia, Africa, back home again, where she met Gordon Roddick, another adventuresome type. Shortly after their marriage, he set off to ride on horseback from Buenos Aires to New York; it would take him two years.

In his absence, with a bank loan of £4,000, Anita opened her first shop. She wanted to sell natural beauty products inspired by some of the remedies she'd seen women using on her travels. It was a gimcrack operation; many of the innovations that later enabled the brand to stand out were driven by necessity. Britain may have been going 'green', but Anita joked that the walls were painted green to hide the mould. As for recycling, she invited customers to bring back the cheap plastic bottles for refills because she could barely afford to buy more of them. She handwrote the labels. Even if she were not averse to advertising, she would never have been able to afford an agency: instead, she became a consummate self-publicist. Her first dose of media coverage came when a local funeral parlour objected to the name of her shop.

Ah, the name. One story goes that Anita borrowed it from a local garage. But there had been a Body Shop before, in Berkeley, California. It opened in 1970. Founders Peggy Short and Jane Saunders hand-labelled all their products and sold them in refillable plastic containers. When Body Shop International entered the US market in 1987, it paid Short and Saunders for the rights to use the name. The Berkeley store changed its name to Body Time, although on its website it still bills itself as 'the original Body Shop' (www.bodytime.com).

There is no doubt that Anita had travelled, and widely. But unless you count cocoa butter, in those days the majority of her ingredients were not sourced from distant lands. 'Roddick's 25 primary products were not so different from those of earlier cosmetic queens; it was the way she sold her Bedouin-recipe moisturizer that was new… [I]f she huckstered anything, it was the history of the ingredients and the anthropology of their cultivators' ('Obituary: Dame Anita Roddick', *Guardian*, 12 September 2007). Writing an obituary in the *Independent* on the same date, Paul Vallely puts it another way: 'Tales of the products and how they were made were displayed alongside photographs of the countries she had visited and the tribes peoples she had met. She was selling the story as much as the product.'

Just like the rest of them, Anita spun us a yarn.

The 'natural' aspect of Body Shop products has often been called into question. The lurid colours alone invite speculation. In fact – like almost every 'natural' product on the market today – they contain a mixture of natural and synthetic ingredients. Don't take my word for it: the ingredients of all the Body Shop's products are fully listed on the e-tail section of the brand's website.

Whatever the origin of its name or its products, the Body Shop was a success: Anita rapidly opened a second branch. When her husband returned from his travels, they set about further expanding the business using a franchise model. This operated in the traditional manner: franchise holders paid a one-off fee and an annual charge for the right to run the business. They agreed to stick closely to the retail and branding template provided by the Roddicks, who helped them to train staff. As the network grew, Body Shop representatives would visit franchises to ensure that they were on-message; franchise holders were also sent newsletters and video updates.

Soon new shops were opening at the rate of two a month. Roddick's convictions seemed to grow along with the retail chain. She billed her products as 'cruelty free', proudly proclaiming with labelling and in-store merchandising that the brand was 'against animal testing'. (There was some ambiguity about this, too: although the products were not tested on animals, it was almost inevitable that some individual ingredients had been.)

By 1984, the year it went public, the company had 138 stores, 87 of them outside the UK. Anita later considered the stock market flotation a mistake, saying that the company could have eventually 'got everywhere we wanted' at a slower pace; shareholders also forced it to tone down its more 'ferocious' campaigns. At first, however, the company's activism continued unimpeded: it launched a 'Save the Whale' window campaign for Greenpeace in 1986. The following year, it started Trade Not Aid, establishing fair trading partnerships with communities like the Pueblo Indians in New Mexico (from whom it sourced blue corn) and the Kayapo Indians of the Amazon river basin (who provided Brazil nut oil). The company was involved in charitable projects from Glasgow to Harlem; in London it helped to finance the launch of a newspaper sold by homeless people, the *Big Issue*. 'The politics of the Body Shop have always been its DNA,' Roddick once said, with a characteristic blend of morality and marketing savvy.

This, then, was the Body Shop brand: the colourful products with their odd names (Banana Hair Conditioner, Dewberry Body Lotion), the ethical business practices, the succession of worthy causes, and corkscrew-curled Anita in the eye of it all, trekking to deserts and rainforests to bring us back new and exotic ways of scrubbing our skin and washing our hair. As Paul Vallely writes, 'it was an extraordinary achievement – she had taken cruelty-free products out of hippie health-food shops and into the high street... she became a key figure in turning the idea of corporate social responsibility... from an idealistic fringe notion into a mainstream concern'.

Roddick was a one-woman PR machine, but that does not mean she didn't rely on outside help. The company established a formal marketing department around the time it moved into the United States; it also hired an advertising agency ('Body Shop creates space for a voice in marketing', *Independent*, 1 July 1995). Its ads maintained an activist tone, however. One of them featured a red-haired plastic doll with a face like Barbie and a plump, Rubenesque figure. 'There are 3 billion women who don't look like supermodels and only 8 who do,' read the tagline, followed by the slogan, 'Love your body'.

The company's seemingly unstoppable growth made Roddick a target for accusations of hypocrisy, but she shrugged off the criticism: 'If you wear a bullseye on your back saying "I'm doing things in a different way", you're going to get shot at.' Instead, she just went right on supporting causes in her own passionate manner, showing up in Seattle to join protests against the 1999 World Trade Organization meeting: one of the rare anti-globalization demonstrators who had founded a multinational business with 1,000 outlets in almost 50 countries.

At times Roddick seemed embarrassed about the fact that she'd created a global brand. 'I have always been deeply sceptical about the whole idea of global brands,' she told a conference in Singapore in 2003.

> There is increasing evidence that people are actually bored to death by brands. People are irritated with the way the big brands are taking over public space, not just on billboards but in their heads. They don't like the bigness, the mental clutter, the sense that somebody is selling to them the entire time. And most of all they don't like their sameness, their mediocrity, their reassuring blandness.
>
> ('Dame Anita Roddick: brands are past their sell-by date', *Independent*, 3 December 2003)

The sentiment jarred with her position, but it may have reflected her state of mind at the time. In 1998 the Roddicks had already begun to relinquish control of the company, appointing a CEO while they became co-chairmen. In 2002 they stepped back to non-executive roles. This enabled Anita to devote herself full time to her many campaigns against things ranging from domestic violence to sweatshop labour. In 2005 she set up the Roddick Foundation, which seems to have been created with the sole aim of giving away her £51 million fortune.

Fans of the Body Shop were stunned the following year when the Roddicks agreed to sell the brand to L'Oréal for £625 million. The move seemed to be contrary to everything Anita claimed to stand for. Writing in the *Independent* newspaper only three years earlier, she had described the global cosmetics industry as 'dull and unimaginative, run by men who create needs that don't exist'. She continued, 'Its primary function is to make women unhappy with what they have; it plays on insecurities and self-doubt by projecting impossible ideals of feminine beauty. It is also racist, rarely celebrating women outside Caucasian culture, and has conspired to leave us alienated from our own bodies' (June 2003, reprinted on 12 September 2007 under the headline 'How Anita changed the world').

And now here she was describing L'Oréal as 'honourable' and saying that she hoped the Body Shop could play the role of a Trojan horse within the group, encouraging it to behave more ethically. Ultimately, the acquisition underlined the central achievement of Roddick's career, which was to make 'ethical and natural' products so desirable that a mainstream beauty company wished to buy her business.

Dame Anita Roddick died of a brain haemorrhage in 2007 at the age of just 64. Despite the fact that many customers had felt betrayed by the sale of the Body Shop to L'Oréal, she remains one of the most admired British businesswomen of all time. Her ethics and that of her company were not as coherent as some might have wished them to be, but her sense of moral outrage was genuine.

And what of animal testing, the cause with which she was perhaps most closely associated? The European Commission banned finished products tested on animals in 2004; a ban on animal-tested ingredients came into force in March 2009, with a further ban on selling these products in the European Union from March 2013. Cosmetics companies are engaged in a race to develop alternative methods of testing – the most promising involve 'growing' discs of artificial human skin in labs from cells harvested after plastic surgery operations.

In other markets there is still work to be done: in the United States animal testing is not banned; the Food and Drug Administration says that it 'supports the development and use of alternatives' to animal testing and that it does not require the use of animals in testing cosmetics for safety, but under the current Federal Food, Drug, and Cosmetic Act (1999, updated in 2006), 'animal testing by manufacturers seeking to market new products may be used to establish product safety'. Were Anita Roddick still here, her fight would have continued; for all her contradictions, she made a positive contribution to the world.

As a friend responded to critics who accused Anita of opportunism: 'How many orphanages have you built?'

GENERATION ORGANIC

In the wake of the Body Shop, ethical and natural brands seemed to spring up like green shoots emerging from a parched earth.

In the United States, one of the brand's contemporaries was Aveda, which had been launched by professional hairdresser Horst Rechelbacher in 1978. Rechelbacher had spent time in India, where he had discovered ayurvedic medicine and herbal remedies. Wanting to share what he'd learned, he began experimenting, mixing a clove shampoo in his kitchen sink. Soon, in time-honoured fashion, he was distributing a range of products to hair salons. Rechelbacher's plant-based ingredients and recycled packaging were ahead of their time, as were the Environmental Lifestyle Store, launched on Madison Avenue in 1989, and the Aveda Spa Retreat – offering clients treatments based on ayurvedic medicine – in 1990. Rechelbacher sold Aveda to Estée Lauder Companies in 1997, but we'll return in a moment to what he did next.

Estée Lauder had already made an incursion into the natural market with Origins, containing natural oils and organic ingredients, which made its debut in department stores in 1990. And we heard earlier from the Australian brand Aesop, launched in 1987, whose founders fully admit that Anita Roddick and the Body Shop were precursors.

The trend for natural and organic products gained impetus after the turn of the millennium, driven by a number of factors. The first was a growing interest in preserving the environment amidst anxiety over climate change. This led consumers to look closely at the chemicals used in a wide range of products, including cosmetics. Concern about the future of the planet was accompanied by a more inward-looking contemplation of health and wellness, as an ageing demographic in the West began considering kinder, gentler lifestyles.

The media amplified these trends with reports about the hidden dangers of cosmetic products. The most dramatic example of this was the parabens scare. Parabens are chemical compounds widely used as preservatives in many cosmetics and toiletries, including moisturizers and shampoo. The source of the scare appears to have been research published in January 2004 in the *Journal of Applied Toxicology* (volume 24, page 5) in the form of an article headed 'Concentrations of parabens in human breast tumours'. As reported in *New Scientist*, the research was led by molecular biologist Philippa Darbre at the University of Reading. 'She says that the ester-bearing form of parabens found in the tumours indicates it came from something applied to the skin, such as an underarm deodorant, cream or body spray' ('Cosmetic chemicals found in breast tumours', 12 January 2004).

Understandably, this information was circulated by other media, and soon it became a given that parabens were dangerous. Some cosmetics companies, including L'Oréal's Vichy, began marketing 'paraben-free' products. However, neither the European Commission's Independent Scientific Committee on Consumer Products nor the US Food and Drug Administration have found any evidence to support the theory that parabens are harmful. The FDA clearly states on its website: 'FDA believes that at the present time there is no reason for consumers to be concerned about the use of cosmetics containing parabens.'

A cosmetics trade journalist I questioned on the issue was brusquely dismissive. 'It did a service to the big beauty companies because it provided them with another claim,' she told me. 'If you take out one chemical preservative, you might as well take them all out. Then you'll have to keep your moisturizer in the fridge; otherwise it will go off in three days.'

This brings us back to Horst Rechelbacher, who could have retired comfortably after selling his brand to Estée Lauder for US$300 million. Instead, when his no-competition clause with Lauder ran out in 2007, he began developing a 100 per cent organic range called Intelligent Nutrients (www.intelligentnutrients.com). The operation is based on his farm in Wisconsin, where he grows his own organic ingredients.

'Pesticides and insecticides make people sick and are destroying the planet,' he told a reporter from the *Telegraph*. 'The whole beauty industry is a cocktail of chemicals.' Rechelbacher uses 'antibacterial and antifungal' essential oils as preservatives; he's something of an expert in this area, having popularized aromatherapy at his Aveda spas. His golden rule is 'Never put anything on your skin that you can't eat.' He's even been known to drink his products at demonstrations. The lipsticks he makes do not have the long-lasting quality of the non-organic variety, but for good reason: 'The stuff they put in lipstick to make it kiss-proof is a plastic coating.' Indeed, he is down on lipstick in general. 'The so-called natural mineral colours are all toxic metals. The colours come from iron, cobalt and lead' ('Aveda founder's mission: to clean up beauty industry act', 23 April 2011).

His products are priced at the higher end of the market: a lip balm will cost you US$12, a 'body elixir' from US$30 to US$80. But customers will pay. Natural and organic will play a big role in the future of the beauty industry. The sector is roughly divided into two categories: 'organic' cosmetics containing certified organic ingredients; and 'natural' cosmetics made from plant extracts and other natural ingredients, blended with synthetic chemicals. Researchers including Mintel and Euromonitor say that the number of cosmetics claiming 'natural' or 'organic' on their packaging has doubled since 2007. The challenge facing consumers, as usual, is the prevalence of spurious marketing claims.

'Natural' is a virtual free-for-all. 'Organic' is becoming more defined. In the United States, the United States Department of Agriculture awards certification to products that meet its standards: those labelled '100 per cent organic' must contain only organic products; those labelled 'organic', 95 per cent organic products; and those labelled 'made with organic ingredients', 70 per cent. In Europe, the situation was confused for some time, with various bodies – Ecocert in France, Natrue and BDIH in Germany, ICEA in Italy and the Soil Association in the UK – all offering certification. However, in June 2010 many of them came together under the COSMOS standard, 'an international and internationally recognized standard for natural and organic cosmetics'. At the time of writing, the European Commission is investigating labelling practices by cosmetic firms with a view to stricter regulation. Until then, the obvious step consumers can take is to check for certification.

The European Commission has already banned more than 1,000 chemicals formerly contained in cosmetics under the EU Cosmetics Directive, revised in 2003. The FDA has banned only a handful, as the industry in the United States is self-regulating, but this is one area in which the globalization of the beauty industry will aid consumers. In addition, the popular movement against chemicals is being abetted by the internet, which has put power into the hands of consumers in the beauty arena just as it has in every other. Numerous websites offer a comprehensive guide to cosmetics and their ingredients, notably the Environmental Working Group's database of 65,000 products, Skin Deep (www.ewg.org/skindeep). The European

Commission has its own database of the ingredients covered by its amended Cosmetics Directive. Health Canada provides an online Cosmetics Hotlist of substances it considers inappropriate for cosmetics use. The 'cosmetic cop' Paula Begoun's 'Beautypedia' is a searchable database of more than 45,000 skincare and make-up reviews, which goes into great detail about ingredients and their potential effects (as well as their effectiveness). New books sounding the alarm about the chemicals contained in cosmetics appear every month.

This may be good news for the beauty industry as well as consumers. Rising demand for natural products is providing an opportunity for cosmetics marketers; it has created a niche for entrepreneurs as well as a new generation of brands that will become targets for acquisition by the global beauty giants; shelf space devoted to naturals and organics is increasing, and there is room for new distribution channels, such as stores devoted entirely to natural beauty. Regions where the trend has not yet fully taken hold – such as Central and Eastern Europe – also offer growth potential. Above all, natural provides a fertile new territory for marketers looking to weave stories and claims.

There is another side to this debate, and one that is worth mentioning: organic products are not necessarily good for your skin. Nature is not gentle. In fact, as we know, it is red in tooth and claw. The natural world swirls with toxins and allergens. A random list of poisonous plants might include deadly nightshade, foxglove, hemlock and henbane. In other words, just because a product is organic doesn't mean it's not going to bring you out in a rash.

CLARINS: NATURAL LUXURY

Can a beauty brand based in a posh Paris suburb, sold in upmarket department stores and promoted with glossy advertisements that are positively weighed down with claims also be ethical and responsible? Clarins thinks so. 'Our vision is based on respect and paying attention,' says Christian Courtin-Clarins, chairman of the privately held company. 'We respect and pay attention to customers. And we respect and pay attention to nature. It's as simple as that.'

He smiles, an amiable smile that creases his sun-tanned face. Courtin-Clarins was the one who told me, when referring to his men's skincare line, that every man secretly wanted to charm. He was certainly including himself in that assessment. He runs the company with Olivier, his brother, who heads the research arm of the operation.

The company was started in 1954 by their father, the late Jacques Courtin, an aspiring surgeon whose medical studies were cut short by the war. Courtin had grown up with a sister and her many friends, which gave him a natural complicity with women, as well as an insight into their health and beauty concerns. While assisting surgeons, he was shocked by how little attention they paid to aesthetic matters when dealing with women: as long as they saved the patient, the size of the scar did not matter. He remembered a doctor brusquely asking a nurse to remove a jar of night cream from a patient's bedside table: for doctors, such products were confidence tricks.

After the war, Courtin looked for a way of putting what he'd learned into practice. The early results of his reflections seem archaic today – a 'breast-firming' device that involved spraying cool water through a pair of cones, a weight-loss machine based on massaging the client with rubber rollers – but they illustrate his lively, questing imagination. His clients seemed to appreciate his methods: Courtin's first beauty institute in the 9th arrondissement attracted a steady stream of saleswomen, actresses and society beauties. He called it Clarins after a role he'd taken in a school play set during the Roman Empire (his sons have since added it to the family name in homage to him).

In the 1960s, Courtin launched six oils to be used during his massage therapies – three for the body and three for the face – made with 100 per cent natural plant extracts. 'He talked about the benefits of natural ingredients decades before the current trend,' says Christian. 'I spent a large part of my childhood exploring botanical gardens with him. What appealed to him was that these ingredients had been used for thousands of years – their beneficial effects were already known.'

'Natural' and 'botanical' are now key elements of the Clarins brand identity. It says it does not use any ingredients of animal origin in its formulas; nor does it test its products on animals. The company engages in fair trade and sponsors a number of environmental projects, such as the Solar Impulse solar-powered plane, and the Alp Action initiative to preserve the biological diversity of the Alpine region.

But Jacques's determination to listen to his customers became a source of anxiety when he began selling his natural oils through perfumeries. 'He liked the idea that he could constantly fine-tune his products based on what people told him,' explains Christian. 'Of course, selling them through a distributor meant he was out of the picture. That's why he began putting cards in each product that the customer could fill in and return. When I first started working here he would give me 10 of them to read the moment I arrived at the office. CRM is deeply embedded in our culture. We created our first serum because customers were asking for it: up until that time, the word was commonly used in pharmacies but not in the beauty industry.'

Another product, Lift Affine Visage, was created to answer a demand among Asian consumers for slimmer, tauter-looking faces. And Jacques Courtin began researching barriers against pollution when customers told him they appreciated how much better their skin looked after spending time outside the city.

Today the company has a club called Clarins & Me that customers can join via its website. They can also sign up to receive a newsletter. Based on the information in its database, Clarins sends out a great deal of samples. 'We encourage the customers to try before they buy. We don't want them to have some kind of allergic reaction: natural ingredients are not necessarily mild.'

Clarins's advertising is both minimalist and bold, combining its bright red logo on a white field with large, soft-focus portraits shot by still-life photographer Guido Mocafico, accompanied by extensive claims in an elegant typeface. Christian says fashion magazines are inevitably the most effective marketing vehicles. 'Each one has a particular readership profile, so we can tailor our messages to them. TV would be a waste. We're also interested in news magazines because they attract opinion leaders.'

Like his father, Christian is inspired by nature, particularly biomimicry – the art of taking inspiration from nature to solve human problems. But the company is careful not to overstate its 'natural' claims in advertising. 'We aim to make products that are effective and safe. When we have the choice, we'll use natural raw materials. If they don't serve our needs, we'll use chemicals. In 90 per cent of cases, we'll favour natural. Of the natural raw materials, we try to ensure that they're grown both locally and organically – but that isn't easy because only a small percentage of cultivated land in

France is devoted to organic farming. So we can't and don't claim to be an organic brand.'

Neither does the brand wish to deceive, says Christian, when it comes to the touchy subject of anti-age creams. 'Look, I believe a woman in her 50s looks more desirable today than she did 15 years ago, and that cosmetics have had something to do with that. But we don't promise miracles. When we're promoting a cream aimed at women in their 50s, we'll take a model in her 40s – not in her 30s – and we won't remove every single line from her face.'

Claims are the territory of Christian's brother, Olivier, who joined the family firm in the 1990s. He spent a great deal of his career as an orthopaedic surgeon, where he specialized in interventions that left minimal scarring. Now he oversees a team of 80 researchers. 'We have never claimed that we can make wrinkles vanish,' he says. 'We can reduce them, to an extent. But what our creams really do is limit future damage. In that way, you could say that we slow down time.'

Christian insists that Clarins products are reasonably priced compared to certain other luxury brands, 'which quite frankly overstep the boundaries of decency'. He smiles once again, aware that the interview is about to return to its point of departure. 'It all goes back to respecting your customers.'

BEAUTY TIPS

✳ Anita Roddick launched the first mainstream 'natural' beauty brand, the Body Shop, by promoting ethical values and a genuine alternative to existing products.

✳ Unable to afford advertising, she relied on her own outspoken personality and engagement with worthy causes to generate media coverage.

✳ Despite accusations of hypocrisy as the company grew, she remained committed to social and environmental causes.

✳ The Body Shop opened the way for a more polished and sophisticated generation of natural beauty brands in the 1990s.

✳ The brand's purchase by L'Oréal confirmed that the natural beauty segment was now big business.

✳ More recently, environmental awareness coupled with consumer alarm about the chemicals in beauty products has elevated the demand for organic brands.

✳ France's Clarins is an interesting compromise between a natural beauty brand and a traditional luxury cosmetics company.

THE NEEDLE
ARTISTS

'We're tattooing doctors and lawyers.'

There didn't seem to be much tattooing going on at The Smile, a hip coffee shop on Bond Street in Manhattan, where I'd heard you could get some skin art along with your carrot cake. I liked the 1900s boarding house style of the place, with its exposed brickwork and scuffed floorboards, dried flowers on the mantelpiece and shelves cluttered with empty bottles of Cutty Sark and old Sclafani tomato cans. I even enjoyed the soundtrack of John Denver singing 'Take me home, country roads'. But I couldn't hear the penetrating whine of the tattooist's needle.

Turned out I was too late: the tattoo parlour had been dismantled, and The Smile was now a straightforward café. This was a shame, as I'd planned to use its existence as proof that tattoos had gone mainstream. No longer underground, or even particularly rebellious, they'd been subsumed by the beauty industry, sported by actresses and models with the same insouciance as jewellery and cosmetics, as easy to come by as hair extensions or false nails.

I wasn't entirely wrong. I had better luck at my next destination, New York Adorned, a combination jewellery boutique and tattoo studio in Williamsburg, Brooklyn.

The operation was founded in 1996 by Lori Leven, who is officially a jewellery designer but also something of a legend in tattoo circles, having always combined the two arts in a single space. 'Tattoos are far more acceptable now than when we started out,' she confirms. 'We're tattooing doctors and lawyers. I think this began with fashion: people like Jean Paul Gaultier and Alexander McQueen putting tattoo prints on clothing. People wore them and felt empowered. A tattoo makes a strong statement. After that, there was a logical next step.'

Leven was born in Queens and is a New Yorker through and through – when she spent some time in Los Angeles, she missed her home town so much that she moved quickly back. She remembers the first tattoo she ever saw up close. 'I must have been eight or nine when my cousin came to dinner at my grandmother's house for dinner with a rose tattooed on her shoulder. Everyone went crazy.'

A few years later, as a teenager hanging out at the beach, she spotted a middle-aged woman with a butterfly tattooed on her hip. *That's what I want*, she thought. Legally, you were supposed to wait until you were 18. 'But I stole my sister's ID and got it done.'

Few people stop at one. Chris O'Donnell, a respected tattoo artist working at New York Adorned when I met him, got his first relatively simple, tribal design as 'a natural progression from skateboarding and punk rock'. He was elated by the experience. 'The first thing I thought of when I woke up every morning was that I had this piece of art on my skin. I wanted to relive that experience. I wanted more – I wanted bigger.'

When Lori Leven returned from her stint in Los Angeles in the early 1990s, she noticed a lot of tattoos around, mostly of the tribal style evoked by O'Donnell. This was interesting, because tattooing was illegal in New York City until 1997 – there were fears that it spread hepatitis. Yet New York had always been a hub of the art. The very first rotary machine was patented in the city. (There are two basic types of tattoo machine: rotary, which uses an electric motor to drive the needle into the skin, and coil, which uses an electromagnetic circuit and is based on the same principle as a doorbell. Coil machines are considered more modern, easier to use and less traumatic, but the rotary models have their fans.)

Leven knew several tattooists – she uses the term 'tattooers' – who were working informally out of their apartments. She rounded them up into a collective called East Side Ink, operating out of a three-bedroom apartment near St Mark's Place. 'I imagined it as a place where people could hang out, exchange ideas, just officialize this whole scene. The landlord hated it because people were always stomping up and down the stairs.' By now, though, Leven and friends knew they were on to something. They opened a jewellery store with, concealed out back, a tattoo parlour: a speakeasy that served ink instead of hooch. Located on 2nd Avenue, it was the first iteration of New York Adorned.

'It must have been the worst kept secret in New York,' Leven laughs. 'Everyone knew about it. We tattooed all the cops in the ninth precinct. They didn't see it as their problem.'

Another famous New York tattoo artist, Jonathan Shaw, opened a shop with a sign outside reading 'Cappuccino & Tattoo'. He stayed in business, which demonstrated the level of concern about the issue. Today, Leven's operation is fully licensed and subject to regular checks by the city's Board of Health.

Despite the fact that she's now legal, Leven continues to design and sell jewellery. Her work sits perfectly alongside the exotic tattoo designs papering the studio, which seem to take their cues from the world's more colourful cultures. She adores India and travels there often. 'People sometimes assume my jewellery is directly related to body piercing, which is not the case. The body piercing trend was at its height in the mid-90s. We had a piercing shop in the East Village and they were doing a hundred piercings a day. But now it's calmed down.'

Tattoos, though, are more popular than ever. At the time of my visit there's a trend for getting text written on the skin. 'Some people ask for entire poems. It's a tricky one because skin is of course an entirely different medium to paper. Try tattooing a verse in copperplate on somebody's ribs, for example.'

As for O'Donnell, he specializes in beautiful, richly coloured Japanese-style tattoos that take up entire blocks of body: imagine golden tigers or giant gem-coloured snakes rippling across a back or a torso. 'But it doesn't have to be big,' he insists. 'I just want to work on things I enjoy. People come in; we talk about their idea. These days, people know the kind of work I do, so they've thought about it beforehand.'

If he doesn't like the sound of your project, he'll politely turn you down. This isn't some backstreet operation where you can get the name of your partner, pet or favourite rock star tattooed on your bicep – or even a Louis Vuitton logo.

TATTOOS COME OUT OF THE PARLOUR

In 2011, luxury brand Louis Vuitton launched an online video featuring tattoo artist Scott Campbell. The three-part 'day in the life of' video was essentially a lengthy advertisement for a collaboration between Campbell and Louis Vuitton menswear designer Paul Helbers, who'd invited the ink maestro to work on prints for scarves, shirts, pants and even bags. Campbell – who is also a contemporary artist – was happy to oblige.

Scott Campbell is often held responsible for the ascension of the tattoo from a symbol of rebellion to one of status. He opened his first studio, Saved Tattoo, in Brooklyn in 2004. He has since tattooed models Helena Christensen and Lily Cole, the late actor Heath Ledger and fashion designer Vera Wang, among others. Marc Jacobs – who designs women's wear for Vuitton – is a regular client: Campbell has inked him with such idiosyncratic adornments as the cartoon character Sponge Bob and a Simpson's caricature of the designer himself. By 2009, when Campbell briefly moved his operation to the basement of The Smile café, he was charging US$300 an hour for his services ('Manhattan ink: tat master Scott Campbell needles the stars', *New York Observer*, 17 March 2009).

Inevitably, Campbell is described as a 'celebrity tattoo artist' – something that doesn't seem to irk him. 'All of a sudden, fashion is appropriating something that's been near and dear to me for so many years,' he told *Papermag*.

A lot of tattoo artists get defensive about it because tattooing is one of those things that you really have to commit to and devote yourself to completely… To have it appropriated by fashion and the mainstream media, there is a part of me that wants to say, 'wait a minute, this is MY world,' but at the end of the day, it's not mine. With more exposure only comes greater understanding and appreciation, and I don't think that could ever be a bad thing.

Campbell must also be given credit for seeing beyond the backroom clichés of the tattoo parlour.

Once I opened my own space and created this environment that was a little more forward-thinking and creative, a lot of these people who always wanted to get tattooed but didn't want to deal with the sweaty biker shops responded to it. If there's one tattoo shop in town that stands out for being different or a little more innovative, people gravitate toward that, especially people in a creative industry.

('The unofficial tattoo artist of the "fashion folks"',
3 September 2010)

In fact, another name may have had even more impact on the adoption of tattoos by the mainstream. In 2004, the French fashion entrepreneur Christian Audigier licensed the rights to produce the Ed Hardy clothing line, inspired by the imagery of a famous San Francisco tattoo artist. Thanks to Audigier's knack for marketing – opening stores in fashionable districts and sending free product to celebrities – tattoo T-shirts were soon cropping up on everyone from Madonna to Paris Hilton.

Don Ed Hardy is a fascinating character in his own right. He studied at the San Francisco Art Institute in the 1960s, where he became skilled at intaglio etching – a printmaking technique that involves engraving images into a metal plate. But he'd been fascinated by tattooing since his childhood in the beach town of Corona del Mar in Orange County, California. 'By ten he was drawing cars and eagles on kids' arms with wet coloured pencils and Maybelline eyeliner', reports the *San Francisco Chronicle* ('Don Ed Hardy's tattoos are high art and big business', 30 September 2006). He borrowed ideas from tattoo catalogues advertised on the back of *Popular Mechanics* and the tattoos he saw on guys in wanted posters on post office walls.

As an adult he learned the trade at an Oakland tattoo shop run by Phil Sparrow, a former literature teacher who'd become a devotee of skin art. It was thanks to Sparrow that Hardy discovered Japanese 'full body' tattoos. In 1973 he became the first Westerner to apprentice with the Japanese master Horihide, where he 'painted and pierced the skins of a number of the Japanese gangsters known as Yakuza'. Hardy also admires the late tattoo artist Norman 'Sailor Jerry' Collins, who earned his nickname conducting tours of the Hawaiian islands in a three-mast schooner. Born in 1911, 'Jerry first tried tattooing as a teenager by hand-poking designs on willing customers with whatever supplies he came across while hitchhiking and hopping freight trains across America. He landed in Chicago in the 1920s and connected with his first formal teacher, the legendary Gib "Tatts" Thomas, who taught Jerry how to use a tattoo machine' (www.sailorjerry.com).

Who taught 'Tatts' I don't know – possibly a pirate. He left his home in New Orleans at the age of 14 to travel the world. There is something about a tattoo that evokes voyage: mariners and drifters, shore leave in the South Pacific. The very word comes from the Polynesian 'tatau'. As Hardy says, 'the oral history of tattoos is fantastic'; he has published a number of books on the subject. He believes the urge to get a tattoo is 'primal': 'Based on the evidence, the frozen mummies, the oldest members of our species had tattoos.'

Tattoos have been used as brands in the most literal sense: the tagging of slaves or convicts; the chill grey procession of Nazi concentration camp numerals. They have also been marks of courage, talismans against the evil eye, and declarations of love. And of course they are tribal, symbols of belonging, which is no doubt why they appeal to the fashion crowd.

Although Hardy still runs the Tattoo City shop in San Francisco, he retired from tattooing some time ago to concentrate on painting and printmaking. His ability to combine the worlds of high and low art, not to mention a savvy sense of branding, helped to bring the intricate craft of tattooing to a wider public.

The notional permanence of tattoos means that getting one is still a radical act. A tattoo hints at daring and creativity. As Scott Campbell implies, tattoos made it into the mainstream via creative professionals and people who wished to emulate them. It's easy to imagine the frisson a doctor or a lawyer might get from the thought of the tattoo secreted beneath a conservative façade. But the ability of a tattoo to shock may be gone within a generation. In 2007, a Pew Research Center survey suggested that 40 per cent of Americans aged between 26 and 40 have a tattoo; and 36 per cent of 18- to 25-year-olds have one. The figures indicate that, for some people, getting a tattoo may be an early manifestation of mid-life crisis.

For those who want to follow the trend without getting ink under their skin, temporary tattoos are everywhere. Even Chanel offers 'exclusive, individual temporary tattoos, referencing iconic Chanel symbols and codes, hand drawn by global creative director of makeup Peter Philips'.

But what if you decide to go for it – to get the real thing? Lori Leven of New York Adorned has words of advice. 'You probably won't get just one, so plan ahead – think about what the end result might be and how you're going to get there. This is not a casual decision; it's going to affect your life, so treat it accordingly. Above all, never be trendy. Always get something tattooed on you that's timeless.'

BEAUTY TIPS

✳ With a salty, rambunctious history, tattoos appeal to rebels. But soon they may not seem rebellious at all: a survey suggests 40 per cent of Americans aged between 26 and 40 have a tattoo. In the UK, the figure is 29 per cent for people aged between 16 and 44.

✳ Models, actors and fashion designers took tattoos out of the back room and into the mainstream.

✳ Tattoo artists believe the trend began with clothing: designers such as Alexander McQueen and Jean Paul Gaultier integrated tattoo-inspired art into their work.

✳ The clothing line Ed Hardy, which licensed the name of a San Francisco tattoo artist, caught on with celebrities.

✳ Tattoo artist Scott Campbell has worked with Louis Vuitton on clothing and bags inspired by tattoo art.

✳ Chanel has launched a range of 'temporary skin art' tattoos.

✳ Fashion magazines have spread the message about the artistry of tattoos and made them more desirable.

✳ A temporary trend for tattoos may die down, but they will remain acceptable adornments.

THE FUTURE

OF BEAUTY

'As human beings yearn to improve themselves, they will be attracted to solutions that give them an edge.'

The Beyond Beauty exhibition in Paris is a beauty bazaar. Or perhaps I should say a 'beauty bizarre'. As I wander around the 500 or so stands in the hangar-like space at Porte de Versailles, I become ever more baffled by the diversity of products that purport to make their users look younger and more attractive.

I pause for a moment by the Re-Age stand, where a demonstrator is squirting a volunteer's face with tiny puffs of air from a metallic handheld device that looks a little like a dentist's drill. I discover that the treatment, called Re-Oxy, uses oxygen to treat signs of ageing. No knives, no injections. The handheld device sends active ingredients deep into the skin with pulses of oxygen. The system has already been installed by a spa in Monaco. Another treatment involves breathing oxygen and essential oils through an inhaler to combat stress.

As I can hardly imagine anything more stressful, I move on. Next I happen across a handheld photon device that emits LED light into the skin to stimulate cells. Such devices were previously the domain of dermatologists and salons, but now 'the last skincare system you will ever need' can be yours for less than 250 euros. Home treatment is going to be the next big thing in skincare, I'm told.

And what else? What will beauty companies be selling us and telling us in the years ahead?

NUTRICOSMETICS

They call them 'neutriceuticals' or 'nutricosmetics': nutritional supplements and functional foods that make us beautiful from within. The trend comes from Japan, where herbal remedies have been linked with beauty for centuries. In more recent years, it has pushed the boundary with products such as collagen-enriched soups and drinks and yoghurts containing hyaluronic acid (which promotes tissue repair) and ceramide (lipids found in the skin's protective upper layer).

The trend crossed to Europe with Danone's Essensis 'skin-enhancing' yoghurt, introduced in France, Spain, Belgium and Italy in 2007. Containing vitamin E and green tea antioxidants, among other ingredients, the product was said to nourish the skin from within. However, it was shelved in France two years later amid flagging sales. This raised the possibility that the potential of functional foods had been exaggerated – but there was also a distribution problem.

Danone placed Essensis next to regular yoghurts on supermarket shelves, where it appeared overpriced and adorned with incongruous beauty claims. When Nestlé launched its beauty drink Glowelle, it sold it in the beauty department of upmarket retailer Neiman Marcus in the United States. 'Consumers at a store like Neiman Marcus are looking for beauty products and have the means to be unconcerned about how they affect their weekly food shopping bill. Sales assistants are also on hand to explain what the new products are and how they work' (Food & Drink Europe, 9 February 2009).

It's unlikely that the failure of Essensis spelled the end of nutritional cosmetics. L'Oréal has a joint venture with Nestlé, called Innéov, to explore this type of product. It produces anti-ageing and firmness pills, as well as tablets that 'detoxify and drain' to combat cellulite, and others that 'preserve and strengthen' hair.

Perricone MD, the skincare brand founded in the United States by dermatologist Dr Nicholas Perricone, promotes a number of 'neutriceutical' dietary supplements. Also in the United States, Walgreens launched Borba Inside Out Beauty Solutions, a range of ingestible beauty products developed by aesthetician Scott-Vincent Borba. They contain a number of antioxidant 'super-fruits' – blueberry, pomegranate, cranberry – and come in playful formats such as Firm & Fit Calcium Chews, Healthy Glow Immunity Drink Mix and Mighty Energy Gummi Mice, as well as vitamin-enhanced Skin Balance Water.

There are a number of obstacles – an uncertain regulatory framework, distribution challengers and consumer scepticism – but the market for beauty from within is ripe for exploration.

NEUROCOSMETICS

If you feel good, there's a better chance that you'll look good. That's a highly simplistic way of looking at neurocosmetics, or beauty products that enhance your mood. Aromatherapy promises similar benefits, but here we're talking about skincare that promotes well-being. Some products claim to generate left–right brain exchange or increase serotonin levels. Others boast active ingredients that stimulate the cutaneous nervous system – the thing that makes you itch – triggering the neurotransmitters that ensure that the skin receives the right balance of nutrients.

One of the names operating in this field is Dr Linda Papadopolous, a British celebrity psychologist who has published a number of books on 'psychodermatology' and has her own skincare line, LP Skin Therapy. Her website says many of her products contain 'nootropics' (www.lpskintherapy. com). These are cognitive enhancers, or 'smart drugs', that stimulate brain activity in a number of ways, from improving memory and concentration to soothing stress; they can also affect production and uptake of dopamine and serotonin.

Papadopolous is not alone in finding this niche interesting. A company called Kroia also specializes in mood-enhancing cosmetics. Its claims are based on 'chromotherapy' – colour therapy – which proposes that certain colours have healing or soothing qualities. Each colour has a different frequency, and the rate at which it vibrates affects the mood of the viewer: compare the times you see red with the mornings you wake up with the blues.

Kroia's founder Karla Farach believes that the deployment of light in skincare, notably the LED treatment mentioned above, as well as the use of minerals, crystals and coloured gemstones in massage therapy, has opened the door for a new form of treatment. Her range of 'active foaming moisturizers', made with ingredients such as natural topaz crystal, neroli flower extract and ginseng, are available in varying colour blends to deliver different results: yellow for energizing, pink for anti-ageing and blue to soothe the mind.

Other beauty companies are undoubtedly studying this area in their constant quest for compelling stories. Look out for more mood-enhancing skincare products, as well as cosmetics that promote confidence and euphoria in a 'scientifically proven' manner.

NANOCOSMETICS

You don't have to probe for too long in the trend forecasting business before things start getting spooky. The very word 'nanotechnology' conjures up science fiction images of subatomic machines capable of reproducing exponentially until they swamp the planet in grey goo. In fact, nanotechnology is concerned with engineering objects and devices from individual atoms and molecules. It has been described as the science of materials that are one billionth of a metre. The cosmetics industry is very interested in nanotech, for reasons I'll explain in a moment, and L'Oréal and Procter & Gamble are among the sponsors of the International Council of Nanotechnology.

The 'grey goo' theory was originally proposed by Eric Drexler, a scientist often referred to as 'the father of nanotechnology'. In his 1986 book *Engines of Creation: The coming era of nanotechnology*, he described a catastrophic scenario in which nanobots with the ability to manipulate matter go out of control and destroy life on earth. Drexler later said he regretted the statement, having merely wanted to outline a theoretical danger of nanotechnology to balance excitement over its potential benefits. 'I also underestimated the popularity of depictions of swarms of tiny nanobugs in science fiction and popular culture' ('Nanotech guru turns back on goo', BBC News Online, 9 June 2004).

Reassuringly, Drexler feels it is extremely unlikely that scientists will ever manufacture a self-replicating nano-machine.

That particular danger may remain in the realm of fantasy, but nanoparticles are being used in cosmetics, and organizations like Friends of the Earth have expressed concern about them. Nanotechnology was first adopted by the makers of sunscreens, which for years had been using titanium dioxide and zinc oxide to block UVB and UVA radiation. These ingredients are not water soluble, meaning that sun creams felt thick and cloying, leaving greasy white streaks on the skin when applied. By using 'nanoparticulate' titanium and zinc, cosmetics companies were able to create thin, transparent, easy-to-apply sunscreens that were much appreciated by consumers.

The question, though, is whether nanoparticles can penetrate the outer layer of the skin and get into the bloodstream, eventually damaging cells or turning up in the lungs, brain and other organs. There have been calls for stricter regulation of nano-ingredients, but at the time of writing these have not been answered by specific legislation. Indeed, there are no rules about labelling products that contain nano-ingredients.

A report in April 2011 by the Nanodermatology Society conceded that, when exposed to UV radiation, nano-sized titanium and zinc generated free radicals and reactive oxygen species – which can damage proteins, DNA and fats within cells. The level of toxicity depended on their size, structure and coating; particles are often protected by swathes of manganese and other materials. Crucially, the report added, 'damage associated with free radical formation is dependent on their ability to interact with living cells'. In order to do so, they first had to penetrate the skin. It concluded formally: 'nano-titanium and zinc do not penetrate the outer layer of human skin, even through hair follicles' and that 'nano-titanium and zinc do not reach living cells, and therefore pose no risk of toxicity' (www.nanodermsociety.org).

But they would say that, wouldn't they?

Unless strict legislation emerges, it is unlikely that cosmetics companies will back away from the use of nanoparticles. They're just too useful. For a start, nanotechnology allows more active ingredients to reach the skin; smaller particles also limit the clogging of pores; and 'nano-encapsuled' active ingredients have a longer shelf life. Hair dye is another area that benefits from nanotechnology: nano-sized colorants penetrate the hair more easily, meaning that the colour lasts longer.

Addressing the annual meeting of the American Academy of Dermatology in March 2010, a dermatologist named Adnan Nasir gave a widely reported speech about the potential benefits of nanotechnology to beauty companies. He said the cosmetic industry led all other industries in the number of patents for nanoparticles, 'which have the potential to enhance sunscreens, shampoos and conditioners, lipsticks, eye shadows, moisturizers, deodorants, after-shave products and perfumes' ('Sizing up nanotechnology: how nanosized particles may affect skincare products', *PR Newswire*, 4 March 2010).

He confirmed that nanotechnology would improve the delivery of anti-ageing ingredients to the skin. But he also raised a marketing issue. 'Since anti-aging products that contain nanoparticles of antioxidants will be harder to make, we expect that these products will cost more than products using traditional formulations... Once these products are determined to be safe, the consumer will have to decide if the increased costs are worth the added benefits.'

L'Oréal, Dior, Shiseido and AmorePacific are among cosmetics companies that openly use nanotechnology in their products. Elsewhere there are blushers, foundations, hair care products and even mascara that claim nano-ingredients – but how many of them just like having the fancy word in their advertising is unclear.

L'Oréal states that it tests all its products for safety. In a sustainability fact sheet from June 2010, the company says that it uses 'nanoemulsions and nanopigments':

Nanoemulsions are in fact macroscopic preparations containing oil and water droplets reduced to nanometric size to increase the content of nutritious oils while preserving the transparency and the lightness of the formulas. Sometimes fragile active ingredients, like vitamins, are protected from air inside nanometre-sized vesicles called nanocapsules™ or liposomes that release the ingredient upon contact with the skin at the time of application.

('The use of nanotechnology in cosmetology',
www.sustainabledevelopent/loreal.com)

Nanotechnology has the potential to transform the beauty industry. The researcher Thomson Reuters confirmed as much in 2009, when it produced a report called 'Can nanotech unlock the fountains of youth?' This quoted James Canton of the Institute for Global Futures, a San Francisco think tank. 'Nanotech is one of the key design tools that will be used to create the largest industry of the 21st century: health enhancement. As human beings yearn to improve themselves, they will be attracted to solutions that give them an edge.'

The report notes that 'the increased presence of specialty chemical manufacturers in the beauty and personal care space is rooted squarely in the development of nanotechnologies derived from other technologies'. It mentions the Astalift cosmetics brand developed by Fujifilm, which ran a TV campaign explaining how nanotechnology originally developed for photography helped its creams better penetrate the skin.

Anxiety over safety may prevent other beauty companies from overemphasizing nanoparticles in their claims, slowing the development of nanocosmetics as a category. But there are others who believe that the future of beauty lies at the intersection of nature and nano.

BEAUTY TIPS

- Functional foods and 'beauty from within' are an emerging category that has not yet been fully exploited.
- Previous attempts mistakenly placed beauty foods alongside mainstream products, disguising their appeal. They may now be marketed with cosmetics rather than on supermarket shelves.
- Mood-enhancing 'neurocosmetics' combine some of the ideas familiar from aromatherapy with skincare products.
- With their gentle façade and faintly New Age claims, they may form a category parallel to the 'organic' market.
- Nanotechnology has already been adopted by a number of mainstream beauty companies – but there are concerns about the safety of nanoparticles.

CONCLUSION

'The consumer is not a moron – she is your wife.'

It would be easy to paint the beauty industry as an outright villain, trafficking unrealistic images of youth and perfection that have blighted the lives of millions of women – and not a few men too. There is plenty of evidence to support such an assertion; many have come to the same conclusion. But the rude health of the global beauty business suggests that the truth is more complex.

Across many ages and cultures, women painted their lips and darkened their lashes. They attempted to whiten their skin long before Fair & Lovely was created. Their desire to appear more beautiful can be attributed to many things – status, sexual selection, even empowerment – but it cannot be entirely ascribed to pressure from male-dominated cosmetics companies abetted by a misogynistic media.

Examples of make-up being used to symbolize emancipation surface time and time again in the history of beauty, from the Greek women who stepped out of the gynaecea to the suffragists Elizabeth Arden saw marching in bright red lipstick. In her (2010) book *Glamour*, Carol Dyhouse mentions Iris Storm, heroine of 'Michael Arlen's cult bestseller of 1926, *The Green Hat*', who 'flaunts all the signs of modernity: she has attitude, sexy clothes, red lipstick and a fast car'. For Dyhouse glamour – and beauty – could 'offer a route to a more powerful and assertive female identity'. The Renaissance women who cooked up alchemical beauty recipes sound hardly less impressive than Iris Storm and her flapper contemporaries.

Many of the skin creams that emerged in the 19th century were based on recipes that had been concocted by women at home and passed down for generations. The industrial revolution allowed for mass production of these creams, while the emergence of the women's magazines provided an ideal advertising vehicle. It was against this background that Helena Rubinstein and Elizabeth Arden created the first global beauty brands.

Rubinstein and Arden were shameless social climbers who successfully turned their own aspirations and desires into packaging, advertising copy, department store counters and salons that invited women into a dream world. Their promises of eternal youth were only part of the mix; progress, science and status were closely intertwined with the allure of their pots of cream. Estée Lauder came from much the same mould. Their communications did not create a new myth of beauty, but rather fuelled and magnified atavistic needs, drumming the message home so often that women became convinced they would be 'letting themselves go' if they did not use cosmetics.

Eugène Schueller, Charles Revson and Max Factor were towering figures in the history of beauty – but some of its most influential names have been women. In the late 1970s, just as feminism was gaining traction, Anita Roddick sold a new kind of status: it was hard not to admire the globetrotting human rights activist, an image that she successfully packaged and sold along with her products.

In her famous (1990) book *The Beauty Myth*, Naomi Wolf hints that the contemporary advertising image of beauty may have been a reaction to feminism itself. 'Feminists… broke the stranglehold on the women's popular press of advertisers for household products, who were promoting the feminine mystique; at once, the diet and skin care industries became the new cultural censors of women's intellectual space… the gaunt, youthful model supplanted the happy housewife as the arbiter of successful womanhood.'

Wolf does not propose that women reject beauty entirely, merely that they embrace a broader definition of it. 'Maybe we will adorn ourselves with real delight, with the sense that we are gilding the lily,' she suggests. She embraces the pursuit of pleasure, even of 'radiance'.

The global expansion of Western beauty companies does present serious issues, however. One might accept that 'paleness' and 'purity' had been associated with beauty for millennia, but the unbending manner in which a narrow, Caucasian vision of attractiveness was sold in markets where it was not the norm is quite distressing. In a related matter, while I was researching this book I was surprised to discover the distasteful political connections of certain beauty pioneers. Eugène Schueller of L'Oréal and François Coty both had close ties with Fascist organizations; Gabrielle Chanel espoused anti-Semitic views and spent the Occupation in the arms of a Nazi officer. It is too much of a reach to connect the attitudes of three individuals with those of the early beauty industry, but that troubling preoccupation with 'purity' ticked away in my mind.

It is fair to say that the beauty brands – helped by Hollywood, television and fashion magazines – successfully globalized standards of beauty. Marketing has made us all aspire to being taller, thinner and fairer. Fortunately, in recent years, the situation has improved. Brands hailing from Asia and Latin America have begun to conquer Western markets; a more flexible approach to product development and marketing at the global giants has led to a wider range of formulations and advertising images. In Europe and the United States, cosmetics brands have begun to more accurately reflect multiracial societies.

Having dealt with sexism and racism, let's consider ageism. Although they can't seem to settle on a figure, researchers agree that anti-ageing products take up the largest slice of the vast global skincare market. To this must be added the growing trend for aesthetic surgery and temporary solutions like Botox and dermal fillers. Once again, the beauty industry did not conjure this demand out of thin air. It merely reinforced the fears of an ageing population. In 2002, during the United Nations Second World Assembly on Ageing in Madrid, it was stated that the number of senior citizens in the world would have risen from 629 million to 2 billion by 2050. At a more micro level, concerns about appearance were exacerbated by the global economic slump, which placed people in their 40s and 50s back on the job market. The beauty industry is cynical, but it panders to our vanities and insecurities.

Do anti-ageing skin creams reduce wrinkles? Yes – but in a way that is barely significant. Do they provide hope, comfort and sensual pleasure? Judging by the number of people who continue to buy them, even though they are well aware they may not work, the answer is, again, yes. It is contemptuous to dismiss consumers as suckers who'll believe anything. As the great adman David Ogilvy said, 'The consumer is not a moron – she is your wife.'

I do not consider my wife a moron. I hope that I am not a moron, yet the moisturizer and soothing under-eye cream are sitting there on the bathroom shelf. Applying cosmetics is a ritual, and rituals ease stress; they represent stability in an uncertain world.

Arden, Rubinstein, Revson, Lauder, Roddick... they were all brilliant storytellers. If the beauty industry has changed the way we look, it has done so chiefly with the written word. In almost every sector, globalization has killed the art of copywriting – a strong logo and a powerful picture cross borders effortlessly – but in beauty, 'claims' continue to fill press and poster advertising, not to mention websites. The words inveigle and caress, skilfully blending poetry with science.

The power of beauty companies to manipulate is waning. The very technology that has allowed them to build vast databases and raise the art of customer relations management to new heights has given the purchasers of cosmetics access to information that they could previously only guess at. Thanks to the internet, consumers can determine the ingredients and effect of almost every tube, pot and tub on shelves today. But something interesting has happened. Instead of recoiling in horror and renouncing cosmetics forever, they have embraced a new generation of natural and organic skincare brands, some of whose claims are as poetic and improbable as those concocted by the global giants.

It seems that, as long as beauty brands carry on telling us stories, we will carry on listening to them.

REFERENCES

Armstrong, John (2005) *The Secret Power of Beauty*, Penguin, London

Aveline, Françoise (2003) *Chanel Parfum*, Editions Assouline, Paris

Basten, Fred E (2008) *Max Factor: The man who changed the faces of the world*, Arcade, New York

Benaïm, Laurence (2002) *Yves Saint Laurent: Biographie*, Grasset, Paris

Burns, Paul (2010) *Entrepreneurship and Small Business: Start-up, growth and maturity*, Palgrave Macmillan, Basingstoke

Burr, Chandler (2007) *The Perfect Scent*, Picador, New York

Collin, Béatrice and Rouach, Daniel (2009) *Le Modèle L'Oréal*, Pearson Education, Paris

Condra, Jill (2008) *The Greenwood Encyclopaedia of Clothing through World History*, vol 2, Greenwood Press, Westport, CT

Drexler, Eric (1986) *Engines of Creation: The coming era of nanotechnology*, Anchor Books, New York

Dyhouse, Carol (2010) *Glamour: Women, history, feminism*, Zed Books, London

Eco, Umberto (2004) *On Beauty*, Secker & Warburg, London

Egyptian State Tourist Department (date unknown) *Beauty Treatment in Ancient Egypt*, R Schindler, Cairo

Iezzi, Teressa (2010) *The Idea Writers*, Palgrave Macmillan, New York

Israel, Lee (1985) *Estée Lauder: Beyond the magic*, Macmillan, New York

Jones, Geoffrey (2010) *Beauty Imagined: A history of the global beauty industry*, Oxford University Press, Oxford

Lorris, Guillaume de and Meun, Jean de (1994 translation), *The Romance of the Rose*, trans Frances Horgan, Oxford University Press, Oxford

McGraw, Thomas K (2000) *American Business, 1920–2000: How it worked*, Harlan Davidson, Wheeling, IL

Macqueen, Adam (2005) *The King of Sunlight: How William Lever cleaned up the world*, Corgi, London

Marseille, Jacques (2009) *L'Oréal 1909–2009*, Perrin, Paris

Mazzeo, Tilar J (2010) *The Secret of Chanel No. 5*, HarperCollins, New York

Mercer, Nigel (2009) Clinical risk in cosmetic surgery, *Clinical Risk*, **15** (6)

Montet, Pierre (1980) *Everyday Life in Egypt in the Days of Ramesses the Great*, University of Pennsylvania Press, Philadelphia

Paquet, Dominique (1997) *Miroir, Mon Beau Miroir: Une histoire de la beauté*, Gallimard, Paris

Schiff, Stacy (2010) *Cleopatra: A life*, Virgin, London

Temporal, Paul and Trott, Martin (2001) *Romancing the Customer: Maximizing brand value through powerful relationship management*, Wiley, New York

Tobias, Andrew (1976) *Fire and Ice: The story of Charles Revson, the man who built the Revlon empire*, William Morrow, New York

Tungate, Mark (2007) *Adland: A global history of advertising*, Kogan Page, London

Tungate, Mark (2008) *Branded Male: Marketing to men*, Kogan Page, London

Turin, Luca (2006) *The Secret of Scent*, Faber and Faber, London

Vigarello, Georges (2004) *Histoire de la Beauté: Le corps et l'art d'embellir de la Renaissance à nos jours*, Editions du Seuil, Paris

Wolf, Naomi (1990) *The Beauty Myth*, Chatto & Windus, London

Woodhead, Lindy (2003) *War Paint*, Virago, London

INDEX